What Your Colleagues Are Saying

When reading Pamela Koutrakos's book, you will feel as though you are talking "word study" with a trusted colleague. Pam is a word study guru who invites you to explore research-based best practices that are meaningful, authentic, and student-centered. In addition, the layout of the book is brilliant—Pam shares not only the "why" behind building an authentic word study practice, but the "how" by "getting you started." However, she doesn't leave you hanging there—she then "keeps you going" by providing all the necessary student minicharts/lessons/conferring forms that will enable your students to grow and become independent in the study of words. Having these ready-made charts/ lessons/forms available at your fingertips will afford you the much-needed time to work with students responsively by providing face-to-face feedback that will ensure student achievement. This book gives teachers comfort in knowing that these word study practices that Pam shares are not just based in theory alone. *Word Study That Sticks* is happening in real schools, with real students, with real teachers. The minicharts/lessons, student work, and student pictures provide authentic examples of engaged, independent students who grew into curious word lovers. These students go on to use what they are learning when reading, writing, and talking with their friends and family. Isn't that what it is all about—always learning to find ways to share our thoughts, ideas, and feelings with one another? Thank you, Pam, for sharing your important work with us—a true gift to all educators.

—Yvonne Mortello, MA, K–5 Literacy Coach, Primary Educator, Hopatcong Borough Schools

Gone are the days of feeling overwhelmed with the planning and organization of word study! In her companion to *Word Study That Sticks*, Pamela Koutrakos seamlessly blends research and resources in one place, making her follow-up book a comprehensive must-have for anyone who teaches word study. With contagious enthusiasm, Pam thoughtfully walks us through how to help students set up, organize, and use notebooks or choice charts for purposeful work and wonderings. She inspires us with suggestions for setting up schedules and spaces that support authentic word learning. Pam infuses each chapter with samples of student work, which serve to remind us how doable a fun and meaningful approach to word study instruction can be. I must admit that what I am most excited about are the gorgeous, student-friendly minicharts that support student choice and agency. How lucky we are that Pam continues to share her love of words with us.

—Heather Frank, Literacy Consultant and Doctoral Candidate, Montclair State University

In *The Word Study That Sticks Companion*, Pamela Koutrakos's can-do stance about word study is contagious when she explains that "you can support students' developing language skills each day with rigor and joy!" It's easy to get jazzed up about word study because Pam's vision and support in this companion text is so clear. As teachers turn the pages, they will be reminded of the research behind word study and ways to put that research into practice. This book is a treasure trove of visuals, step-by-step explanations, routines, and resources that are timely and invaluable.

—Julie Wright, Instructional Coach, Educational Consultant, and Coauthor of *What Are You Grouping For?*

Pamela Koutrakos has hit a homerun with her companion book to *Word Study That Sticks*. The original book is a game changer and now with the companion, teachers have the research, procedures, and tools at their fingertips. Together these books are game changers and easily implemented in both primary and intermediate classrooms. I totally understand why teachers were clamoring for Pam's charts and structure. While

I can rave over this new book, the best review comes from my fourth-grade students who are engaged and excited about word work. As one of them stated so brilliantly, "I wish we had had these books a long time ago." Wise words. Wise advice. Thank you, Pam! All of our elementary students deserve the wonder of words. I recommend that teachers bring Pam into their classrooms and let her guide you using both her books in tandem!

—Leslie Blauman, Teacher, Speaker, and Author of *Teaching Evidence-Based Writing: Fiction* and *Teaching Evidence-Based Writing: Nonfiction*

With *Word Study That Sticks: Best Practices* serving as a firm foundation, Pamela Koutrakos's companion text gives busy teachers, like you, ready-to-use student resources to help launch and sustain a vibrant word study community in your classroom. After your students learn the what, why, and how of each word study routine, the handy minicharts (over 100 of them!) will guide them toward independence. With additional classroom-tested tips on using word study notebooks or choice charts in kindergarten, you are holding in your hands everything you need to inspire curious and independent word learners.

—Maria Walther, First-Grade Teacher and Instructional Specialist, Indian Prairie District 204, Aurora, IL, and Author of *The Ramped-Up Read Aloud: What to Notice as You Turn the Page*

Handing learners tools to help them grow can be tricky—any checklist or form can quickly become disconnected from meaningful practice. Yet with this book, Pamela Koutrakos succeeds beyond a time-pressed teacher's wildest dreams, offering more than 100 word study minicharts that help students become independent. Each chart explains the purpose in child-friendly terms, lists the needed materials, and provides a visual reminder of what the routine looks like (and I love that Pam shares versions for K–2 and versions for Grades 3–6). Meaning routines, phonemic awareness and phonics routines, spelling pattern routines, habit and hybrid routines, check-in/assessment routines—these are the tools that are going to help you transform word study in your classroom and free you up to confer and teach. At every turn, Pam shows you how they connect to meaningful word study experiences.

—Gravity Goldberg, Author and Consultant

If you have any concern about how your students are spelling words, pick up this book! Pamela Koutrakos is revolutionizing word study here, through streamlined approaches that make word learning more effective, playful, and joyful. You WILL see a difference in students' use of phonemic awareness, phonics, spelling, *and* vocabulary. This collection is a set of tools that stands on a strong foundation of research that practicalizes language learning for the reality of the classroom. This book is a game changer!

—Patty McGee, Author of *Feedback That Moves Writers Forward*

Pamela Koutrakos helps teachers understand the urgency of word study and the ways in which they can fold word study into their daily teaching easily. Her book is rich with hands-on, practical lessons that can be accomplished in only a few minutes a day. This book is more than a "companion" to her first word study book; it's an instructional playbook for teaching students to own their reading and find joy and wonder in words.

—Nancy Akhavan, Author of *The Big Book of Literacy Tasks* and *The Nonfiction Now Lesson Bank*

The Word Study
That Sticks Companion

To Colby and Peyton
Thanks for reminding me every single day that love is all we need.

The Word Study That Sticks Companion

Classroom-Ready Tools for Teachers and Students, Grades K–6

Pamela Koutrakos

CORWIN Literacy

A SAGE Publishing Company

FOR INFORMATION:

Corwin

A SAGE Company

2455 Teller Road

Thousand Oaks, California 91320

(800) 233-9936

www.corwin.com

SAGE Publications Ltd.

1 Oliver's Yard

55 City Road

London EC1Y 1SP

United Kingdom

SAGE Publications India Pvt. Ltd.

B 1/I 1 Mohan Cooperative Industrial Area

Mathura Road, New Delhi 110 044

India

SAGE Publications Asia-Pacific Pte. Ltd.

18 Cross Street #10-10/11/12

China Square Central

Singapore 048423

Acquisitions Editor: Tori Bachman

Editorial Development Manager: Julie Nemer

Senior Editorial Assistant: Sharon Wu

Production Editor: Jane Martinez

Copy Editor: Megan Markanich

Typesetter: C&M Digitals (P) Ltd.

Proofreader: Talia Greenberg

Indexer: Judy Hunt

Cover Designer: Candice Harman

Graphic Designer: Gail Buschman

Marketing Manager: Brian Grimm

Library of Congress Cataloging-in-Publication Data

Names: Koutrakos, Pamela, author.

Title: The word study that sticks companion : classroom-ready tools for   teachers and students, grades K-6 / Pamela Koutrakos.

Description: Thousand Oaks, California : Corwin, [2019] | Includes bibliographical references and index.

Identifiers: LCCN 2019010745 | ISBN 9781544361628 (pbk. : alk. paper)

Subjects: LCSH: Reading—Phonetic method—Study and teaching (Elementary) | English language—Orthography and spelling—Study and teaching (Elementary) | Language arts (Elementary) | Student-centered learning.

Classification: LCC LB1573.3 .K69 2019 | DDC 372.465—dc23
LC record available at https://lccn.loc.gov/2019010745

This book is printed on acid-free paper.

19 20 21 22 23 10 9 8 7 6 5 4 3 2 1

Contents

PART I: LAUNCHING CURIOUS, CREATIVE WORD STUDY

PART II: TOOLS TO FOSTER ENGAGEMENT AND INDEPENDENCE

PART III: EXTENDING WORD LEARNING

Visit the companion website at
http://resources.corwin.com/wstscompanion
for downloadable resources.

Acknowledgments

Com·mu·ni·ty /kə'myo͞onədē/

Noun: *A feeling of fellowship with others, as a result of sharing common attitudes, interests, and goals.*

Margaret Wheatley (2002) tells us that *nothing* exists in isolation and that relationships are central to everything in the universe. I am infinitely fortunate for the personal and professional relationships that enrich each day of my life.

My Home Community

In order to promote equity in "book acknowledgement recognition" I am intentionally listing names in reverse this time around: *Peyton*, *Colby*, and *Ike*, you are my center. Our home is my happy place, and there is nowhere I would rather be than in my PJs hanging with you. Our family is a hub of selfless and steadfast love, safety, and acceptance. You inspire me to try, fail, grow, succeed, and find joy in each of these endeavors. Michele, Tim, Liam, Linda, and Ron, the gratitude I feel for each of you is limitless. The support and encouragement you all provide is felt every day. Our seemingly complicated and strange family compilation is actually quite simple . . . in the most imperfectly beautiful of ways.

My Core Work Community at Gravity Goldberg, LLC

I get to be a part of a fabulous team: Gravity Goldberg, Patty McGee, Laura Sarsten, Sarah Fiedeldey, Heather Frank, Dana Clark, Julie McAuley, and Wendy Murray are truly "it." I am filled up and energized by what we have the opportunity to do together. I am tremendously grateful to be a part of our group that is committed to not only the heart, joy, and practices of learning but also each other's successes. On this team, meetings become celebrations, inspiration and ideas come to life, and sharing is second nature.

My Corwin Community

Tori Bachman, from the first time we talked, I felt connected. Your guidance, advice, feedback, counsel, and cheerleading are woven into every page of this book! One of the very best parts of this entire process has been having the opportunity to build a new friendship. Sharon Wu, you are a rock star. Thank you for your guidance each step of the way. Lisa Luedeke, the way you inspire, lead, and support is a model for us all. Thank you for inviting and welcoming me to the Corwin Literacy family. Much gratitude goes to Julie Nemer and Jane Martinez for making this entire process so smooth and fun! Candice Harman, your cover design reflects the joy and playfulness inherent in word exploring. Megan Markanich, Brian Grimm, Deena Meyer, and so many others—thank you, thank you, thank you.

My Extended Professional Community

The acts of generosity from educators who have welcomed me into schools and classrooms continue to be overwhelming. There is true reciprocity in the relationships developed with teachers, administrators, and students in the school communities I am lucky enough to partner with! To Viviana Tamas, Rebecca Johnson, Ellen Calamito, Dina Bolan, Katie McGrath, Nancy Costanzo, and Jessica Boyle, your altruism and willingness to help me bring the ideas of this book to life are so appreciated. The communities of Ward School, Jefferson School, Central School, Hamilton School, and West Brook School facilitated wonderful learning opportunities as ideas were tried out, learned from, and captured. To the many hardworking educators I partner with—in person and digitally—you inspire me, and I am incredibly grateful for all you do to make this world an even better place to learn, work, and live.

My Past—but Always With Me—School Communities

The schools where my mom dedicated her heart became early places of inspiration for me: Happy Time Cooperative Nursery School became my first "home away from home" and provided precious play-based memories that brought forth a love of school and learning. The active inclusion of families and connection with caregivers that were central to the core values of this school made a lasting impression. Everyone at Hewlett Elementary School, led by Dr. Mildred David, made me feel like a full-fledged member of a school community even when I was school-age myself! Here, I explored the role of teacher: helping in classrooms, partner reading with students, and discussing the latest and greatest books with teachers across all grades. The poetry collection housed at Hewlett Elementary that honors my mom's legacy and her love for words inspired me to explore and prioritize the inherent beauty and power of words myself.

When I later became legit in my teaching practice and certifications, Dresden Elementary in ATL showed me the excitement and joy of being a part of a multifaceted and multilingual classroom community. Here every perspective and idea I held was challenged and enriched. Deirdre Spollen-LaRaia and the entire Teaneck school community provided the collaboration and experiences that continued to broaden my educational and life perspectives. Everyone at Allendale schools embodies what it means to be a welcoming community and I continue to be inspired by the culture of continuous, ongoing professional learning found here. A special shout-out goes to the Hillside Language Arts Committee members and our exploration of ways to help students become more independent in word study. Our early notebook brainstorming helped inspire me to continue to grow those ideas and experiment with new ways to support learners of *all* ages!

Thank you to the students, colleagues, and families in each of these communities . . . for helping me see and understand what it means to be an educator.

I look forward to creating new connections and continuing to learn from logophiles near and far:

Twitter: @PamKou

Publisher's Acknowledgments

Corwin gratefully acknowledges the contributions of the following reviewers:

Nancy Akhavan
Associate Professor
Fresno State University
Fresno, CA

Melissa Black
Associate Dean, Second-Grade Teacher
Harlem Village Academy and Two
 Rivers Elementary School
Washington, DC

Leslie Blauman
Teacher, Author, Consultant
Cherry Creek School District
Centennial, CO

Helen S. Comba
Consultant
Rutgers University Center for Literacy
 Development
Westfield, NJ

Viviana Tamas
Reading Teacher, Literacy Coach
William B. Ward Elementary School
New Rochelle, NY

Introduction

Dear Teachers,

Thank you for being a part of our incredible community of educators. Our work is not only important but essential. I stand in awe of my peers and the ideas, passion, and dedication brought to classrooms each day. I am inspired to be a part of a larger, global community of educators who dedicate themselves to making a real difference and creating a future filled with promise and possibility. I see and recognize your thoughtful approach to teaching and learning.

You do an incredible amount to support the students you learn beside. I know the time you put in before and after each school day. I admire your professionalism, expertise, and constant interest in growing. I understand your desire for guidance, ideas, and conversation—not a script—to jump-start and propel classroom learning. I hear you when you say that there is more you could do and would want to do—if you had the time and resources. This book is here to lend a hand. Across these pages, you will find resources to help you implement a stepped-up approach to word learning. Cover to cover, you will find materials that support thoughtful decision making and instructional choices. In the pages to come, you will find tools to help students drive their own learning and create their own successes. As a result, your time in the classroom will not be spent intervening to provide reminders and redirection. Instead, you will be freed up to spend those precious minutes providing meaningful feedback and modeling next steps. I hope after reading about best practices in *Word Study That Sticks* that you find these additional go-to resources help you create, customize, and carry out a more playful, collaborative, and inquiry-driven approach to word study.

Enjoy the active exploration of words with classroom learners! Let me know how it goes!

With great respect and admiration,
Pamela Koutrakos

PART I

Launching Curious, Creative Word Study

CHAPTER ONE

Building Vision for Word Learning

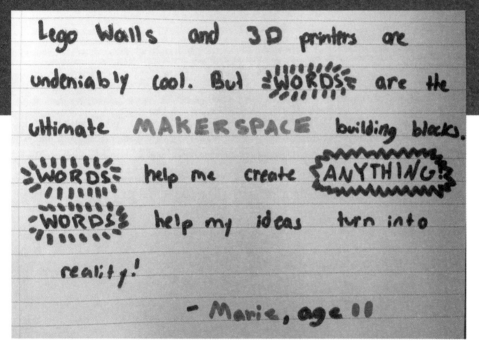

Lego Walls and 3D printers are undeniably cool. But WORDS are the ultimate MAKERSPACE building blocks. WORDS help me create ANYTHING! WORDS help my ideas turn into reality!

— Marie, age 11

When we set up rich opportunities for word exploring and support student independence, students start to feel differently about words.

Word study instruction embedded in best practices and relevant for students today? It does exist! We've learned that traditional approaches (the isolated spelling lists and spoon-fed vocabulary definitions, and rote drills of yesteryear) don't help learners progress. They don't stick. They don't elicit collaboration, deep inquiry, engaging conversation, or a playful stance. Now is the time for word study routines that are collaborative, curiosity-driven, and designed for learners to take to the next level. With *Word Study That Sticks* (Koutrakos, 2018), and this companion book, I set out to prove that you *can* have your cake and eat it too. We *can* support students' developing language skills each day with rigor and joy!

- Step 1: Learn about the research, ideas, and approach to this stepped-up approach to word study in *Word Study That Sticks*.
- Step 2: Use this book, *The Word Study That Sticks Companion*, to clear the path, pave the way, and help you put this approach into practice!

Get ready, get set, now is the time to GO.

Teaching and Tools Make for a Purposeful Partnership

Teaching tools will not be the answer to every problem you face in your classroom, nor will they all by themselves create rigor and independence just by being in your students' hands. You will also need good teaching practices, a strong curriculum, and solid relationships with your kids. But . . . teaching tools are powerful assistants along the way. (Roberts & Beattie Roberts, 2016, p. 5)

Here is a not-so-secret secret: Most programs don't support meaningful, personalized, authentically engaging learning. Tools alone also won't do the trick. *You* are the expert on the students you observe, talk with, laugh with, and learn alongside. Colorful, boxed materials and cutesy, downloadable "stuff" could never replace you or your expertise. Teaching and learning are built upon connection, relationships, and responsiveness. Working alongside students takes tremendous patience, creativity, experimentation, and flexibility. It is our practiced skill set, commitment to continual professional growth, and knowledge of each unique group of learners that guide strong teaching and responsive decision making.

This companion text contains a plethora of resources to support the stepped-up approach to word learning presented in *Word Study That Sticks*. But please remember that tools alone are unable to provide a complete picture of what word learning looks like, sounds like, and feels like. Perhaps most important, resources (even those of high quality) do not share the complete "why" teachers crave to back up their instructional decisions and practices. As Kate and Maggie Beattie Roberts share in the quote above, tools are there to assist. **When used in conjunction with the strong instruction outlined in *Word Study That Sticks*, these resources will amplify student learning and increase independence and success**.

To that end, in *this* book, you will find the following:

- Advice to make rolling out word study more successful than you had originally hoped
- Resources to greatly minimize the time you spend preparing, creating, and revamping
- Tools that will help students empower themselves and create more of their own successes

Multifaceted Word Study

Many people think of word study as spelling. Although spelling plays a critical role in word study, this view ignores the bigger picture and important factors such as the role of orthographic knowledge in reading and writing, the importance of oral language and vocabulary knowledge for reading and writing, and the interrelatedness of reading and writing. (Ganske, 2014, p. 4)

Word study is not just one thing. The study of words includes nurturing phonemic awareness, building a strong phonics foundation, studying word parts and patterns, and studying actual words. I believe that anything learned in isolation stays there. As such, for word study to stick, we need to integrate different facets of word study into our instruction. Furthermore, we also need to study words throughout the day, not just in a tiny window of our day labeled *word study*.

Vocabulary building is a key component to word study. Students need a strong handle on the meaning of words (including lesser-known definitions), contexts for using

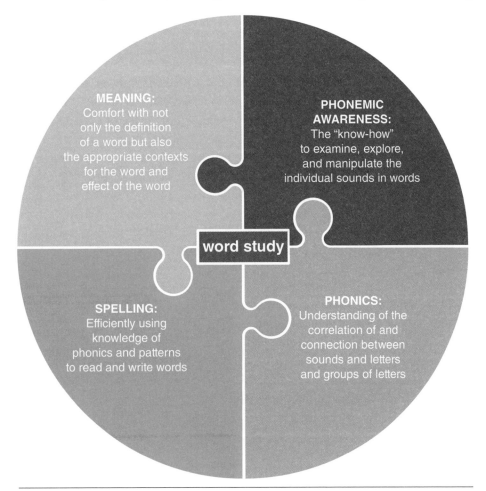

MEANING:
Comfort with not only the definition of a word but also the appropriate contexts for the word and effect of the word

PHONEMIC AWARENESS:
The "know-how" to examine, explore, and manipulate the individual sounds in words

word study

SPELLING:
Efficiently using knowledge of phonics and patterns to read and write words

PHONICS:
Understanding of the correlation of and connection between sounds and letters and groups of letters

Each facet of word study is essential and, furthermore, interrelated.

Source: Koutrakos, P. (2018). Word Study That Sticks. Thousand Oaks, CA: Corwin.

words, and opportunities to use words (and their knowledge of how words work) in authentic conversation, reading, and writing. This is as much a part of word study as studying how words look and sound and the why behind these visual and auditory features.

However, perhaps more than anything else, a truly student-centered approach to word study most emphasizes teaching the mindset, habits, and behaviors of one who is curious about and interested in discovering more and more about words. This is what's laid out in *Word Study That Sticks*—structures, lessons, and routines that promote inquiry-based, joyful word learning.

Organizing Our Time: Creating a Cycle of Word Learning

A1: Many Ts say time is the challenge, but if we view our schedule by the week rather than just day . . . there is always time. #G2Great. (Howard, 2018)

Teachers and schools have made the thoughtful choice to move away from one size fits all instruction. However, even when we trust and believe in this approach to teaching, it can feel overwhelming to organize our time and provide equitable support to all classroom learners. In word study, as we plan to meet with small groups of learners, it is helpful to think in cycles as opposed to a daily or even a Monday through Friday schedule. Cycles help us organize our time with greater efficiency and less stress. By using a cycle model (like those shown below), teachers are freed up to meet with different learners on different days. As a result, all learners get equal billing in the classroom. Learners receive appropriate and meaningful instruction. Learners grow and progress. *And* learners experience greater success. When we make the time to observe what is happening in classrooms, listen to, and meet with students, we become truly student-centered in our approach. Cycles help us make this all happen!

I have often found having a "mentor text" to lean on helps me feel ready and inspired to consider how a new practice might look. Building my vision of how others have done this work enables me to feel more prepared and ready to start. To that end, I have included three different examples of cycles I have used in word study at different points in my career. I invite you to look over these mentor texts. Consider your style of teaching and the personalities and next steps of the group of learners you currently work with. Then, tweak and twist the following starting suggestions.

PRIMARY

	Day 1	Day 2	Day 3	Day 4	Day 5
Routine	Meaning intro	Meaning practice center	Pattern intro Pattern practice	Pattern practice: Fluency center	Phonemic awareness and phonics center

ELEMENTARY

	Day 1	Day 2	Day 3	Day 4	Day 5	Day 6
Routine	Meaning intro	Meaning practice	Pattern intro Pattern practice	Pattern practice	Pattern practice with emphasis on fluency	Extra phonemic awareness and phonics routine

UPPER-ELEMENTARY AND MIDDLE GRADES

	Day 1	Day 2	Day 3	Day 4	Day 5	Day 6	Day 7
Routine	Meaning intro	Meaning practice	Pattern intro Pattern practice	Pattern practice with emphasis on fluency	Additional meaning, spelling, or hybrid practice	Transfer work	Assess and/ or reflect

Source: Koutrakos, P. (2018). Word Study That Sticks. *Thousand Oaks, CA: Corwin.*

Schmoker (2001) offers poignant words of advice in his article "The Crayola Curriculum." He reminds us that the reality is that many classrooms have way too much stuff taking the place of meaningful literate activities. Often, the problem is not how much time we have but we how we spend that time. When more time is not possible, we have two choices: Wish and hope . . . or make a new choice. Worksheets and word search puzzles take up precious minutes that can be spent engaging in more dynamic word-centered practices. We can always rethink the status quo and make a different choice about what stays and what goes. Looking for a win-win scenario? These kinds of choices about how we spend our classroom time often mean a whole lot less "correcting" done during prep periods and more in-the-moment feedback that makes a real difference to learners.

Find It

Several additional examples of five-, six-, and seven-day cycles across all grade levels are included in *Word Study That Sticks.* Check out both Chapter 2 and Appendix E for even more ideas!

Minichart Essentials

No quick fix exists. Worksheets and workbooks aren't a necessary evil. We don't need pages of fill-in-the-blank exercises designed to cram language into a tidy black-and-white package tied up with a chevron bow. (Anderson & LaRocca, 2018, p. 2)

This book contains a variety of helpful tools and resources (the antidote to worksheets and workbooks) to bring about greater independence and success in word study. A core feature of this book is the over 100 minicharts. A *minichart* is a student-friendly reminder of the why, what, and how of a word study routine. A *word study routine* is a practice students use regularly in word study. Routines are how students explore the why, what, and how of letters, sounds, patterns, and words: playfully making sense of and deepening their ideas about words. **The routines suggested and supported in this text can be used with *any* set of words, as they transcend any one pattern, program, philosophy, or approach to word study.** By infusing these routines into classroom practice, teachers can start up or step up their approach to word study, feeling confident their instruction reflects research-based best practices. Essentially, here is how it goes:

1. The teacher introduces a new routine (way to actively study words) to the class or a small group of learners.

2. The teacher models *how* to do the routine.

3. The students practice carrying out the routine with teacher support.

4. The class reflects on their interest in and understanding of the routine.

5. The teacher provides a minichart (a student-friendly reminder of how to do the routine) for each student, and this chart gets glued into a student's word study notebook (or added to a digital notebook).

6. In the future, whenever a student chooses to use a specific routine to explore words, they can look back to the minichart to see what it is, what materials are needed, how to do it, and even "how it looks."

It is quite simple: By using the process of gradual release (I GO, WE GO, YOU GO), students become confident in their daily word study practice. Because students feel comfortable using taught routines, their competence also increases. If, at any point, the student wavers in their confidence or even "forgets" how to do a routine (we know this happens to every student at one time or another), they have these mini-chart resources to lean on. As a result, instead of coming to us, students get *themselves* unstuck. The students feel proud of their independence and success. And, our teaching time becomes freed up. Instead of managing materials and reteaching the same thing time and again, we can instead provide meaningful feedback to students to help them take next steps. Minicharts help us feel prepared to begin and ready to trust that students will become more independent and successful.

Getting Started: A Successful Launch for a Year of Word Learning

Today, we are a whole lot smarter about classroom design, learning styles, and student preferences. We know our classrooms need to be arranged in ways that make a variety of whole-class, small-group, partner, and individual work a natural and manageable part of the day. We know kids need chances to connect and interact easily and frequently. . . . (Yates, 2015, p. 13)

Very often, the toughest and most exhausting part of the school year is setting up the structures and routines for a year of productive learning. Explicit instruction in "the getting things going" is essential and yet is usually not taught in college or included in district curriculum. In *Word Study That Sticks*, I outlined a why, what, when, and how of getting word study up and running in kindergarten through Grade 6 classrooms. It goes something like this: Before the school year even begins, teachers look at their schedules and carve out the actual space for word learning. Next come gathering, creating, or finding ways to purchase needed materials. Together, teachers and students ponder and co-create a plan for facilitating student ownership of getting, respectfully using, and cleaning up these materials. Once time, space, and materials are organized, it is time to officially launch word study.

The launch of word study happens in the first few weeks of school. During this time, the structures and inner workings of a fluent, independent, smooth-running word study classroom are taught. The core baseline routines that students can use to study words are practiced. These early routines incorporate developmentally appropriate aspects of word study: phonemic awareness, phonics, spelling pattern work, and meaning work. Additionally, during these early weeks, there are prioritized lessons on talking with partners, setting up and organizing word study notebooks, reflecting, and staying accountable. In *Word Study That Sticks*, you will find lists, ideas, suggestions, tips, and the actual lessons to launch word study. It is here, in this companion book, that you will find ready-to-go tools students can use during and after this "whole-class launch" to keep themselves independent, accountable, and progressing all year long. In the chapters ahead, you'll gain access to materials that will help you take the first steps with confidence and keep your motivation and "I can do this" mindset high all year.

Building Repertoire: Active and Engaged Word Learning All Year

Talk to your students about the joy of being truly engaged. Differentiate between compliance, participation and collaboration, motivation, and engagement. Describe how all are important for learners but that, as a proportion of time, you would like them to spend

increasing periods of time engaged rather than in compliance as the school year goes on.
(Keene, 2018, p. 31)

As the year progresses, I recommend teaching students additional routines for exploring and studying words. After the launch is complete, students will be ready to dig in and expand their repertoire for studying words. These new routines can be taught whole class or small group. By peppering in new routines throughout the year, we sustain tried-and-true comfort with the original routines taught while also adding in a regular dose of new and fresh. This keeps word study from becoming mundane and keeps classroom word exploring active and exciting. This also nurtures the continued progress and growth of classroom learners.

Checking In: Noticing Growth and Maintaining Progress

If we truly believe a growth mindset is vital for children's positive growth and development, then we can't just teach about it, we also have to assess children across the curriculum with growth in mind. Assessment conversations that look at growth in learning are very different from those that look only at finished products. . . . A child can move across the continuum, and we as teachers can help her get there with helpful strategies and support. (Mraz, Porcelli, & Tyler, 2016, pp. 101–102)

What are the first words that come to mind when you hear "spelling test"? If your initial reaction brings grumbles or face contortions, then it might be a sign you recognize *how* we check in on student progress in word study needs a face-lift. Traditional spelling tests do let us know if a student (today . . . this minute) can spell a few identified words. However, these types of assessments are not reliable indicators of a student's understanding of why a word is spelled that way. They also do not prioritize the application of word knowledge: how students can use learned word parts to decode and encode infinite other words. Traditional spelling tests are often not even predictive of whether a student will remember how to spell that word on Monday morning!

As we help students expand their repertoire for studying words, we might also want to revamp how we, as educators, check in on that learning. In *Word Study That Sticks*, I introduced several different methods for goal setting, reflection, celebration, *and* assessment. In that core resource, the ins and outs of each assessment method are provided in detail. Often when our assessments become more of an "*un*assessment," we end up gleaning more useful information about what students have learned—and guidance for our next instructional steps. To get students more involved, this companion text includes minicharts for students to promote greater ownership of goal setting, reflection, celebration, and—yes—even assessment!

Partners demonstrate applying their gained word knowledge by first identifying pattern words in a text and then chorally reading that book with accuracy, fluency, and comprehension.

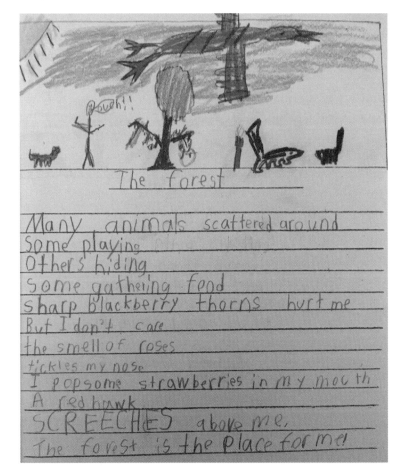

This student demonstrates gained word knowledge by using pattern words in his writing. After finishing a word study unit centered on inflectional endings, he worked to apply learning to his poetry writing.

How to Navigate This Book

I imagine readers might first quickly skim this book cover to cover to get the lay of the land but then use the included resources in bits and pieces, selecting the right parts at the right time. It is very likely that teachers will use many of the same resources year to year. However, in our effort to nurture the unique next steps of each special group of learners, responsive educators may also find that they end up using different tools to support different learners in different ways and different times—and that this looks different period to period and/or year to year. Here's the lowdown on what's included and how to easily and quickly find what you need.

WORD STUDY NOTEBOOKS AND CHOICE CHARTS

Chapter 2 provides a visual tour of the word study notebooks used in Grade 1 and up. Each notebook section is shown, and the purpose is explained. Additionally, you'll find ideas for digital word study notebooks and read advice for when and how to infuse digital tools into daily practices. Furthermore, you'll gain an introduction to kindergarten choice charts so even the youngest word explorers can feel ownership of their daily practices.

RESOURCES TO LIGHTEN THE LOAD

In Chapter 3, you will find plentiful resources to support robust word exploring. Whether your district has the minimal necessities or full-blown access to all the supplies and materials you could imagine (where do you work, by the way?), here is where you can find tools to crystalize priorities, organize instruction, and make student learning stickier. Checklists, look-fors, planning guides, and record-keeping forms are just a few of the many valuable tools found here.

MINICHARTS, MINICHARTS, AND MORE MINICHARTS

This text is heavily saturated with minicharts for a reason: Teachers love them, and students love them! It is a win-win situation.

There are five chapters dedicated to minicharts:

- Chapter 4: Meaning Routines

- Chapter 5: Phonemic Awareness and Phonics Routines

- Chapter 6: Spelling Pattern Routines

- Chapter 7: Habit and Hybrid Routines

- Chapter 8: Check-In and Assessment Routines

All these chapters contain minicharts that "summarize" routines in each area of word study. Each minichart starts with the why, briefly explaining the purpose and value of the routine. Then, the needed materials and the how of the routine are listed. The charts end with a visual example, tip, or reminder of what the routine looks like. Each chapter contains both primary-grade minicharts, which are appropriate for students in kindergarten through Grade 2, and upper-elementary minicharts, which are for students in Grades 3 through 6. The primary minicharts have icons that accompany steps and support learner understanding. The upper-elementary charts include the same basics but look a bit more sophisticated for older students. You will find that some routines overlap because there are both primary and upper-elementary versions. You will also find routines unique to each grade-level band. These reflect more developmentally appropriate practices appropriate for students in specific grades.

STRETCHING THE LEARNING EVEN FURTHER

We want to do all we can to support students and their growth. Partnering with care-givers is essential in making this happen. Chapter 9 offers tips, ideas, and resources to connect school to home. These tools help the important people in a child's life feel informed and included.

Additionally, Chapter 10 of this book is dedicated solely to the twenty lessons that introduce the twenty new bonus routines included in this book. These additional lessons build confidence and readiness to support all classroom learners. They also yield excitement about word study from the start of school through the end.

FINDING IT SNAPPY

This is the kind of professional text that makes us love and appreciate the table of contents and index. Looking for a new way to support students' vocabulary development? Peruse the options in the meaning chapter, and turn right to that page. Looking for playful ways to get kids hearing and noticing sounds in words? Check out the table of contents to find pages filled with minicharts that support phonemic awareness. It really is that simple!

FEATURE KEY

Recurring Feature	Purpose
Find It	Signals where to find an accompanying lesson or additional useful information in *Word Study That Sticks*
Bonus	Signals that an accompanying introductory lesson for this routine is available in Chapter 10 of this book
Tech Tip	Signals how to use this resource digitally and/or options to digitally enhance this practice
Word Wall	Signals that this routine can also be done with high-frequency words and word wall words
eTool	Signals that there are related downloadable and reproducible resources available on the companion website: resources.corwin.com/wstscompanion
Tying It Together	Synthesizes and summarizes information and ideas presented in the chapter

GETTING THE FULL PICTURE OF THE WHY, WHAT, AND HOW

REFER

Refer to *Word Study That Sticks* to build a vision for a more purposeful and productive approach to word study. You will find research, lessons, and ideas that reflect best practices in all facets of word study. In this companion book, you will find coordinated resources that support student success and independence in *all* aspects of word study.

USE

Use the table of contents to help you quickly and easily find resources that match learner readiness, interests, and passions. Use the recurring Find It and Bonus icons for guidance in where to find lesson details that accompany each included resource.

REMEMBER

Remember that tools are not intended to teach. As Kate and Maggie Beattie Roberts (2016) write in *DIY Literacy*, "Tools are not enough—we need to explicitly teach strategies, tricks, tips, and small steps to help students progress along a certain skill" (p. 20). The tools and resources in this book are intended to be used as *part* of a thoughtful, planned approach to instruction to help students become independent and successful word explorers.

CHAPTER TWO

Visual Tour of a Word Study Notebook and Kindergarten Choice Chart

My notebook is special. Although I don't use it all the time, the word wonder and collection section is my favorite. Some of the words I have collected so far include melancholy, superstitious, fastidious, and perseverate. Whenever I use one of my new words, People look at me like they are surprised and impressed.

In Chapter 1, we reviewed tips for using this book in conjunction with *Word Study That Sticks*. Now, we begin to pave the way to word study success by refining our vision of the methods, tools, and resources that help students become more independent in their daily practice. First, we take a walking tour of the word study notebooks described in *Word Study That Sticks*—with the goal of clarifying how these notebooks are set up and defining the purpose of each recommended section. Next, we delve into digital notebook options for teachers who have 1:1 classrooms. Finally, although many early childhood classrooms enjoy using meaningful word centers as an efficient management structure, kindergarten choice charts are introduced as a second option. I present each of these possibilities so that you can make thoughtful choices and decisions regarding the tools and methods that best align with the personalities and developmental readiness of the students with whom you work each day.

Word Study Notebooks

Reading notebooks are used as tools to deepen comprehension, not as assignments to prove to the teacher the students did the reading. Students choose when to write about a book and how to write about a book. . . . This is all modeled by Pam first so students understand how to make these choices. (Goldberg, 2016, p. 65)

Above, Gravity Goldberg describes the purpose and "nonnegotiables" of reading notebooks. The same can be said of word study notebooks. Our notebooks hold many of our word quests! I highly recommend that teachers create word study notebooks alongside students, as it helps us model the why, what, and how of notebooks in a truly authentic way. A notebook helps us not only talk the talk but also walk the walk of someone who explores, studies, and collects words. Furthermore, students understand that everyone in the classroom (teacher included) is part of the learning community. Students are not told to do "assignments." Instead, everyone partakes in word exploring in meaningful and rich ways. Likewise, as we grow our own notebooks, they also become coveted teaching tools that can be used as we model and provide feedback.

I recommend four sections for word study notebooks:

1. *Resources:* This section holds routine minicharts and first samples of each word study routine.

2. *Routines:* This is the largest section of the word study notebook. Students record any written work in this section of the word study notebook.

3. *Word Wonders and Collections:* This small section makes the space for students not only to collect and pursue investigations about their "word wonders" but also provides prioritized space for collecting new, unusual, and exciting words students collect throughout their explorations.

4. *Goals and Reflections:* This last section is dedicated to goal setting, reflection, and celebration. Students work toward personalized goals, reflect on progress toward goals, and celebrate these metacognitive endeavors.

Check out the visual tour of a couple of my word study notebooks shown in the photos that follow:

Just like we might personalize reading and writing notebooks, we can also take the time to personalize our word study notebooks.

I often use quotes about words, favorite quotes from books, and even some of my own favorite words to personalize my word study notebooks.

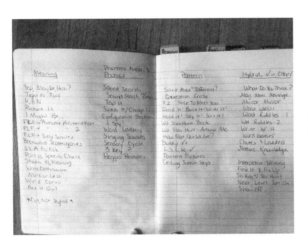

Students can keep a running list of all word study routines taught (categorized by type of routine).

Students keep a copy of their word study schedule close by in their notebooks. Having the schedule available at all times helps students work independently and stay accountable. Word study schedules sometimes change. Whenever we make a change to the schedule, I provide a new schedule to students. Reproducible cycle templates are available online at **resources.corwin.com/wstscompanion**.

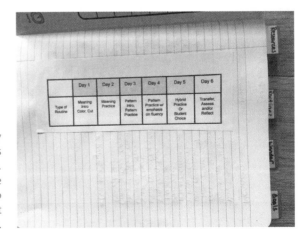

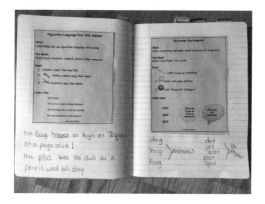
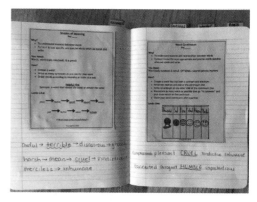

The first fifteen to twenty-five pages of the notebook are dedicated to resources. This is a key part in building independence in daily practice and lasting success. In this section, we glue in the minichart reminders of why we engage in a specific routine, what we need, and how we do it. I like to copy each type of minichart onto colored paper to help students choose the correct type of routine at the correct time. As shown here, the meaning routines are copied onto pink paper. The pink paper shows that these are meaning routines students can choose on "meaning" days of the word study cycle.

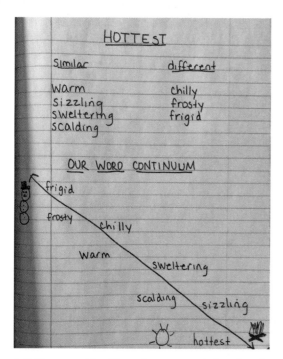
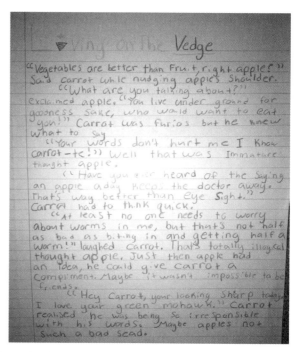

Left: The second (and largest) recommended section of a word study notebook contains routines. This is where students jot written routines. Note: Not all routines have a writing component, but if they do, the work goes in this section of a word study notebook. Shown here is a page from the Routines section of my teacher notebook. This work sample was created in the moment during small-group instruction. Whenever possible, I try to build my notebook while working with students. This provides the students vision for what it looks like to complete a routine. It also helps me practice "teacher self-care"—by building entries during instruction, I protect a bit more of my free time outside of work!

Right: Here is a student work sample. This playful fourth grader created a fantasy story (the characters are talking vegetables) using word study pattern words. This work was included in the Routines section of their word study notebook.

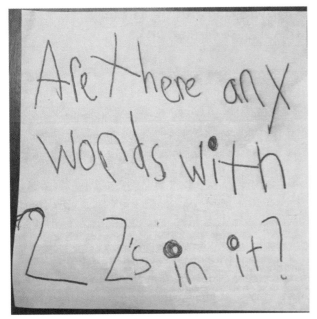

Wondering is essential. I recommend including a small section with word wonders and collections as notebooks are set up. On these five to eight pages, students can collect their wonders about words (shown here on a sticky note). These are a great source for class, small-group, partner, and individual inquiry investigations.

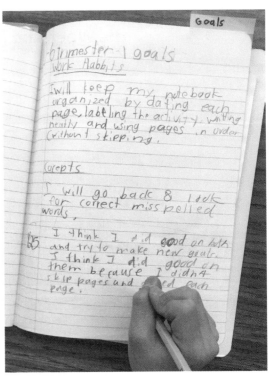

The last section of a word study notebook is dedicated to goal setting, reflection, and celebration. Often, students use checklists to help them set work habits and concepts goals.

Students use their notebook as a tool for thinking, talking, experimenting, discovering, reflecting, and sharing.

Balanced Use of Technology: Thinking Through the When and Why of Digital Notebooks

Classroom practice that empowers students is deliberate, intentional, and often filled with choices that were made after the thoughtful consideration of who the students are, their learning goals, and the methods [that] are best suited for these specific students at this specific time. When you invite students to co-create the environment in your classroom that values independent thinkers and problem solvers, there are clear benefits for both you and your students. (Rami, 2014, p. 78)

I trust we all understand and agree that technological proficiency is an integral part of the profile of a 21st century learner. I work actively and diligently to embed and integrate technology in thoughtful and meaningful ways to enhance learning. That said, just because something *could* be done with technology does not mean it *should* or *must* be done with technology. Tech gurus and educational mentors like Meenoo Rami (quoted above) advocate for this kind of thoughtful contemplation around classroom use of technology. The benefits of purposeful technology integration are very clear. Here are just a few:

- Diverse platforms—with a plethora of accessibility features—that encourage more inclusive collaboration and creation

- The capability to communicate with a wider audience

- Increased engagement for a subset of classroom learners

- Opportunities to share ideas using an ever-growing range of exciting formats

- Saving trees—less paper being used and copied on a daily basis

We also know that youngsters are spending more and more time in front of a screen every day, and this may yield problematic results. This leaves caregivers and educators wondering about how to balance classroom practice and how to be mindful of recreational screen time. Yalda et al. (2017) shared research on how too much screen time hinders school-age children's understanding of nonverbal emotional cues. Dunckley (2017) reports on "Electronic Screen Syndrome," where a child's nervous system becomes overstimulated and hyperaroused from moderate yet regular screen time. According to her research, this results in the brain being in a chronic state of stress that essentially short-circuits the frontal lobe, which regulates emotions and stress levels. And there is research that shows that when school-age children spend seven or more hours a week on computers or mobile devices, it may triple their risk of myopia (CBS News, 2017). Moreover, recent research, like that of Mueller and Oppenheimer (2014), shares the benefits of note-taking using pen and paper as opposed to a digital device and Baron (2016) of reading from a "hard copy." These include better concentration, decreased distraction, deeper processing, and—in many studies—even better performance on "conceptual" types of test questions.

Furthermore, although digital reading and note-taking save trees, the environmental benefits may be considered a wash when we consider the resources needed to man-ufacture, run, and recycle digital products. As thoughtful consumers of research, we are empowered when we learn more about the benefits *and* drawbacks, so we gain a wider perspective and feel confident in the subsequent decisions we make. As with most things in life, balance is key.

It is very possible to wholeheartedly embrace technology in the classroom; inte-grate it in meaningful ways; and teach students to make choices about where, when, and how to integrate technology. We want school screen time to be engag-ing and purposeful—and for digital devices to represent one of the *many* types of tools students might choose to use to solve problems, think more about wonders, and present ideas—without taking the place of face-to-face conversations for a significant amount of the school day. As Rami writes, we can invite students to co-create their environment, provide a balanced range of opportunities, and have ownership of many of these choices—including when and how to use technology. Dr. Stephanie Affinito (2018), professor and author of a professional text on inte-grating technology in professional learning, summed it up perfectly in a recent Twitter chat:

Dr. Stephanie Affinito
@AffinitoLit

Follow

A7: Privilege pedagogy over technology. We must model how and when to use technology to support learning, as well as how and when to choose not to use it as well. We need to teach students how to make intentional decisions behind their screen time and technology use. #ILAchat

All that said, we may be working toward equity in access, but we are not yet there. I have worked in schools that have abundant access to the latest and greatest in technology and other schools where the technology available was not too different from what was present back when I was in school! Regardless of the scenario in your district, there are infinite opportunities to incorporate what's available in balanced, meaningful, and purposeful ways during word study.

When choosing apps, websites, programs, and tools for technological infusion, it is helpful to consider the following:

- Amount of personal information required

- Effectiveness

- Support and improvement of instruction and learning

- Cost

- Ease of use and accessibility for all classroom learners

- Ability to work on different platforms

Essentially, we want to spend time asking ourselves the following: Is the privacy of students protected? Will this *better* enable students to reach goals? Does this provide equitable access for *all* learners? Is it in the budget? Is it "worth" our precious learning time? Can students use this tool on a variety of types of devices and from a variety of locations?

By taking the time to think through our choices, instruction and learning remain the focus. When we first consider student goals and then match these anticipated outcomes to technology, technology use remains purposeful and intentional.

Tech Tip

Some classrooms prefer to set up digital notebooks or use a "hybrid approach" to notebook work. Here are some screenshots of how teachers have used digital platforms to house word study materials.

4K RESOURCES: Meaning Routines

Shades of Meaning
Day ____

Why?
- To understand nuances between words
- To learn to use specific and precise words when we speak and write

You Need:
- Words
- Word study notebook
- Pencil

How?
- Choose a word.
- Write as many synonyms as you can for that word.
- Order words according to intensity (a little to a lot).
- *Hint:* A synonym is a word that means the same or almost the same.

Looks Like:

press → flatten → squish → squash → smash
yell ——— holler ——— shout ——— scream

*Word study words are underlined.

Word Continuum
Day____

Why?
- To understand nuances and relationships between words
- To learn to use the most appropriate and precise words possible when we speak and write

You Need:
- Word study notebook
- Pencil
- *Optional:* Colored pencils/markers

How?
- Choose a word that has both a synonym and antonym.
- Write the word on one side of the continuum line.
- Write an antonym on the other side of the continuum line.
- Brainstorm as many words as possible that go "in between" and plot those words on the continuum.
- Share your word continuums with a partner.

Looks Like:

Here is an example of how one class kept digital routine minicharts. This slide presentation was posted for all class members and acted as a shared Resources notebook section. All students, interventionists, and caregivers could access the minicharts for taught routines whenever and wherever needed.

PAIGE'S WORD STUDY NOTEBOOK
DATE: 10/4   PATTERN: -EL, -LE, -AL

table	kettle	recycle	triple
			X3
buckle	pedal	squirrel	vowel
			a e i o u (y w)

Here, we see Paige's digital version of Picture It, which uses free-for-use clip art images. In this class, students use options within the G Suite to create and maintain their digital word study notebooks. These digital notebooks can be shared with partners, group members, and/or teachers. They can also be submitted online. Teachers can provide digital feedback in addition to in-person, face-to-face feedback. No more bringing home a heavy bag of student notebooks!

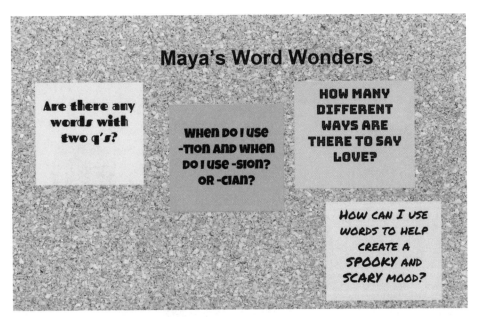

Maya's Word Wonders

Are there any words with two q's?

WHEN DO I USE -TION AND WHEN DO I USE -SION? OR -CIAN?

HOW MANY DIFFERENT WAYS ARE THERE TO SAY LOVE?

HOW CAN I USE WORDS TO HELP CREATE A SPOOKY AND SCARY MOOD?

Students can create personal word wonder boards or the class can share a digital "wonder wall" using online platforms such as Padlet. Here, we see Maya's wonders about words. Some of these questions have quick answers; some require more research and investigation. These wonders present options for student-driven inquiry.

Jahquan's Trimester 2 Goals

CONCEPT GOAL:
I want to work on using my word learning to help me spell pattern words correctly in math, social studies, and science.
I am now good at remembering to do this when I write. But in other subjects, I usually rush or forget.

HABIT GOAL:
I plan to work on taking the lead when I work with a group. I have a habit of letting other people do a lot of the work. My group is getting annoyed with me. I need to start to do my part. Mrs. K—can you help me with this? Any tips or ideas for an action plan?

Different classrooms use different options for online goal setting and reflection. Some teachers prefer students use an online document or notebook to record and reflect on goals. In other classrooms, students use blogging and vlogging platforms so there is added accountability and peer encouragement. Google Forms present another possibility that many teachers have found great success with. When using Google Forms, student responses and input can be viewed regularly and used formatively by the teacher.

Notebooks are helpful learning tools *and* helpful teaching tools. Here, I use my notebook to help me model during small-group instruction. The students in this sixth-grade class use digital word study notebooks. Even when classes use digital notebooks and platforms to house word work, teachers continue to meet with students in person.

NOTEBOOK KNOW-HOW

WHY?

Notebooks help students maintain independence (Resources section) and provide space for students to hold their work and ideas about word study.

WHAT?

Notebooks are thinking, learning, *and* teaching tools.

WHEN?

Students will personalize, set up, and start using their notebook in the launch to word study. Notebooks are used regularly across the year.

HOW?

Gather notebooks as well as tabs, dividers, and/or sticky notes to mark each section. Find clip art, words, and quotes to personalize the cover. Personalize notebooks. Begin filling up the Resources section each day during the word study launch.

Kindergarten Choice Charts

We need to look for, listen for, and feel the heartbeats in our students. That's where the energy is, for us and for them. (Graves, 2004, p. 90)

So much has been said about working from student strengths and passions. Everyone's favorite mentor, Donald Graves, reminded us of the vitality of learning that results from tuning into our students and building instruction from what we see in these young learners. Many will agree that kindergarteners are fans of and experts in play. As educators, we can capitalize on this asset and use it to drive learning. In *Purposeful Play* (Mraz, Porcelli, & Tyler, 2016), the ever-brilliant authors frame the way reading partners work together as "partner games." This tried-and-true best practice can be tweaked, twisted, and then used in word study!

In *Word Study That Sticks*, I recommend that teachers begin using notebooks in first grade. In kindergarten, word exploring sometimes happens in meaningful centers driven by the routines outlined in both *Word Study That Sticks* and this text. Choice charts can be used in conjunction with centers or as a stand-alone practice. Choice charts help students make choices about which word study routines they want to try each day. Because we have classrooms of introverts and extroverts—and we want to nurture and nudge all kinds of dispositions—these word study choice charts offer options for quiet, individual practice and more collaborative routines. In word study, learners have regular opportunities for quiet time that stirs the imagination and time to be a part of more chatty and collaborative think tanks.

Kindergarteners engage in many of the same kinds of word study routines as other elementary students. The facing page shows a small selection of student favorites.

Choice chart options are word study routines, here presented as "word games." Kindergarteners use their choice charts to stay independent and become successful! Word study is playful in nature, and the word games provided as choice chart options help students to feel excited to explore and learn about letters, sounds, and words.

To help you better visualize and understand how choice charts work, look through the photos on pages 30–31. Please notice that there is not one "perfect" way for these choice charts to look or be used. These examples intend to highlight the different ways choice charts have been customized to fit classroom learners.

Suggestions for Independent Choice Chart Routines

Find and Fix Up	Students look back for specific letters and words in their writing—and "fix up" any errors using their new learning.
Hunt	Students look for letters and words in environmental print and class texts.
I Spy!	Students look around them for specific letters and words.
Picture It	Students create a sketch that shows the meaning of a word.
Read It! Build It! Write It!	Students use letter manipulatives to build words.
Reggio Routines	Students engage in constructivist, experiential letter and word learning consistent with the Reggio Emilia process.
Sound Search	Students segment a word (separate and isolate each sound in a word).
Tap It!	Students segment words and tap out each sound.
Word Webs	Students create a simple semantic map with each "bubble" showing their knowledge of the word.

Suggestions for Collaborative Choice Chart Routines

Act It Out	Students use their bodies to kinesthetically show their understanding of a word (charades).
Hold It, Say It, Sort It	Students hold different objects (one at a time), segment the sounds in the name of the object, and then sort the objects based on their starting or ending sounds.
Partner Prompting	Students check in with a partner to informally assess their knowledge of a word.
Sort It! Alike or Different?	Students sort and categorize picture, letter, or word cards.
Sound Search	Students segment a word (separate and isolate each sound in a word).
Sound Snapshot	Students use iPads and/or cameras to take photos of objects that start or end with specific letters or sounds.
Switch It, Change It	Students manipulate phonemes in familiar words to make new words.
We Spy	Students look around them for specific letters and words.
Word Games	Students play a simple word game together.

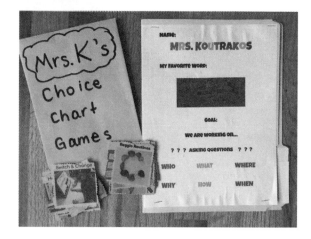

The front of a choice chart folder aims to keep class goals front and center! Goals and action plans are co-created by the class. When students appear ready, they can create partner goals.

Shown here are the covers of a student folder and a group folder.

Here are the "insides" of two of my own word study folders. On one side of the folder, choices for independent word study practices are displayed on the choice chart. On the other side, choices for partner and small group are displayed. In this model, Velcro helps choices "stay put" on the folder. Between uses, choice chart "game cards" are stored in envelopes.

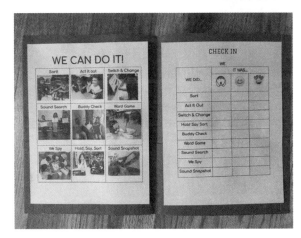

The I Can Do It! side of a choice chart folder helps students choose routines they want to do independently. Just because students are quiet and working on their own does not mean the practice is not playful. In this model, choice chart options are inserted into a clear sheet protector, and students use dry erase markers to check off which routines they have completed.

The We Can Do It! side of a choice chart folder provides support for partners in making fair and *fun* decisions about how they will spend collaborative word study time. When working together, partners take turns choosing which word games they will play together.

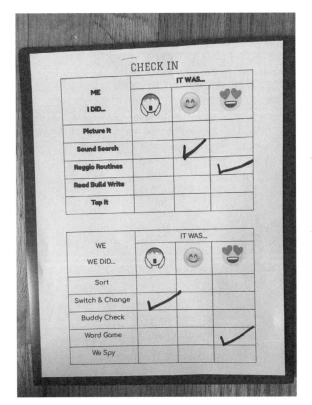

The choice checklist promotes reflection and self-accountability. Here, students check off the routines they tried and how they went. Teachers can use the checklist to kick off conferring conversations. These checklists are also used as tools to model and encourage whole-class reflection. Teachers may provide a new checklist each word study cycle or laminate a checklist to be used time and time again.

eTool *Reproducible choice chart tables can be found on the companion website. Additionally, separated, printable choice chart icons can be found on the companion website. A larger teacher set ("pocket chart"-sized versions) of each of the choice chart options can also be found online:* **resources.corwin.com/wstscompanion.**

TAKING CHARGE OF CHOICES

WHY?

Even the youngest of learners wants (and is capable of) choice in practice. Making thoughtful choices is not only empowering but it also elicits engagement and is a critical life skill.

WHAT?

Choice charts are a developmentally appropriate alternative to word study notebooks. They guide the time and practices students use to study words on a daily basis.

WHEN?

Create choice charts for yourself and students. Use a class choice chart to model and then collaboratively set goals, make choices about daily practices, and check in to reflect on choices. Later, as students become ready, they will use their own folders to stay independent, engaged, and accountable.

HOW?

All of us are better together! Have a choice chart setup party. Collaborate with grade-level colleagues. Chat and connect while you work. Use the templates provided in Chapter 3 and online to make this task easier and snappier. If you are looking to earn extra credit in personalization and creativity, you might consider using the provided icons as a reference—and then take similar photos of the students *you* work with. These more personalized photos could also serve as choice chart icons.

NOTEBOOKS AND CHOICE CHARTS IN ACTION

Notebooks are safe spaces for students to learn about words.

Photo by Linda Day

Word study notebooks are teaching tools *and* learning tools.

Photo by Linda Day

Choice charts, like centers, help students become independent during word study.

Choice charts help students feel in charge of their learning.

A kindergartener chose Picture It to practice -*at* family words.

A kindergartener chose Find and Fix Up to transfer his recent word study learning to writing.

CHAPTER THREE

Resources to Lighten the Load

Checklists and other tools help us feel in control of our learning. When we set goals we care about, working toward them doesn't even seem like work. Everytime we reflect, it feels like a celebration. I appreciate that our teacher supports us and the goals we feel are most important.

Instruction is successful when it is responsive, purposeful, and keeps students front and center. The tools in this full-bodied chapter aspire to help you do this—with confidence and efficiency. There are a plethora of tools, templates, and resources ahead to help you feel prepared and ready to start up and step up high-impact word learning all year long.

First, I provide tools to walk you through setting up a safe and comfortable learning space and creating word study cycle schedules.

Next, I share a multitude of options for looking at both formal and informal assessment. These tools help streamline and simplify a process many feel is cumbersome and ineffective. There are also planning and feedback forms to help you turn these noticings into teaching.

Last, you will find tools to foster independence and help students reflect on progress toward set goals and self-assess their own learning.

Look through the samples ahead and check out the aligned templates online. I do not anticipate that anyone will want to use all these tools, but I do know we all like having options! Choose to try the tools that you believe have the greatest purpose and value. And know that when one tool falls flat or does not seem to fit you or your priorities, there are numerous other possibilities available. If I was to provide any unsolicited advice it would be this: Think of this part of the process as play. Experiment, tinker, and try out different ways to go about this important work with the goal of finding a method that makes the most sense for you.

Creating Inviting Learning Spaces

As naturally curious creatures, they will find what they are looking for, and I don't have to stop what I'm doing to direct them. The responsibility to take initiative is back where it belongs: on the students. They accept this responsibility gladly. . . . And since students aren't waiting on me to find or pass out supplies, independent and group work is more productive and efficient. (Kirr, 2017, p. 41)

I understand the joy of setting up a classroom. Even now, as I write this book, I *long* for the days when I went to school well before the year officially began to start setting up the space. The idea of a fresh start, new supplies, and materials organized like they are ready for a photo shoot (aka before they are actually used) has always been super exciting! That said, just like it is impossible to know exactly what words and patterns we might teach before meeting a group of learners, it is just as impossible to fully set up a space before meeting those learners. Collaborative communities are fostered when there is discussion and some shared decision making around what can be used, where those things go, and where someone can work. Our experience in the classroom helps us outline a space . . . considering traffic patterns, sight lines, and general accessibility. But a space can't be truly and fully created until everyone is present! Classroom spaces will likely evolve and change over time—sometimes in unpredictable ways. This is likely why, while in the classroom full time, I didn't only rearrange seating . . . I often observed classroom happenings, asked for student input, and overhauled classroom setups multiple times throughout the year. Just when I thought I had it just right, the students would surprise me. Attraction to different materials change, seating preferences change, needed points of access change, favored spots to wonder and connect with others change, and where and how I choose to support learners often change too. Included in the upcoming pages are checklists to help create and sustain student-run classroom spaces as well as photos that show possibilities for evolving and flexible classroom spaces.

Find It

Find blueprints of different classroom setups in Chapter 2 of *Word Study That Sticks*. In this same chapter, you will also find "shopping lists" for needed essentials through dreamworld wants. Additionally, there are tips and photographs related to storage of supplies and materials.

Create the Space Checklists

Points to Consider Before the Year Starts:

✓ Class meeting area

✓ Small-group and partner meeting areas (different kinds of spaces to collaborate)

✓ Independent work areas

✓ Comfortable, relaxing workspaces

✓ Adequate lighting

✓ Low shelves to store materials safely

✓ Clear spaces that will display student wondering, thinking, and work (in progress and celebrated)

✓ Clear sight lines to/from different areas of classroom

✓ Safe "traffic pattern" and cleared walkway to exit(s)

✓ Accessibility to different classroom spaces

✓ Books, books, and more books—*representative* books and texts across genres!

✓ Purchased, collected, or created "essentials" for word study (the basics: folders, notebooks, writing materials, word building manipulatives, scissors, glue sticks . . .)

Wonders Once the Year Is in Full Swing:

✓ Is there anything in the classroom environment preventing students from working to their capabilities?

✓ What parts of the classroom most encourage students to work toward and exceed set goals?

✓ Does the class meeting area provide adequate space for all class members?

✓ Do the planned spaces invite collaborating in different types of ways? Do students gravitate to certain areas more than others? Have learners found or created any of their own meeting spaces?

✓ Are students able to stay on task and focused when working independently?

✓ Does there seem to be relaxed breathing room or do we feel packed in?

✓ Do students have a strong understanding of where supplies go and how they are safely stored?

✓ Are students often waiting in lines and clusters to get and put away materials?

✓ Are there materials that students often ask for assistance in retrieving or cleaning up?

✓ Are there materials that are used much more than others? Much less?

✓ Are students navigating supplies and spaces with independence?

✓ Are there spaces that encourage a productive buzz and others that offer peaceful quiet?

✓ Am I able to see what's happening all around the room as I travel to meet with different learners?

✓ What additional choices and responsibilities are students showing a readiness to take on?

(Continued)

(Continued)

Questions to Ask Students:

✓ How could our classroom space become to feel more inviting?

✓ How could our classroom space become a hub of productivity?

✓ Do you feel a part of the classroom and the way it runs?

✓ Where do you most like to work alone? With a partner? In groups?

✓ How could we manage materials more easily?

✓ Are there supplies that are difficult for you to get or put away?

✓ How could we better utilize different areas of the classroom?

✓ What big ideas do you have about changes we could make to our classroom space?

Flexible seating options help students create—and continuously recreate—the learning spaces that match their goals.

Classroom setups are constantly evolving: the common denominator is that we now co-create learning spaces with a wide variety of students and learning processes front and center in our minds.

Setting Up Schedules That Encourage Independence

We have so much time and so little to do. Strike that, reverse it.

—*Willy Wonka and the Chocolate Factory* (Stuart, 1971)

Schedules help us make sense of time and prioritize what is most important. Schedules ensure that we spend time where it matters most and where it will yield the greatest results. Many of us feel there is not enough time in the day, and this may be true. However, when we try to put too much learning into too little time, we work at a pace that can't be sustained long term—by the students or us. We all end up cranky, stressed, and anxious.

Thankfully, word study does not require a great deal of time, but it is crucial for word study to happen as consistently as possible. Create and try on a word study cycle with your students in mind. After the launch, reevaluate how the schedule is working for you and the students. Adjust as necessary—nothing is written in stone. Use the forthcoming examples of *student-friendly schedules* and the online *schedule templates* to help students build greater awareness of their choices in word study. This creates greater independence in carrying out daily practices. There are options included for five-, six-, and seven-day word study cycles. If using notebooks, students can glue a copy of the cycle schedule in their notebooks. For those using digital notebooks, the word study schedule can be posted on Google Classroom or the classroom website. Whether in a notebook or online, having the cycle schedule at their fingertips helps students work with greater independence.

Find It

In Chapter 2 of *Word Study That Sticks*, sample daily schedules are provided for primary, elementary, and middle-grade classrooms. You will also get information about how to schedule word study—whether you have five minutes a day or thirty minutes a day! Appendix E also provides several additional word study cycle "mentor texts" for primary, elementary, and middle-grade classrooms.

FIVE-DAY WORD STUDY CYCLE SAMPLES

As demonstrated here, students can fill in the routine "choices" that can be done each day of the cycle. As new routines are taught, students can add these additional choices to their schedules.

1	2	3	4	5
Meaning	Meaning	Pattern	Phonemic Awareness and Phonics	Hybrid

Day	1	2	3	4	5
Focus	Meaning	Meaning	Pattern	Phonemic Awareness and Phonics	Hybrid
Choices	Yep! Maybe …Huh?	Picture It More or Less? I Might…	Sort It! Alike or Different? Nice to Meet You!	Sound Search With Letters Tap It! Switch It, Change It	Word Webs Word Games Nature Knowledge

1	2	3	4	5
Meaning	Meaning	Pattern	Hybrid	Check-In

Day	1	2	3	4	5
Focus	Meaning	Meaning	Pattern	Hybrid	Check-In
Choices	None to Some Cut, Not Styled	Talkin' the Talk Word Family Trees Backward Scattergories	Guess the Pattern Now I Know!	Word Riddles Write With It Word Share	Find and Fix Up Show Off

eTool *Find reproducible word study cycle templates on the companion website:* **resources.corwin.com/wstscompanion**.

What Words Will We Use?
Matching Students to Words

We all know the feeling of teaching a lesson when the realization hits that this is the wrong work for the class. . . . To avoid this unfortunate mismatch, assess before a unit begins. Knowing what skills this year's class needs can supercharge the curriculum, aligning the teaching in class to the kids' needs. (Roberts, 2018, p. 36)

In your school, you may craft curriculum that's active, fluid, and constantly evolving. However, you may also be one of the many other professionals leaning on a district-approved resource—and then tweaking and/or refining daily implementation to respond to the unique areas of readiness shown by classroom learners. Regardless of whether you are given a source for words or not . . . words are not hard to come by! Our professional know-how will help us ascertain quality of the abundant choices available: Virtually every educational publisher offers possible patterns and words to study. There are hard copy and digital books of word lists out there for the taking. Quick and efficient Internet searches yield free and fruitful results. Moreover, if we take mere minutes, we will be able to recall words with identified sounds, letters, and patterns. **What matters more than where the words come from is matching *students* to the words. And what matters the most is what we *do* with the words, the practices we use, and habits we develop as ones who actively explore and study words.**

Students benefit from having skilled, creative, and caring professionals (us!) tailor classroom teaching and learning to the goals, next steps, interests, and curiosities of those currently in the classroom. We also know that these qualities vary not only class to class and year to year but sometimes day to day! Boxed curriculum and workbooks sometimes offer ideas for differentiation as if it was a "thing" and as a result often fall short of the intended results. Being in particular classrooms with particular learners is what helps us plan and implement thoughtful, personalized instruction. The intentional decisions and adjustments teachers make are driven by what is seen and heard in the classroom. Meaningful differentiation happens when educators use this firsthand knowledge and couple it with research-backed best practices. This kind of pedagogy aims to prepare students for real life. When we use ongoing, authentic, and meaningful formative assessment as a *process,* we feel confident in our decisions regarding which words to use.

Find It

Well-documented research supports the idea of developmental stages of reading, writing, and spelling development. As educators, we can use these findings to help us match students to developmentally appropriate words and patterns. Page 15 of *Word Study That Sticks* includes a one-page "at a glance" chart that summarizes the stages of spelling, reading, and writing development.

Find It

Common spelling inventories are listed in Appendix B of *Word Study That Sticks*. Multiple "mentor text" scope and sequence maps for possible ways a year of word study *could* go are shared in Appendix A of *Word Study That Sticks*.

Find It

There are printable letter, blend, digraph, prefix, suffix, and root cards to support word building and exploring across a wide range of grade levels and instructional settings available on the companion website. Additionally, a template to customize word lists can also be found online. All of these helpful, reproducible tools can be found online at **resources. corwin.com/wstscompanion**.

There are countless quality spelling inventories and standardized assessments that provide some of the picture. The results of these assessments provide a snapshot of a student's knowledge at any one moment in time. We also have access to abundant student work and the near-daily opportunity to observe and converse with students. When both formal and informal assessment are used together and used formatively, we feel ready to make cognizant, intentional decisions about what words we will use. In this next section, I first provide a framework/protocol for looking at student work and assessments that help us apply these research-backed ideas. These tools aid us in finding strengths in place, getting curious about patterns and discrepancies, and deciding on instructional priorities. Next, I share a small sampling of tools to help streamline and summarize noticed whole-class trends, small-group patterns, and individual goals. Each of these resources enables us to provide follow-up, responsive instruction that makes sense.

Remember this: The behaviors and habits of learning itself supersede the content of any one unit we might teach. Many of the tools in this chapter (and throughout this entire book) can help you carry out a well-rounded, active, and meaningful approach to word study. They support building the practices used by motivated, curious, and invested learners.

PROTOCOL FOR LOOKING AT STUDENT WORK AND ASSESSMENTS (WRITTEN)

Teachers can use assessment formatively and make responsive instructional decisions based on what they see students doing. By doing so, our instruction becomes aligned to the next steps students are most ready for. An example of a teacher's jots using the written protocol form is on page 43.

Student: *Dylan* **Date/Window:** *Winter (2 of 3)*

	Formal Assessment	Observations, Conversations, and Student Work
Noticings Patterns I see are . . . Discrepancies I see are . . . What stands out is . . . *(Hint: Focus on the positives)*	Dylan shows a strong understanding of blends, digraphs, and short vowel sounds. What stands out is that Dylan is trying to make sense of long vowel sounds and other vowel sounds. He is actively using strategies and trying something at the point of confusion.	Dylan can segment and separate sounds in words and consistently identify which consonant(s) make which sounds. Dylan uses short vowels conventionally in his writing. Dylan often adds an e to the end of words when he hears a long vowel sound.
Wonders and Ideas Patterns I am curious about are . . . Could it be . . . Discrepancies I am curious about are . . . Perhaps . . . I'm interested to find out if . . .	I am curious about what Dylan knows about "vowel teams" and unusual vowel patterns.	
Identified Strengths ____ is able to . . . What seems to be in place is . . . ____ has a solid grasp on . . .	Dylan has a solid grasp on letter/sound correspondence. He knows that sometimes two consonants work together to make a new sound (digraphs). Dylan understands that something is done to make a long vowel sound.	
Prioritized Next Steps Given what's in place, a logical next step would be . . . because . . . What appears most important to focus on next is . . . because . . .	Given what is in place, I believe Dylan is in the Within Words stage of spelling development. A logical next step would be to focus on different long vowel patterns.	

Plan Briefly outline immediate, short-term, and long-term plans to support student in reaching and exceeding identified goal. *(Hint: List actionable steps.)*	**Immediate** Share strengths and next steps with Dylan.	**Short Term** Choose prioritized patterns for the next few word study cycles.	**Long Term** Prioritize phonics practices in word study cycle. Provide feedback during practice and in writing workshop. Regularly reflect on work toward this goal.

Reflections Steps actually taken: Progress noted: Celebrations:	Dylan worked on long a, e, and o vowel patterns. He is making consistent growth (cycle assessments and informal observations of student work). Stay the course! Continue long vowel pattern work for the remainder of the trimester.
Looking Ahead Preliminary thoughts, wonders, and ideas regarding priorities for next unit:	How might I encourage Dylan to begin to remember and use word study learning while writing . . . not only checking after writing is complete?

eTool *Find a reproducible, ready-to-go version of this protocol online:* **resources.corwin.com/wstscompanion.**

PROTOCOL FOR LOOKING AT STUDENT WORK AND ASSESSMENTS: A CONVERSATION WITH COLLEAGUES

Arrange for a time to meet with grade-level or department colleagues. Bring a class set of formal assessments and/or student work to this meeting. Use the questions and prompts below to guide conversation about noticings and next steps. Jot brief notes about the class, small group(s), or individual student(s).

Noticings in formal assessments and student work:

✓ Patterns I see are . . .

✓ Discrepancies I see are . . .

✓ What stands out is . . .

(Hint: Name what is seen, and try to avoid judgment and labels.)

Wonders and Ideas

✓ Patterns I am curious about are . . . Could it be . . .

✓ Discrepancies I am curious about are . . . Perhaps . . .

✓ I'm curious about why . . . I'm interested to find out if . . .

Identified Strengths

✓ ____ is able to . . .

✓ What seems to be in place is . . .

✓ ____ has a solid grasp on . . .

Prioritized Next Steps

✓ Given what's in place, a logical next step would be . . . because . . .

✓ What appears most important to focus on next is . . . because . . .

✓ My immediate, short-term, and long-term plans to support this student/these students in reaching and exceeding identified goals are:

(Hint: List actionable steps.)

CLASS AT-A-GLANCE FORMATIVE ASSESSMENT TOOLS

It can be challenging to make sense of assessment information. As we look at formal and informal assessments, we practice many of the skills we teach readers, including determining importance, synthesizing, and using patterns to grow theories. Each of the following examples is intended as an *option* for teachers who would like some support in synthesizing assessment information and easily seeing whole-class trends, small-group patterns, and possible individual goals. Check them out, and see if one of these matches your own personal goals in this work.

Bonus

Check out Appendix B for examples of patterns to prioritize when you notice different strengths and areas of readiness in classroom learners.

This Class at-a-Glance makes it easy to see whole-class trends and small-group priorities. Using this information to plan responsive instruction is a natural next step.

The colors used in this chart make patterns pop right out. Here, green means something is solid, yellow means a student is working toward greater consistency in this area, and pink means the student is not yet showing a consistent or strong understanding of this kind of work.

eTool *Downloadable and reproducible versions of these templates (and other similar versions) are available online at* **resources .corwin.com/wstscompanion**.

TEMPLATES FOR USING ASSESSMENT

The forms that follow are truncated views of the full-sized reproducible tools that teachers may decide to use to document how they plan to use the results of formal and informal assessment in upcoming instruction. (All of these tools can be downloaded from **resources.corwin.com/wstscompanion**.) Here are things to notice and remember about all of the "making sense of assessment" tools that follow:

- Each chart asks teachers to note strengths and what is in place.

- Each chart supports teachers in prioritizing goals and next steps that are based off strengths and in a student's zone of proximal development.

- Each chart aims to help teachers use information from formal and informal assessments so it becomes formative and actionable.

A word of caution: Once completed, these charts record snapshots of observations. These are not stagnant and could never represent all there is to know about a student and their interests or even all about their areas of readiness. Students are continuously changing, growing, and progressing . . . a chart could never capture all that happens in the classroom day to day, but these can help guide decision making.

Using Assessment Information to Build Upon Class Strengths

Class Strengths (Widespread Patterns)	Class Priorities (Next Steps)	Plan/Resources Needed to Address Next Steps
Enthusiasm for word study Getting started each day	Sustained focus and ability to keep going during word study	Use the engagement lesson on pages 140 and 141 of Word Study That Sticks whole class. Co-create a class tool (like those pictured). Use the if/then talk conferring tips on pages 158 to 160 of Word Study That Sticks to help students support one another in more sustained word study practice.
Spelling pattern words	Using pattern words in conversation and writing	Teach additional meaning routines (in Chapters 6 and 7 of Word Study That Sticks), and provide students with the meaning minicharts in Chapter 4.

Using Assessment Information to Build Upon Small-Group Strengths

Group Members	Current Stage of Development	Strengths in Place	Instructional Priorities	Resources/Tools
Jay, Simone, Pauley, Simon, David, Angelina, Aly, Bar	Syllables and Affixes	Inflected endings secure and consistent	Syllabification—Open and closed syllables, accented and unaccented syllables (with the why!)	Prioritized sorts and word lists from district document
Emma, Todd, Addison, Jalen, Cruz, Harmony, Carolina	Derivational Relations	Suffixes that indicate parts of speech	Meaning-rich prefixes	Look for or create word lists and sorts that include these prioritized prefixes: pre-, post-, fore-, after-, micro-, mega-, super-, hyper-, inter-, intra-.

eTool *A full-sized downloadable and reproducible version of this template is available online at* **resources.corwin.com/ wstscompanion**.

Using Assessment Information to Build Upon Individual Strengths

Class Member	Strengths in Place	Prioritized Goals (1 or 2)
Jay	Engagement, focus, work completion	Material management
Simone	Attention to detail, organization, material management	Conversation and teamwork
Addison	Material management, conversation, teamwork	Application: Remembering and using word learning in the content areas
Jalen	Engagement, focus, material management	Conversation and teamwork

eTool *A full-sized downloadable and reproducible version of this template is available online at* **resources.corwin.com/ wstscompanion**.

Student Action Plan

___Angelina___ 's Action Plan

What is ___Angelina___ already doing with proficiency?

Angelina is motivated and enthusiastic about word study. She gets started right away every day. She loves the vocabulary work.

What is ___Angelina___ ready to work on as a next step?

Angelina is ready to work on staying motivated and engaged on all days, not only the meaning days.

What observable strategies does ___Angelina___ use?

- Looks at her word study schedule at the start of each session.
- Quickly looks through the Resources section of notebook to choose an aligned routine.
- Gathers needed materials quickly.
- Shares materials with group members.
- Supports team members as they work, asks questions of team members when feeling stuck.

What are ___Angelina___ 's interests and priorities?

- Angelina is social and loves collaborating with peers.
- She loves using letter manipulatives and concrete materials. Anything involving art is of interest.

eTool *A more complete, comprehensive, and full-sized version of this template is available online at* **resources.corwin.com/wstscompanion**.

Responsive Instruction and Feedback Support Success

I like to think of feedback as rooted in the Renaissance construct of apprenticeship. Think about it: Masters like Titian, Raphael, and others learned their craft through apprentice-ships. Imagine the feedback in the midst of their learning! (McGee, 2017, pp. 29–30)

Feedback matters! John Hattie (2009, 2012) synthesized more than 900 meta-analyses and reported that feedback is one of the most high-impact practices that influence student learning. Back in 1985, Elawar and Corno found that students who received diagnostic comments (feedback) instead of grades learned twice as fast as the control group. In addition, the achievement gap between those identifying as male and female disappeared, and student attitudes improved. Several studies echo these ideas and show that feedback has more of an impact than a grade—and feedback alone yields more statistically significant results than both feedback and grades given together (Butler 1987, 1988; Deevers, 2006; Pulfrey, Buchs, & Butera, 2011). The power of feedback is indeed formidable.

The type of feedback we provide also matters! In *Mindset and Moves* (2016), Gravity Goldberg shares the 4Ms model for providing asset-based feedback. In this four-step process, we start by uncovering what *is* in place and what the student *is* doing well. We then say back to the students what we noticed. We carefully choose student-centered language, recognizing and attributing the student as owner of these efforts and outcomes. By intentionally starting with the word *you* instead of the phrase "I like . . ." we reframe and strengthen the feedback we provide. Next, we explicitly model a next step related to this identified strength. Finally, we coach students through a first—or follow-up—try of this process, preparing students to continue to approximate and practice on their own. This type of feedback can be used in a variety of settings and across all subject areas.

Feedback comes in many forms! I like to think of *all* strong, responsive instruction as formative feedback: First, see what students are doing, and think through next steps (which can be related to readiness, interest, and/or student-set goals). Then, find ways to support student growth in these identified areas. Voila! Responsive instruction! There are times this utilizes more inquiry-driven methods and times that call for the explicit and direct instruction of a strategy. Moreover, feedback can also be used to encourage students to apply and transfer what they know to help them get themselves unstuck and move ahead—without our interference! Remember, our end goal is independence. We want students to make the conscious choice to start, sustain, and succeed on their own. Feedback powers the release of scaffolds and increases student independence.

The pages ahead include tools to help teachers confidently follow through and use information from both formal and informal assessment. The *small-group planning forms* help you turn noticings and instructional priorities into responsive teaching. The included *record-keeping templates* identify student goals, monitor student progress, and keep track of teacher feedback. Finally, the Word Study Look-Fors help you self-assess the current state of affairs and set short- and long-term goals. This look-for guide is also a helpful resource for administrator visits and teacher-led learning walks. These tools enable us to streamline the decision-making process and use the resources in this book with greater intention. For example, these tools prepare you to select the types of routines that will best support identified goals and next steps of each student. By combining our knowledge of students and expertise in content, we naturally differentiate learning and support learners in ways that make sense. To sum up, the resources in this section (and collectively throughout this book) support all aspects of the ongoing and continuous formative assessment-instruction-feedback loop.

Tech Tip

Many teachers like to plan online using tools like Planboard and PlanbookEdu. I have personally tried (and really enjoyed) *free* digital record keeping using Evernote and Google Forms. For those who may not feel ready to dive into these arenas but are driven by the desire to be more environmentally friendly, simple digital documents can help you write plans and keep conferring notes online. All of the resources provided in the next section can easily be brought to a digital platform. For those interested or curious, I invite you to do so.

SMALL-GROUP PLANNING FORM

Once we decide on an instructional goal for a small group of learners, it is time to get going and start carrying out our plan for responsive instruction. Below is an example of how teachers can turn observations into teaching.

Small-Group Planning Form	
Students: Emma, Todd, Addison, Jalen, Cruz, Harmony, Carolina Working on prefixes	**Shared Strengths:** Creative, hardworking, enjoying current work focused on prefixes **Goal:** Use taught patterns—starting with using pattern words in conversation
Model of Instruction: Small-Group Inquiry Group Observation With Feedback (Introduction of New Routine) Strategy Group—Concept Strategy Group—Habit Other	**Needed Materials:** Current pattern word cards (micro- & mega-) Devices/digital notebooks **upload minichart for Talkin' the Talk routine **Process:** Lesson for introducing Talkin' the Talk is on p. 154 of Word Study That Sticks
Notes: Able to engage in conversation when I generated context/topic of conversation—had a trickier time thinking of different topics of conversation.	
Next Step: Check in with group when they next try this routine—coach and provide feedback as needed.	

eTool   *A full-sized downloadable and reproducible version of this template is available online at* **resources.corwin.com/ wstscompanion**.

RECORD-KEEPING FORM

Record keeping helps us keep track of the instruction and feedback we have provided. It also helps us note student progress toward identified goals. Additionally, record keeping helps us reflect on recent classroom experience and feel better prepared for parent–teacher conferences, administrator meetings, and report cards. Below is a sample of teacher record keeping in word study:

Student: Cruz

Unit: Prefixes

Student Goal	Teacher Goal
Work successfully with word study group members.	Application: Use taught patterns.

Date	Interaction	Strengths Observed	Instruction?	Possible Next Step?
12/9	(Kid watching) Conversation Small group Student work Other	Cruz helped his group set up, made a suggestion for the routine they would work on, and contributed ideas throughout the work session	Named what I saw Cruz doing well…role-played a scenario of what to do if the group members were talking over him/not listening	Keep reinforcing the positive acts I see while Cruz is working in a group
12/12	Kid watching (Conversation) Small group Student work Other	Hardworking throughout recent word study sessions, enjoying current work focused on prefixes	Introduced Talkin' the Talk routine	Check in to see how group does with more independence—especially with creating topics for conversations
12/16	(Kid watching) Conversation Small group Student work Other	Group got to work quickly, chose "related" word for a conversation, and worked together to try to come up with a topic for their conversation	Used the words to help generate conversation topics (not randomly throwing out topic ideas)	Thirty-second group reflection—how is the routine going?

eTool *A full-sized downloadable and reproducible version of this template is available online at* **resources.corwin.com/wstscompanion**.

WORD STUDY LOOK-FORS

Category	Guiding Questions	What We Might See or Hear
Workplace and Materials	Why did you choose to work here? How are these materials supporting your work today? Why did you choose this ____? How does it help you?	• Students self-select seating. • Students self-select resources. • Students navigate the workspace. • Students access their choice of materials. • Students co-create charts. • Students create tools to support their own learning. • Clearly defined spaces are outlined for whole-class, small-group, partnership, and individual learning.
Energy and Engagement	What is most interesting and exciting about what you are working on? What is the purpose behind what you are doing? How does it help?	• Students explore/study words with energy and agency. • Students focus attention on the chosen learning routine. • Students (and teachers) collaborate in different ways. • Students act as resources for one another.
Goals, Reflection, and Self-Direction	What are you working toward? How did you decide on your goal? How are you doing with your goal?	• Students set goals and explain why this goal was chosen. • Student goals are displayed. • Students set intentions for the day's work and share how it supports work toward goals. • Students self-start (choose a method/strategy/routine). • Students share what is going well and what is challenging.
Personalization	How are you being supported in your work toward your goals? What choices have you made in this work? Why?	• Student strengths and areas of readiness drive small-group work and conferring conversations. • Students engage in diverse and meaningful learning routines at any given time. • Students play an active role in work choices.
Application	How does your word knowledge help you? How do the habits, strategies, and/or learning from word study help you?	• Students transfer word learning into other content areas. • Students apply learning consistently and over time. • Students use knowledge and expertise to problem solve with independence.

Source: Created by Pamela Koutrakos. Adapted from the series Balanced Literacy Look Fors, *created by Gravity Goldberg, LLC.*

Fostering Independence

This way of thinking about motivation is radical because it does not locate "the problem" in the teacher or the learner but in the match between challenge and capability . . . if we see motivation not as a cause but as an outcome, an emergent property of getting the match between challenge and capability right, then if the student isn't motivated, that's just a signal that the teacher and learner need to try something different. (Wiliam, 2011, p. 150)

Csikszentmihalyi (1990) explains this idea of motivation being not the cause but the consequence of achievement. He talks about the situations where we become so completely absorbed in what we are doing that we are *completely* engaged. Csikszentmihalyi feels that when challenge and capability are both high, a state of "flow" results. I am a strong believer in the capabilities and potential of all classroom learners, and I also trust in the idea that learners want to be challenged. We crave these opportunities, especially when they match goals we are intrinsically motivated to achieve. One thing that feels true for me when I read about the ideas of Wiliam, Csikszentmihalyi, and so many others is that engaging students, building motivation, creating a strong sense of ownership, and fostering independence in practices require us to *know* students and make responsive decisions. There is not a simple if/then algorithm . . . different students respond to different approaches. As Wiliam writes above, if we do not see the results we hope for, we can go back to the drawing board and try a different approach.

The resources included in this next section include *goal-setting templates* and *reflection protocol templates*. These all aim to help students navigate their own paths toward greater independence. Even the youngest learners benefit from being immersed in these kinds of metacognitive practices. The chart on the facing page provides a sneak peek of what's ahead . . . and when and why you might choose to use it in the classroom.

Find It

Chapters 6 and 7 of *Word Study That Sticks* provide information and ideas for differentiating word study instruction. Chapter 8 includes numerous ways to make reflection and celebration a regular feature in the classroom. Appendix F is *filled* with student-facing checklists for primary, upper-elementary, and middle-grade learners. These checklists help students set "habits" and "concepts" goals, and each set reflects the developmental readiness of classroom learners.

Resource	Time, Place, and Purpose
Goal-Setting Templates (Primary and upper-elementary)	Students often glue these templates into the goal section of their notebooks. They can also be accessed online as a Google Form if using digital notebooks. Once students are familiar with the structure, they may choose to recreate this template themselves. These templates help students articulate goals and create an action plan to meet goals.
Reflection Protocol (Kindergarten)	Reflection checklists are often stapled on the back of choice charts or laminated and kept inside choice chart folders. Students use these checklists to reflect on a daily or near-daily basis.
Reflection Protocols (Primary and upper-elementary)	Students often glue reflection protocols into the goal section of their notebooks. They can also be shared online as a Google Form if using digital notebooks. Once students are familiar with the structure, they may choose to recreate these forms themselves. These help students think about their progress toward goals and decide if the action plan needs to be modified or changed. This type of formal reflection happens about once a month. Informal reflection happens much more frequently.

Tech Tip

Chapter 2 listed several options for digital options for goal setting, reflection, and celebration online. The forthcoming goal-setting and reflection tools can also be utilized in digital forums.

Goal-Setting Templates (Primary)

I can:

I want to:

My goal:

I can:

My goal:

My plan:

1.

2.

3.

Goal-Setting Templates (Upper-Elementary and Middle Grades)

Word Study Habit Goal	
I have been successful in . . .	
A worthwhile next step might be . . . because . . .	
A goal I am interested in working toward is . . .	
I plan to accomplish this goal by . . .	

Word Study Concepts Goal	
A success I am celebrating is . . .	
A worthwhile next step might be . . . because . . .	
A goal I am interested in working toward is . . .	
I plan to accomplish this goal by . . .	

eTool *A full-sized downloadable and reproducible version of this template is available online at* **resources.corwin.com/ wstscompanion**.

Reflection Protocol Templates (Kindergarten)

CHECK-IN
ME

I did . . .	It was . . .		
	😱	😊	😍
Find and Fix Up			
Hunt			
I Spy!			
Picture It			
Read It! Build It! Write It!			
Reggio Routines			
Sound Search			
Tap It!			
Word Webs			

eTool *A full-sized downloadable and reproducible version of this template is available online at* **resources.corwin.com/ wstscompanion**.

CHECK-IN
WE

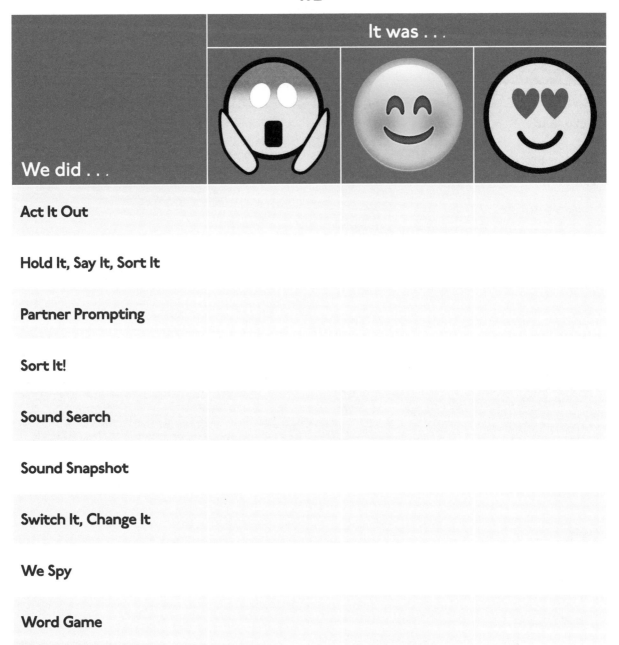

We did . . .	It was . . .		
Act It Out			
Hold It, Say It, Sort It			
Partner Prompting			
Sort It!			
Sound Search			
Sound Snapshot			
Switch It, Change It			
We Spy			
Word Game			

eTool *A full-sized downloadable and reproducible version of this template is available online at* **resources.corwin.com/ wstscompanion**.

CHECK-IN
ME

I did . . .	It was . . .		
	😱	😊	😍
Picture It			
Read It! Build It! Write It!			
Reggio Routines			
Sound Search			
Tap It!			

WE

We did . . .	It was . . .		
	😱	😊	😍
Buddy Check			
Sort It!			
Switch It, Change It			
We Spy			
Word Game			

Reflection Protocol Template (Primary)

WORD STUDY GOAL REFLECTIONS

My Goal:

Check-In 1	Check-In 2	Check-In 3	Check-In 4

Final Reflection:

 A full-sized downloadable and reproducible version of this template is available online at **resources.corwin.com/ wstscompanion**.

Reflection Protocol Template (Upper-Elementary Grades)

My Goal:

Check-In 1:

Check-In 2:

Check-In 3:

Check-In 4:

Final Reflection:

RESOURCE ROUNDUP

CO-CREATE LEARNING SPACES

Use your knowledge and experience to put together the outline of a productive learning space, and carve out consistent time for exploring and studying words. Commit to being flexible in your thinking, and adjust space and plans to accommodate classroom learners and foster shared ownership of word study materials and practices. The Create the Space Checklists and various templates for student-friendly schedules will support shared (and informed) decision making. The Word Study Look-Fors provide guidance and support in building a strong community of word learning across a classroom, building, or district.

START WITH STUDENTS

There are infinite resources from which you can access patterns and word lists. Prioritize using a healthy balance of formal and informal assessments to make informed choices and support student learning. Use the word card templates and the letter, blend, digraph, affix, and root cards (available online at **resources.corwin.com/ wstscompanion**) to bolster meaningful learning with selected patterns and words. Check out Appendix B for a helpful if/then chart to help connect the dots and guide you to patterns that match student goals.

USE ASSESSMENT FORMATIVELY TO YIELD RESPONSIVE INSTRUCTION

No one assessment (whether formal or informal) tells us all there is to know about a learner and where they are headed. The written and conversational protocols for using assessments formatively help teachers look at and discuss student work and assessments with colleagues. The planning and record-keeping forms turn these noticings into responsive teaching—*and* keep track of student progress as that teaching and learning are happening.

INCORPORATE TOOLS TO PROMOTE CHOICE, GOAL SETTING, REFLECTION, AND SELF-ASSESSMENT

Students deserve and need our trust! With modeling, guidance, and instruction, students will develop metacognitive thought processes and learn to make purposeful choices. When introduced and supported in meaningful ways, the goal-setting templates and reflection forms included in this chapter will help make this happen!

TEACHER AND STUDENT TOOLS IN ACTION

Small-group planning forms help make personalized instruction more efficient.

Record-keeping forms help teachers keep track of the feedback they provide.

Reflection forms help learners feel invested in learning.

Photo by Linda Day

Teachers and students can use the tools and resources from this chapter to personalize word learning.

By using the results of formal and informal assessment, our instructional next steps become personalized and "just right" for classroom learners.

PART II

Tools to Foster Engagement and Independence

CHAPTER FOUR

Meaning Routines

> We talk a lot about the meaning of words in word study. Knowing so many new words totally helps me when I read and write. But the best part is now I am the Scrabble champion in my family. No one can beat me!

The minicharts included in this chapter reflect routines that help students develop rich, comprehensive understanding of words—not only that, but they have been teacher tested and student approved. These minicharts provide a needed reminder of diverse practices that are playful as well as promote discovery and, quite often, enhance meaningful collaboration. Which will you first teach to the learners you work alongside?

Why Is Meaning Work Important?

Consider this: It is futile to learn to spell a word if you are unclear of what it means or how, where, or when to use it. Without a strong sense of meaning, students will not use the word in conversation, write with the word, understand when others use the word, or comprehend a text that uses that word. So, meaning is an integral element of a strong, well-balanced word study diet. The meaning-based practices we use in word study are vocabulary stepping stones. They pave the path to rich word discovery.

It is critical that each new cycle of word study starts by emphasizing the meaning of the words. By making the simple tweak of spending the start of each word study cycle focusing on enriching student vocabularies, we lift the level of all that follows. This is essential because research tells us that vocabulary is an indicator of school success (Baker, Simmons, & Kame'enui, 1997)—but even further, "life success" (Marzano & Pickering, 2005). In *Bringing Words to Life*, Beck, McKeown, and Kucan (2013) talk about the instructional potential of words and ask us to consider teaching words that are "more than one-dimensional and offer a variety of contexts and uses to explore" (p. 28). Even seemingly simplistic CVC words often have more than one meaning, context, and/or connotation. Phonetically simple words offer more than meet the eye. Word study is a time to explore all facets of words, and by starting with meaning-based practices, students get in-depth knowledge of the what, where, and when of words.

How Does Meaning Work Fit a Range of Learners?

Early-elementary students are excited and motivated to learn new words. By taking the time to explicitly teach not only letters, sounds, and patterns but also words, we set up students for success in more ways than we might initially imagine. The primary meaning-based routines and coordinating minicharts reflect developmentally appropriate, research-backed practices.

Upper-elementary and middle-grade learners want to be seen—and heard. They want those around them to understand precisely what they are saying and often spend a great time trying to convince others why they are right, why something is just (or unjust), or why or why not something should happen. The deep study of words enables students to do just this! By learning about affixes and roots, we open a world of possibilities and opportunities for students. There is no doubt these meaning-based practices are not only empowering but also essential to the work we do with all students. There are infinite ways to make these practices accessible to the diverse cross-section of learners we support and admire.

> **TEACHER TIP**
>
> Sometimes, teachers working with students acquiring English or those with language-based learning disabilities prefer using the primary minicharts with learners who are beyond the primary grades. The icons and more direct language provide greater accessibility for students when working independently. Other times, teachers use the upper-elementary minicharts and after modeling and practicing the routine together ask the students to create and add in their own icons or visual reminders.

When Do Learners Engage in Meaning Work?

Meaning lays the foundation of word work. Without an understanding of what words mean, every routine is simply an assignment and holds little value for students. Even if students can decode, pronounce, or encode words, they will not be able to attain the ultimate goals: rich comprehension of texts, appropriate use in oral conversation, and conventional use in writing. Below are two of the infinite examples of how a word study cycle might look. Regardless of how you structure the cycle, remember to always start with meaning. Also note that meaning is often, but not always, included in other cycle practices.

Day 1	Day 2	Day 3	Day 4	Day 5	Day 6
Meaning	Meaning	Pattern	Pattern	Hybrid	Check-In/ Transfer

Day 1	Day 2	Day 3	Day 4	Day 5	Day 6
Meaning	Meaning	Pattern	Pattern	Phonemic Awareness and Phonics	High Frequency

Meaning Day: Word Intro

Yep! Maybe . . . Huh?

Why?

To learn new words!

You Need:

Word study folder

How?

1. Listen to the teacher.

2. 💭 Think: Do I know this word? How well do I know this word?

Looks Like:

Ear: openclipart.org/CCX; Thought cloud: openclipart.org/rejon.

Find It *The accompanying lesson can be found on page 59 of* Word Study That Sticks.

Word Wall *This routine can also be done with high-frequency words.*

Meaning Day: Word Intro
Tight to Two

Why?

To learn new words!

You Need:

Word study folder, scissors, and a crayon

How?

1. 👂 Listen to the teacher.

2. 💭 Think: Do I know this word? How well do I know this word?

Looks Like:

Find It *The accompanying lesson (a variation of None to Some) can be found on page 74 of* Word Study That Sticks.

Word Wall *This routine can also be done with high-frequency words.*

Ear: openclipart.org/CCX; Thought cloud: openclipart.org/rejon.

73

Picture It

Why?

To show understanding of new words

You Need:

Word study notebook and a pencil (colors optional)

How?

1. ⬇ Choose a word.
2. ☁ Think: What does this word mean? What could I draw?
3. ✏ Make a sketch that shows you know what the word means.

Looks Like:

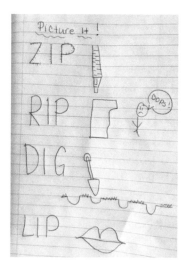

Find It *The accompanying lesson can be found on page 123 of* Word Study That Sticks.

Word Wall *This routine can also be done with high-frequency words.*

Arrow: openclipart.org/GD]; Thought cloud: openclipart.org/rejon; Pencil: openclipart.org/pascallpalme.

Act It Out

Why?
To show understanding of new words

You Need:
Word study notebook and a pencil

How?

1. ↓ Choose a word.
2. 💭 Think: How can I act out this word?
3. 🤸 Use your body to show what the word means (act it out).
4. ❓ Can a partner guess which word you are acting out?

Looks Like:

Bonus *The accompanying lesson can be found on page 220.*

Arrow: openclipart.org/GDj; Thought cloud: openclipart.org/rejon; Jump rope: openclipart.org/johnny_automatic; Question mark: openclipart.org/jean_victor_balin.

I Might . . .

Why?

- To think about all the ways and places we can use new words

- To use word learning when we talk and write

You Need:

Words and *maybe* a word study notebook and pencil

How?

1.  Choose a word.
2. Think: When might I do this, use this, or feel this?
3. Say or jot your ideas.

Looks Like:

Arrow: openclipart.org/GDJ; Thought cloud: openclipart.org/rejon; Speech bubble: openclipart.org/PrinterKiller.

Find It *The accompanying lesson can be found on page 124 of* Word Study That Sticks.

Talkin' the Talk
(Word Conversations)

Why?

- To use the words we are learning
- To practice speaking and listening

You Need:

Word cards and partner

Optional: iPad, paper and pencil for tally

How?

1. 👀 Look at words. Choose two to five words.

2. 💭 Think: What topic can we talk about using these words?

3. 💬 Talk to your partner using those words.

Looks Like:

Find It *The accompanying lesson can be found on page 154 of* Word Study That Sticks.

Word Wall *This routine can also be done with high-frequency words.*

Tally: openclipart.org/rejon; Eyes: openclipart.org/Prawny; Thought cloud: openclipart.org/rejon; Speech bubble: openclipart.org/PrinterKiller.

Homophones, Homographs, or None (Nun)

Why?

To use words correctly

You Need:

Word study notebook, a pencil, and crayons

How?

1. ◉◉ Look at a word.
2. 💭 Think: Does this word have a homophone or homograph?
3. ✏️ Jot a sketch to show what you know.

Looks Like:

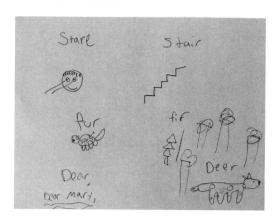

Helpful Hint

Homophone: Sounds the same, looks different
  Example: to, too, and two

Homograph: Looks the same, sounds different *or* looks the same, means something different
  Example: read and read

Eyes: openclipart.org/Prawny; Thought cloud: openclipart.org/rejon; Pencil: openclipart.org/pascallpalme.

 Find It The accompanying lesson can be found on page 121 of Word Study That Sticks.

Word Wall *This routine can also be done with high-frequency words.*

Part-of-Speech Chart

Why?

To use words correctly when speaking and writing

You Need:

Word study notebook, a pencil, and/or other resources

How?

1. 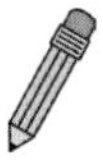 ✏️ List words.
2. 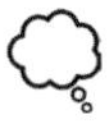 💭 Think: What is the part of speech of this word?
3. 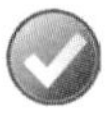 ✅ Put a check or X in the correct column(s).

Looks Like:

Word	Noun	Verb	Adjective	Adverb
Green			X	
Team	X			
Teeth	X			
Clean		X	X	

Bonus *The accompanying lesson can be found on page 219.*

79

Backward Scattergories

Why?

To make connections between words and grow our vocabulary

You Need:

Word study folder and words

How?

1. 👀 Look at your words.

2. 💭 Think: Which words fit together? What is the category or topic for this group of words?

3. 💬 Meet with your partner: Can he or she guess your categories?

Looks Like:

CAT
RAT
BAT

What do these all have in common?

They are all animals?

Find It   *The accompanying lesson can be found on page 75 of* Word Study That Sticks.

More or Less?

Why?

To use the best words when we speak and write

You Need:

Word study notebook and pencil

Optional: Crayons

How?

1. ✏️ Choose a word. Write it down.

2. 💭 Think of a "more" word, and write it on one side of your word.

3. 💭 Think of a "less" word, and write it on the other side of your word.

4. 💬 Share with others in your group.

Looks Like:

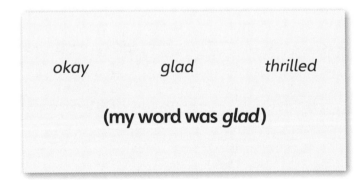

okay   glad   thrilled

(my word was *glad*)

Find It   *The accompanying lesson (a variation of Shades of Meaning) can be found on page 79 of* Word Study That Sticks.

Pencil: openclipart.org/pascallpalmr; Thought cloud: openclipart.org/rejon; Speech bubble: openclipart.org/PrinterKiller.

Shades of Meaning

Why?

To use the *best* words when we speak and write

You Need:

Word study notebook, pencil, and crayons

How?

1. ⬇ Choose a word.
2. ☁ Think: What words have a similar meaning?
3. ✏ Order the words—a little to a lot.

Helpful Hint

Synonym: A word that means the same or almost the same

Looks Like:

good → cheery → <u>glad</u> → joyous

blue → <u>sad</u> → gloomy → weepy

Find It *The accompanying lesson can be found on page 78 of* Word Study That Sticks.

Arrow: openclipart.org/GDJ; Thought cloud: openclipart.org/rejon; Pencil: openclipart.org/pascallpalme.

Word Continuums

Why?

- To explore words with similar and different meanings
- To use the best words when we speak and write

You Need:

Word study notebook, pencil

Optional: Crayons

How?

1. ↓ Choose a word.
2. ☁ Think of a synonym. Think of an antonym.
3. ☁ Think: What words might go "in between"?
4. ✏ Write the words from least to most.

Looks Like:

Find It *The accompanying lesson can be found on page 79 of* Word Study That Sticks.

Arrow: openclipart.org/GDJ; Thought cloud: openclipart.org/rejon; Pencil: openclipart.org/pascallpalne.

83

Figurative Language Fun: Awesome Alliteration I

Why?
To understand and use playful, poetic language

You Need:
Word study notebook and a pencil

How?

1. ↓ Choose a word.
2. ☁ Make up a funny tongue twister using that word.
3. 💬 Share with a partner. How many times can you say your "awesome alliteration" sentences fast?

Looks Like:

Awesome Alliteration

BUG:
Billy <u>bugged</u> out when the balloon burst.

SUN:
Shiny, sparkly <u>sunshine</u> soothes Sam's soul.

RUG:
Reggie ripped the red <u>rug</u>.

CHALLENGE: Use more than one studied word in your tongue twister.

Arrow: openclipart.org/GDJ; Thought cloud: openclipart.org/rejon; Speech bubble: openclipart.org/PrinterKiller.

Find It *The accompanying lesson can be found on page 125 of* Word Study That Sticks.

Figurative Language Fun: Awesome Alliteration 2

Why?

To understand and use figurative language

You Need:

Word study notebook and a pencil

How?

1. Choose a word.

2. Create and write a tongue twister using that word.

3. Share with a partner. How many times can you say your "awesome alliteration" sentences fast?

Looks Like:

CHALLENGE: Use more than one studied word in your tongue twister.

RUG
Reggie ripped the red <u>rug</u>.

BUG
Billy <u>bugged</u> out when the balloon burst.

Arrow: openclipart.org/GDJ; Pencil: openclipart.org/pascallpalme; Speech bubble: openclipart.org/PrinterKiller.

Find It   *The accompanying lesson can be found on page 125 of* Word Study That Sticks.

Figurative Language Fun:
Silly Similes

Why?
To understand and use figurative language with words

You Need:
Word study notebook and a pencil

How?

1. ⬇ Choose a word.
2. ✏ Write a simile using that word.
3. ✎ Illustrate your silly simile.

Looks Like:

Silly Similes

The sun is as bright as Albert Einstein.

The little bug was as scary as a zombie.

The rug was as itchy as 45 bug bites.

Find It *The accompanying lesson can be found on page 125 of* Word Study That Sticks.

Arrow: openclipart.org/GDj; Pencil: openclipart.org/pascallpalme; Crayons: openclipart.org/Dug.

Word Introductions
None to Some

Day ____

Why?

- To fully understand the meaning of the words
- To prepare to use our knowledge of words

You Need:

Your eyes and ears

How?

1. Listen and look at the word being shared.
2. Think: How well do I *really* know this word?
3. Use the appropriate hand signal to show your understanding.
4. Listen for more word information.

Looks Like:

Photo by Linda Day

Find It *The accompanying lesson can be found on page 74 of* Word Study That Sticks.

Word Wall *This routine can also be done with high-frequency words.*

Word Introductions

Yep! Maybe . . . Huh?

Day ____

Why?

- To fully understand the meaning of the words
- To prepare to use our knowledge of words

You Need:

Your eyes and ears

How?

1. Listen and look at the word being shared.
2. Think: How well do I *really* know this word?
3. Use the taught signals to show how well you know the word.
4. Listen for more word information.

Looks Like:

Find It *The accompanying lesson can be found on page 59 of* Word Study That Sticks.

Word Wall *This routine can also be done with high-frequency words.*

Backward Scattergories

Day ____

Why?

- To create connections between words
- To develop our vocabulary

You Need:

Word cards and word study notebook

How?

1. Look at your words, and choose a few that have something in common (based on the *meaning* of the words—*not* how the words look or sound).

2. Look at the group of words, and ask yourself this: What do these words have in common? What is the topic or header for this group of words?

3. Meet with your partner/group, and try to guess what the words have in common. Explain your thinking and ideas.

Looks Like:

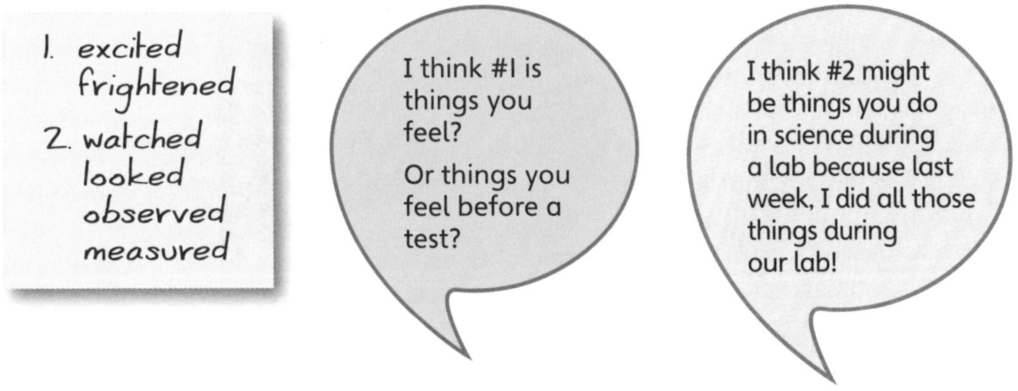

1. excited
   frightened
2. watched
   looked
   observed
   measured

I think #1 is things you feel?

Or things you feel before a test?

I think #2 might be things you do in science during a lab because last week, I did all those things during our lab!

Find It *The accompanying lesson can be found on page 75 of* Word Study That Sticks.

Picture It

Day ___

Why?

To show off understanding of words

You Need:

Word study notebook and a pencil

Optional: Coloring supplies

Digital: Google Docs and Google Drawings

How?

1. Choose a word.

2. Think: What does this word mean? What could I sketch to show this meaning?

3. Make a quick sketch that demonstrates your understanding of that word.

4. Repeat with other words.

Looks Like:

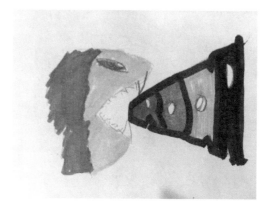

Find It *The accompanying lesson can be found on page 123 of* Word Study That Sticks.

Tech Tip *Many students enjoy a digitized version of Picture It, with online drawing tools, such as Google Drawings, Adobe Illustrator, Sketchpad, and Tux Paint.*

Word Wall *This routine can also be done with high-frequency words.*

I Might . . .

Day ___

Why?

- To better understand the "when" behind how we might use words
- To extend our word learning to our talking and writing

You Need:

Word study notebook and a pencil

How?

1. Choose a word.
2. Think: When might I feel this? Do this? See this? Use this? . . .
3. List different times and/or examples (contexts).

Looks Like:

```
I MIGHT FEAR . . .              I MIGHT PEER AT . . .

 - Seeing a snake               - My dad wrapping presents

 - Getting in trouble           - The new student

 - Falling off the beam in      - The answers to a crossword
   a competition                  puzzle

 - Making a big mistake         - Anything interesting!

 - Getting lost
```

Find It *The accompanying lesson can be found on page 124 of* Word Study That Sticks.

Shades of Meaning

Day ___

Why?

- To understand nuances between words
- To learn to use specific and precise words when we speak and write

You Need:

Words, word study notebook, and a pencil

How?

1. Choose a word.

2. Think: What other words do I know that have a similar meaning? Write as many as you can.

3. Order words according to intensity (*a little* to *a lot*).

Helpful Hint

Synonym: A word that means the same or almost the same

Looks Like:

press → flatten → squish → squash → smash

yell → holler → shout → scream

Find It The accompanying lesson can be found on page 78 of Word Study That Sticks.

Tech Tip *Any routine that can be done in a notebook can also be done digitally.*

Word Continuums

Day____

Why?

- To understand nuances and relationships between words
- To learn to use the most appropriate and precise words possible when we speak and write

You Need:

Word study notebook and a pencil
Optional: Colored pencils/markers

How?

1. Choose a word that has both a synonym and antonym.

2. Think: What are a few different synonyms and antonyms for this word? What are some other words that might go "in between"?

3. Plot words on the continuum—moving from one extreme to the other.

4. Share your word continuums with a partner.

Looks Like:

Find It *The accompanying lesson can be found on page 79 of* Word Study That Sticks.

Tech Tip *A user-friendly site is www.wordhippo.com. Other popular student choices are www.kidthesaurus.com and www .wordsmyth.net.*

Homophones, Homographs, or None (Nun) of the Above

Chart Version

Day ____

Why?

- To deepen our understanding of words
- To clarify the differences between commonly confused words
- To become confident using the correct, intended word

You Need:

Word study notebook and a pencil

How?

1. Create a chart (like below). List words being studied in the first column.
2. For each word, think: Does it have a homophone? A homograph? Neither?
3. Mark if a word has a homophone, a homograph, or neither.

Helpful Hint

Homophone: Words that are pronounced the same but differ in meaning and spelling

Example: there, they're, their

Homograph: Words that are spelled the same but are not necessarily pronounced the same and have different meanings and/or origins

Example: read and read

Looks Like:

Word	Homophone?	Homograph?	Neither?
Maul	X		
Fault		X	
Draw	X	X	
Bawl	X		
Haul	X	X	

Find It *The accompanying lesson can be found on page 121 of* Word Study That Sticks.

Tech Tip Any *written routine that can be done in a notebook can also be done digitally.*

Word Wall *This routine can also be done with high-frequency words.*

Homophones, Homographs, or None (Nun) of the Above

Sketch or Write Version

Day ____

Why?

- To deepen our understanding of words that look or sound the same but may have different spellings or meanings
- To clarify the differences between commonly confused words
- To know when to use the correct form of the word

You Need:

Word study notebook and a pencil

How?

1. Choose a word that has either a homophone or homograph.
2. Think: What could I sketch to show I know the difference between each word?
3. Sketch an image or icon for each word. Repeat.
4. Optional: Talk or write with the words, further showing your understanding.

Helpful Hint

Homophone: Words that are pronounced the same but differ in meaning and spelling

Example: there, they're, their

Homograph: Words that are spelled the same but are not necessarily pronounced the same and have different meanings and/or origins

Example: read and read

Looks Like:

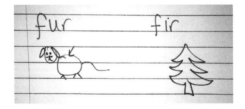

 The accompanying lesson can be found on page 121 of Word Study That Sticks.

 See student-friendly digital drawing ideas listed with the Picture It routine.

Word Wall This routine can also be done with high-frequency words.

Talkin' the Talk
(Word Conversations)

Day _____

Why?

- To practice using words in context
- To help internalize the meaning of words being studied
- To apply word learning: get comfortable noticing/hearing pattern words when others speak and using pattern words more frequently when speaking

You Need:

Word study notebook or word cards

Keeping track: Record each time you use a word (tally marks or actual words)

How?

1. Choose a few words.
2. Think: When would I use these words? What might our conversation be about?
3. Start a conversation with your partner about that topic, and use the selected pattern words (and other pattern words) as much as possible.
4. Remember to use words appropriately! Challenge: How many times did you use pattern words?

Looks Like:

 Find It *The accompanying lesson can be found on page 154 of* Word Study That Sticks.

 Tech Tip *Apps such as Skype, FaceTime, or Google Hangouts make this fun to do with other class members or kids in other classrooms.*

Word Wall *This routine can also be done with high-frequency words.*

Synonym and Antonym Chart

Day ____

Why?

- To create connections between words
- To grow our vocabularies

You Need:

Word study notebook and a pencil

How?

1. Create a simple chart in your word study notebook. List all words being studied in the first column.

2. Brainstorm synonyms and antonyms for as many words as possible.

3. List synonyms and antonyms on the chart. Consider the part of speech. Adjectives, verbs, and adverbs work best for this routine. Remember, some words do not have a synonym or antonym.

Looks Like:

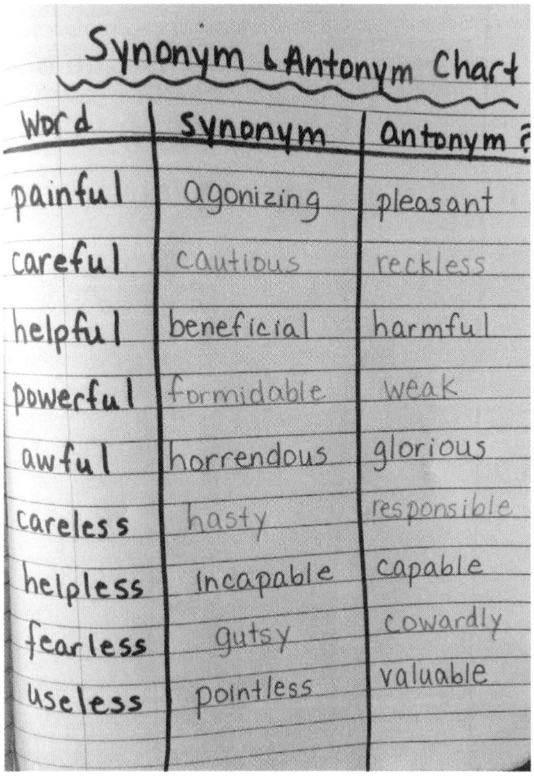

Word	Synonym	Antonym?
painful	agonizing	pleasant
careful	cautious	reckless
helpful	beneficial	harmful
powerful	formidable	weak
awful	horrendous	glorious
careless	hasty	responsible
helpless	incapable	capable
fearless	gutsy	cowardly
useless	pointless	valuable

Bonus *The accompanying lesson can be found on page 221.*

Word Family Trees

Day____

Why?

- To see connections between words

- To recognize and appropriately use different forms of words when we read, speak, and write

You Need:

Word study notebook and a pencil

How?

1. Choose a word. Write the base word on the tree trunk.

2. Think of different forms of the word (consider affixes).

3. Jot these "word relatives" on branches of the tree.

Looks Like:

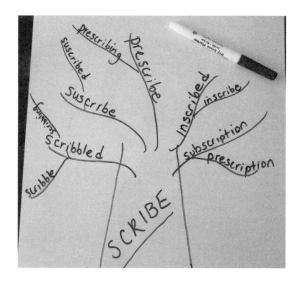

Bonus *The accompanying lesson can be found on page 222.*

Tech Tip *Students can do different versions of Word Family Trees digitally by creating mind maps, word splashes, and word clouds using apps such as MindMaple, Sketchboard, Wordle, and ABCya!*

Part-of-Speech Chart

Day ____

Why?

- To deepen our understanding of the different words being studied

- To explore the different meanings of words and contexts where these words might be used

You Need:

Word study notebook and a pencil

How?

1. Create a five-column chart. In the first column, list all words being studied.

2. For each word, think this: What is the part of speech? Does this word have more than one meaning—and perhaps another part of speech?

3. Check off if each word is a noun, verb, adjective, and/or adverb.

4. Extra time? Start a conversation, or do a little writing with these words.

Looks Like:

WORD	N	V	ADJ	ADV
geography	X			
geographic			X	
geology	X			
geometry	X			
geode	X			
geographer	X			
geographically				X

Bonus *The accompanying lesson can be found on page 219.*

Figurative Language Fun

Day____

Why?
- To become more playful with words
- To better understand how to use words in creative and interesting ways

You Need:
Word study notebook and a pencil

How?
1. Choose a word (or a few words).
2. Think: How can I use this word in a more poetic and playful way? (Some examples of figurative language include similes, metaphors, idioms, puns, personification, and alliteration.)
3. Use each of your chosen words to create playful examples of figurative language.
4. Challenge ideas:
   - Choose one word, and use that word in several different examples of figurative language.
   - Choose a few words, and try to include those words in a short piece of writing that includes multiple examples of figurative language.
   - Choose a few word study words, and include those in your writing entries, reading entries, math writing, social studies writing, or science writing . . . using figurative language—and in a way that makes sense!

Looks Like:

The flowers danced in the breeze.

Frank flew the flowers from Florida to Frankfort for the fashion show.

The children were flowers, growing and blooming with each passing day.

The flowers were as bright as a jewel and reminded me of a sapphire.

Find It *The accompanying lesson can be found on page 125 of* Word Study That Sticks.

Creating Connections
(Analogies)

Day _____

Why?
- To deepen our understanding of the different words being studied
- To create connections between words

You Need:
Word study notebook and a pencil

How?
1. Study the word list, carefully looking for words that have identifiable synonyms, antonyms, uses, etc.
2. Think: What kind of analogy might I create? What analogy structure works with what I know about this word?
3. Create an analogy. Repeat with other words.
4. Challenge: Include more than one word being studied into the same analogy!

Looks Like:

Common Formats of Analogies

A: B:: A: B
Word 1: Word 2:: Synonym for word 1: Synonym for word 2
Word 1: Word 2:: Antonym for word 1: Antonym for word 2

A: A:: B: B
Word 1: Synonym for Word 1:: Word 2: Synonym for Word 2
Word 1: Antonym for Word 1:: Word 2: Antonym for Word 2

Other Common Types of Relationships Include:
Part: Whole   Tool: Use   Cause: Effect   Object/Place: User

Bonus *The accompanying lesson can be found on page 223.*

Concept S-T-R-E-T-C-H

Day ____

Why?

- To deepen understanding of the different words being studied
- To explore other contexts for using words
- To apply word learning to other subject areas

You Need:

Word study notebook and a pencil

How?

1. Choose a word. (Hint: If necessary, change or add a suffix to the word—adjectives work best for this routine.)
2. Think of a concept—ideally something you are studying that can be described this way.
3. Discuss, list, and/or sketch your ideas.

Example: If the word was *dangerous*, you might consider books you read with dangerous characters or settings and discuss these characters and settings. You might also discuss dangerous people, places, or times from history and think, talk, sketch, or write more about the dangers present.

Looks Like:

```
Characters who are inquisitive:

 - Curious George

 - Ada Twist from Ada Twist, Scientist

 - Ruby from the Ruby and the Booker Boys series

 - Hermione from Harry Potter

I noticed that although being inquisitive is a good
thing, it sometimes gets these characters into trouble!
```

Bonus *The accompanying lesson can be found on page 224.*

MEANING MASTERY

LAUNCH

Think of your current group of students. Consider their strengths, interests, and areas of readiness. Teach two or three responsive meaning routines.

LATER

Teach additional meaning routines (about one per month) to the class or to small groups of students. Choose routines to match the strengths, interests, and areas of readiness of different classroom learners.

TIP

Find ways to authentically incorporate meaning routines (with word study pattern words) into the content areas. This helps us use time efficiently and promotes greater transfer.

TIP

Use meaning routines to explore content area vocabulary. Because students already know how to explore the meanings of words, there's no need to take the time to reteach these methods or create additional routines. This is another way to use our time efficiently!

MEANING ROUTINES IN ACTION

Photo by Holly Bruni

This fourth-grade reading partnership discusses recent reading . . . *and* tries to use word study pattern words in that conversation.

Photo by Viviana Tamas

A third-grade student writes (and then solves) a math word problem that includes word study pattern words!

Fifth-grade students work together to craft poems that include recent word study pattern words.

A second-grade student uses recent learning from word study to help decode and clarify the meaning of a word while reading.

The Picture It routine is a favorite for students of all ages.

CREATING CONNECTIONS
WHO CAN SOLVE THESE?

1. <u>preseason</u> : _ _ _ _ _ _ _ _ _ _ _ : : <u>predate</u> : _ _ _ _ _ _ _ _ _ _

2. <u>preapprove</u> : deny : : _ _ _ _ _ _ _ _ : assist

3. law school : <u>postgraduate</u> : : racial bias : _ _ _ _ _ _ _

WORD BANK:

prejudice   postseason   prevent   postdate

Older students enjoy Creating Connections (Analogies).

CHAPTER FIVE

Phonemic Awareness and Phonics Routines

> I have goten good at hearing and seprading the sounds in words. This helps me read new words and write new words.

Phonemic awareness and phonics are essential aspects of word study. The minicharts included in this chapter help students practice related strategies in meaningful and fun ways. Here you'll find minicharts to help students explore and study sounds and letters in words. When the focus is on separating, blending, or manipulating sounds, students engage in practices that increase phonemic awareness. By simply adding visual cues (letters) to this work, many of the routines naturally transition to also building phonics power.

Why Is This Phonemic Awareness and Phonics Work Important?

In *Essential Strategies for Word Study*, Rasinski and Zutell (2010) remind us that word study includes not only the direct study but also the exploration of words. They share that "when we store words in our brain, the sound, spelling, and meaning are usually consolidated. When we view a word on a printed page, we access the sound, spelling, and meaning simultaneously and immediately" (p. 6). The importance and relevance of phonemic awareness and phonics can't be underestimated. They are essential aspects of word study—and, of course, becoming a proficient reader and writer.

In 2000, the National Reading Panel named phonemic awareness one of the five crucial components of teaching reading. Young children developing phonemic awareness are learning to notice and separate sounds (phonemes) in words and manipulate these sounds. Through developmentally appropriate and *fun* wordplay, we teach how to isolate, add, delete, blend, segment, and substitute sounds. And, man, do we have a blast rhyming! Children delight in hearing, repeating, rhyming, chanting, singing, and playing around with sounds in words—and this joy has a big impact. Research shows early literacy learning is highly predictive of a child's later ability to read (Ehri et al., 2001; Lonigan, 2003; Snow, Burns, & Griffin, 1999; Storch & Whitehurst, 2002). Some of this phonemic and phonologic groundwork is laid before students even enter school. There is plenty of research available that documents the educational impact of a student's home literacy environment (Evans, Shaw, Bell, & Can, 2000; Lonigan, Dyer, & Anthony, 1996; Payne, Whitehurst, & Angell, 1994; Phillips & Lonigan, 2005, 2007; Sénéchal & LeFevre, 2002). However, as educators we know that there are vast differences in the early literacy experiences of young students, and because of this, we will likely need to double down on our efforts to include short, regular snippets of strong instruction that bolster the phonemic awareness of all classroom learners. The mini-charts in this chapter that support phonemic awareness routines aim to do just that!

Phonics is the knowledge of the relationship between letters and sounds and how they are used in reading and writing. Believe it or not, phonics instruction is regarded as a somewhat controversial topic. There are a lot of brilliant and passionate educators, researchers, and leaders with very different perspectives on phonics and how this component of word study is best approached. As with most things in life, I believe different perspectives are an asset—and by listening, reading, sharing, and discussing research findings, we can integrate the plentiful research out there in a way that makes sense. My own core phonics beliefs are balanced and are represented in instruction that includes the following:

- Inquiry and discovery to ignite and build interest

- Expertly planned instruction of letter-sound relationships

- Practice in how to study sounds in *real* words

- Opportunities to hear, see, and notice similarities and differences in *real* words

- An emphasis on developing connections between the letters and sounds in different words

- Consistent application and use of this knowledge while reading and writing

I have often referred to the work of Donald R. Bear, Isabel Beck, Wiley Blevins, Irene Fountas, J. Richard Gentry, Marcia Invernizzi, Francine Johnston, Gay Sue Pinnell, Tim Rasinski, Deborah Reed, and Sandra Wilde to get ideas about what works and how to support learners with different areas of expertise and readiness. The practices represented in the following routines highlight what I've learned from all these greats.

How Does Phonemic Awareness and Phonics Work Fit a Range of Learners?

Primary-grade students greatly benefit from explicit phonemic awareness and phonics instruction. It makes sense to consistently prioritize time to study sounds and letters and the way they "work" in words. Moreover, phonemic awareness and phonics also need to be embedded into reading and writing instruction so students understand and learn (from the start) *why* this learning matters and *how* to apply concepts where it counts. We empower students to understand these fundamentals by providing a wide range of opportunities to watch, hear, manipulate, and play with letters and sounds in real words. Students learn by trying, seeing, and applying their knowledge in authentic contexts. These are needed and precious minutes. However, please remember that students benefit from a well-rounded approach to word study. In the primary grades, phonemic awareness and phonics have a prominent role but are not *all* that are needed to build a strong foundation.

Even as a teacher of *middle school students*, I encouraged students to reflect and ask themselves these questions: Does that look right? and Does that sound right? We don't stop using our phonemic awareness and phonics knowledge after second grade. These facets of word study become more closely aligned to spelling pattern work but are still included as part of instruction and learning.

Some students identified as having language-based learning disabilities benefit from integrating a multisensory approach to instruction. Teachers of students acquiring English also often find success with incorporating phonics into classroom instruction. Rest assured that many educators who work as interventionists, language experts, and special education professionals have tried out the phonemic awareness and phonics routines supported by the tools in this chapter. They have seen and shared the benefits and joy that results. When used alongside carefully planned and personalized instruction, the tools in this chapter help bring independence and success to *all* who study words.

When Do Learners Engage in Phonemic Awareness and Phonics Work?

Here are two of the infinite examples of how a word study cycle might look. Please note that phonemic awareness and phonics are sometimes included in other cycle practices. Many primary teachers also prioritize infusing short snippets (thirty seconds to five minutes) of phonemic awareness and phonics throughout the day; morning meeting, shared reading, and transition times are perfect opportunities for this efficient practice.

Day 1	Day 2	Day 3	Day 4	Day 5	Day 6
Meaning	Meaning	Phonemic Awareness and Phonics	Pattern	Pattern	Check-In/ Transfer

Day 1	Day 2	Day 3	Day 4	Day 5	Day 6
Meaning	Meaning	Pattern	Pattern	Phonemic Awareness and Phonics	High Frequency

Sound Search

Why?

To listen for and hear all the sounds in words

You Need:

Sound boxes and counters

How?

1. 💬 Say the word. S-T-R-E-T-C-H the word.

2. 🧩 Separate the sounds.

3. ⚫⚫⚫ Count the sounds.

Looks Like:

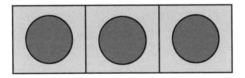

Speech bubble: openclipart.org/PrinterKiller; Jigsaw puzzle: openclipart.org/ben.

Find It   *The accompanying lesson can be found on page 68 of* Word Study That Sticks.

Sound Search With Letters

Why?

To learn about letters, sounds, and words

You Need:

Sound boxes and counters

How?

1. 💬 Say the word. S-T-R-E-T-C-H the word.

2. 🧩 Separate the sounds.

3. ⚫⚫⚫ Count the sounds.

4. C - A - T. Replace each sound with letters.

Looks Like:

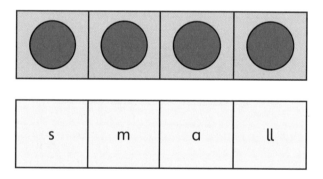

Speech bubble: openclipart.org/PrinterKiller; Jigsaw puzzle: openclipart.org/ben.

Find It *The accompanying lesson can be found on page 68 of* Word Study That Sticks.

Tap It!

Why?
To learn about letters, sounds, and words

You Need:
Something to tap with and something to tap on

How?

1. 💬 Say the word. S-T-R-E-T-C-H the word.
2. 🧩 Separate the sounds in the word.
3. ⬤⬤⬤ Tap the sounds you hear.

Looks Like:

Find It *The accompanying lesson can be found on page 117 of* Word Study That Sticks.

Rounded speech bubble: openclipart.org/demiki; Jigsaw puzzle: openclipart.org/ben.

Hold It, Say It, Sort It

Why?

- To hear the different sounds in words
- To compare sounds in words

You Need:

Set of items

Optional: Sorting mats

How?

1. Hold the item.
2. Say the word. Listen for sounds.
3. Sort the item based on the sounds you hear.

Remember: Clean up!

Looks Like:

Find It *The accompanying lesson can be found on page 118 of* Word Study That Sticks.

Hands: openclipart.org/GDJ; Speech bubble: openclipart.org/PrinterKiller; Stacks of papers: openclipart.org/hmproulx.

Jumping Beans

Why?

- To hear the different sounds in words
- To separate the sounds in words

You Need:

Large "sound boxes" (stepping stones or taped-out boxes on the floor)

How?

1. 💬 Say the word. S-T-R-E-T-C-H the word.
2. 🧩 Separate the sounds, and jump once for each sound.

Remember: Be careful with your body. Work safely.

Looks Like:

Photo by Rebecca Johnson

Speech bubble: openclipart.org/PrinterKiller; Jigsaw puzzle: openclipart.org/ben.

Find It *The accompanying lesson can be found on page 147 of* Word Study That Sticks.

Switch It, Change It

Why?

- To learn new words
- To see how words are the same and different

You Need:

Word cards

Choice: Magnetic letters, slates, letter tiles, or letter/blend cards

How?

1. 💬 Say the word.

2. 👂 S-T-R-E-T-C-H the word. Listen for sounds.

3. 🔄 Switch one letter or sound to make a new word.

4. 💡 Challenge: How many new words can you find?

Looks Like:

Speech bubble: openclipart.org/PrinterKiller; Ear: openclipart.org/CCX; Switch: openclipart.org/bnielsen; Idea: openclipart.org/ousia.

Find It *The accompanying lesson can be found on page 119 of* Word Study That Sticks.

Configuration Station

Why?

- To visualize the shape of a word
- To use the known shape of a word to help spell the word

You Need:

Word study notebook and a pencil

How?

1. Write a word neatly in one color.
2. Outline the shape of each letter using rectangular boxes in another color.

Looks Like:

Bonus *The accompanying lesson can be found on page 226.*

Word Wall *This routine can also be done with high-frequency words.*

Pencil: openclipart.org/pascallpalme.

I Spy!

Why?
To notice learned sounds and letters in words all around us

You Need:
Curious eyes and mind

How?

1.  Say: *I am learning about ___.*

2. ◉◉ Look: What do you see that has these letter(s) and sound(s)?

3. Say: *I spy with my little eye . . . a word with ___. It is ___.*

Hint: Look for written words or "things" that have the sounds you are studying.

Looks Like:

Speech bubble: openclipart.org/PrinterKiller; Eyes: openclipart.org/Prawny

Bonus *The accompanying lesson can be found on page 227.*

Word Wall *This routine can also be done with high-frequency words.*

Word Ladders

Why?

- To think about the sounds and letters in words
- To study what's the same and what's different about words

You Need:

Word study notebook and a pencil

How?

1. 👀 Look at the word at the bottom of the ladder. Read the clue on the next rung.

2. 💭 Think: What word is being described? What letter(s) need to change?

3. ✏️ Write the new word. Keep going up the ladder!

Challenge: Create your own word ladder.

Looks Like:

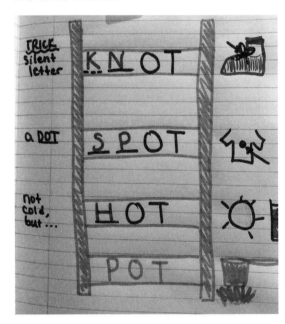

Eyes: openclipart.org/Prawny; Thought cloud: openclipart.org/rejon; Pencil: openclipart.org/pascallpalme.

Singing Sounds

Why?

To read pattern words fluently

You Need:

Text (song, poem, rhyme, short text)

How?

1. Listen to the text being read.

2. Look for pattern words. Circle or underline these words.

3. Reread the text many times. Say the pattern words in different voices.

Voices to try: Whisper, shout, spooky, cheerleader, bored, excited . . .

Looks Like:

I had a silly <u>dream</u>
Where an elephant danced on a <u>beam</u>.
And when he tumbled, he fell on top of his <u>team</u>.
I had a VERY silly <u>dream</u>.

Ear: openclipart.org/CCX; Eyes: openclipart.org/Prawny; Redo: openclipart.org/PERCE-NEIGE.

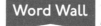
Find It *The accompanying lesson can be found on page 149 of* Word Study That Sticks.

Word Wall *This routine can also be done with high-frequency words.*

Sensory Cycle

Why?
To use our five senses as we learn

You Need:
Word cards and different sensory tracing materials

How?

1. 👀 Look at the word.
2. 💬 Say the word.
3. 👂 Listen to your partner say the word.
4. 👆 Trace the word.

Looks Like:

Bonus *The accompanying lesson can be found on page 228.*   **Word Wall** *This routine can also be done with high-frequency words.*

Reggio Routines

Why?

To discover more about sounds, letters, and words

You Need:

Loose parts

How?

1. 👀 Read the "letter" or "word" invitation.
2. 👀 Look at and explore the different loose parts.
3. 💡 Create letters, words, and learning using the materials.

Looks Like:

Photo by Ellen Calamito

Eyes: openclipart.org/Prawny; Ear: openclipart.org/CCX.

Bonus *The accompanying lesson can be found on page 229.*

Word Wall *This routine can also be done with high-frequency words.*

Sound Search With Letters

Day _____

Why?

- To explore sounds, word parts, and words
- To think about the letters that make particular sounds

You Need:

Words and sound boxes

How?

1. Say and S-T-R-E-T-C-H a word.

2. Separate and count the number of different sounds (or perhaps syllables).

3. Replace each sound with letter(s). Then repeat!

Looks Like:

(sleepy is divided by sound)

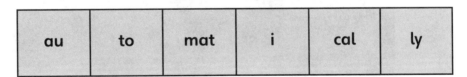

(automatically is divided by syllable)

Find It *The accompanying lesson (this is an adapted version of Sound Search) can be found on page 68 of* Word Study That Sticks.

Tap It!

Day ____

Why?

- To help us hear *all* the different sounds in words
- To help us spell words correctly

You Need:

Word cards or list, something to tap on, and something to tap with

How?

1. Choose a word, and say it aloud. Stretch out the word by saying it slowly.

2. Segment (separate) the sounds in the word, *tapping* something each time you hear a different sound.

3. Say the word again.

Looks Like:

Find It *The accompanying lesson can be found on page 117 of* Word Study That Sticks.

Switch It, Change It

Day ___

Why?

- To see the similarities and differences between words
- To provide a reminder of how we can use what we already know to help us spell other new and challenging words

You Need:

Words/word cards

Optional: Word-building manipulatives

How?

1. Choose a word and say it aloud.

2. Identify a pattern in the word. Think: What other words do I know that have this pattern? What letters and sounds can I change to make other words?

3. Jot all the words you can think of—use known word parts to help you spell each word.

Looks Like:

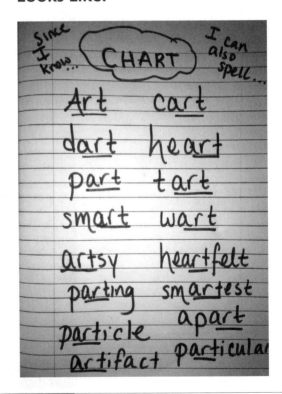

Find It *The accompanying lesson (this is an adapted version) can be found on page 119 of* Word Study That Sticks.

Tech Tip *Remember, any routine that can be written in a notebook can also be written on a digital document or submitted digitally.*

I Spy!

Day ____

Why?

- To transfer learning about words
- To look for and explore pattern words out in the real world—*not* on a list!

You Need:

Access to the pattern being studied and a place (in person or digital) to search and spy

How?

1. Look over words, and briefly discuss the pattern being studied.

2. Look around. Search for actual words—or items—that include the pattern being studied.

3. Say *I spy* ____. See how many different words or items can be found.

Looks Like:

Bonus *The accompanying lesson can be found on page 227.*

Tech Tip *Students can also search for specific sounds, letters, or words following a pattern in digital texts, video clips, and podcasts.*

Pattern Pictures

Day ____

Why?

- To transfer learning about words

- To look for and explore pattern words out in the real world—*not* on a list!

You Need:

Access to the pattern being studied and a camera or device with a camera

How?

1. Look over words, and briefly discuss the pattern being studied.

2. Look around. Search for actual words—or items—that include the pattern/sound(s) being studied.

3. Snap a photo of each found word and item.

Looks Like:

Bonus *The accompanying lesson can be found on page 230.*

Tech Tip *Students can also create a visual compilation of their pattern pictures by posting the photos on a class bulletin board (wall space or digital) or sharing a photo slideshow.*

Tying It Together

PHONEMIC AWARENESS AND PHONICS FUNDAMENTALS

HIGH IMPACT!

Phonemic awareness and phonics are core aspects of word study, and high-quality practice is essential for success in reading, writing, and word know-how!

NOT ONLY KINDERS!

Phonemic awareness and phonics are more prevalent features of the school day in the early grades. However, many students across a larger range of grades benefit from these types of word study practices.

A LITTLE GOES A LONG WAY!

Short, consistent snippets of phonemic awareness and phonics instruction make a huge difference in competence. In the primary grades, teachers often benefit from including this type of instruction *throughout* the day. Additionally, one to two days of the word study cycle are often dedicated to these types of practices.

REMINDER

Phonemic awareness and phonics are not the only aspects of word study. Highlight these practices, and *also* incorporate meaning, spelling pattern, and hybrid practices to build the foundation students need. This integrated approach includes a wide range of best practices and yields more high-impact results than a worksheet packet ever could!

PHONEMIC AWARENESS AND PHONICS ROUTINES IN ACTION

A kindergartener uses knowledge of letter-sound relationships while doing the Sound Search With Letters routine.

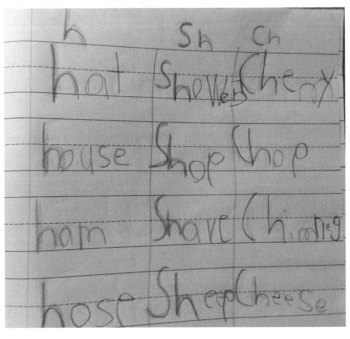

This first grader is showing off recent learning about digraphs.

Photo by Linda Day

Young learners appreciate having choice and enjoy deciding which phonemic awareness and phonics routines they will complete each day.

A motivated learner is proud of a first try of Configuration Station.

A primary learner uses sound boxes to help switch and change the onset of one word to make many other words.

An elementary student enjoys Sound Snapshot outside, finding examples of different blends in the school garden (plant).

Photo by Viviana Tamas

CHAPTER SIX

Spelling Pattern Routines

My writing has gotten so much better. I used to pick easy words that I knew how to spell. My writing was kinda boring. Now that I know so much more about ~~words~~ how words work, I am not scared to try to spell more interesting words. I am really proud of my work. I feel like I have grown as a writer and a speller.

So far in Part II, resources have been provided so that students can study the meaning of words, sounds in words, and the letters that each of these sounds makes—with greater ease and independence. We are now ready to peruse and select tools to support students as they practice applying their knowledge of spelling patterns. This work is essential in a well-rounded approach to word study. The tools on the following pages invite students to engage in spelling routines that are hands-on, student-centered, and fun. The provided charts promote independence as students seek out information about patterns within and between words; forge connections; and engage in significant discussion about what they see, wonder, think, and now understand.

Why Is Spelling Pattern Work Important?

English spelling is frustrating only when we expect it to be something it's not (i.e. a pure alphabetic system). If we see it for what it is, we can appreciate it for representing a lot of information about sound, a fair bit about meaning, and a little about etymology and history. (Wilde, 1992, p. 17)

Sandra Wilde explains why we can't teach spelling "rules" and absolutes in word study. Consequently, our lens shifts to finding joy in the fascinating, multifaceted nuances of our complex language. Our invitation to students to study words comes with this celebratory footnote.

Developmental stages and progressions (Bear, Invernizzi, Templeton, & Johnston, 2003; Gentry, 1982; Read, 1971) help us understand the increasingly complex knowledge required to think about, read, and write words conventionally. In word study, we explore patterns, noticing how words look and how they sound. We refine our understanding of these patterns as we look across words, noticing similarities and differences. We generalize our understandings and use these "big ideas" about how words work to help us decode and encode words fluently. Barron (1980), Chomsky (1970), Horn (1954), and Nolen and McCartin (1984) informed us years ago that phonics alone will not help students become conventional spellers; students need to internalize spelling patterns instead of rules. Much more recently, Fountas and Pinnell (2017) have prioritized the instructional goal of getting students "interested in words-seeking patterns, looking for connections, thinking about parts and what they mean" (p. 10). I always appreciate Fountas and Pinnell's way of breaking down deeply conceptual ideas into lingo we can all grab on to and understand. The goal of our instruction, then, is to have students integrate *all* their knowledge about words— and to have a bit of fun doing it.

What all this research has in common is this: Pattern-focused exploration, discussion, and practice aim to develop this understanding and drive it to become internalized. *This* is how our approach to instruction becomes more rich, full-bodied, and comprehensive. The resources in this chapter support students in these pursuits.

How Does Spelling Pattern Work Fit a Range of Learners?

Primary and upper-elementary grade learners in *all kinds* of instructional settings benefit from spelling pattern work. The developmental stages noted by aforementioned researchers guide our choices on the types of spelling patterns we prioritize for different groups of learners across settings and grades. Most ideally, we use a spelling inventory, look at authentic student work, *and* observe students reading and writing to help us make responsive instructional choices. By using formal and informal assessment to help match students to appropriate spelling pattern work—and then make ongoing adjustments—we use best practices that yield the high-impact results we most want for learners. Spelling pattern

Bonus

Check out Appendix B for a helpful if/then chart that helps us match students to prioritized patterns.

work, when integrated with other aspects of word study, empowers learners with infinite word-related opportunities.

When Do Learners Engage in Spelling Pattern Work?

Spelling pattern work begins mid-cycle, after students have been introduced to the meaning of words and have had time to explore words using meaning-based routines. Here are two of the many possibilities of how a word study cycle might look. Please note that spelling pattern practice is often but not always included in other cycle routines.

Day 1	Day 2	Day 3	Day 4	Day 5	Day 6
Meaning	Meaning	Pattern	Pattern	Hybrid	Check-In/ Transfer

Day 1	Day 2	Day 3	Day 4	Day 5	Day 6
Meaning	Meaning	Pattern	Pattern	Phonemic Awareness and Phonics	High Frequency

Sort It! Alike or Different?

Why?

To think about how words look and sound and notice patterns

You Need:

Word study folder, notebook, and words

How?

1. ๏๏ Look at the words: letters and sounds.

2. ☁ Think: How are these words alike? How are they different?

3. 💬 Sort words and share. "I did this because . . . "

Looks Like:

Find It *The accompanying lesson can be found on page 64 of* Word Study That Sticks.

Eyes: openclipart.org/Prawny; Thought cloud: openclipart.org/rejon; Speech bubble: openclipart.org/PrinterKiller.

Question Craze

Why?
To help us look at words, notice more about words, and make connections between words

You Need:
Word cards and question list

How?

1. 👀 Look at sorted words.

2. 💭 Think about what you see. How are the groups the same? Different?

3. ❓ Ask your partner a question, and talk more about the words.

Looks Like:

> **QUESTIONS WE CAN ASK OUR PARTNER WHILE LOOKING AT WORDS**
>
> How are these words alike?
>
> What is the same?
>
> How are these words different?
>
> Do you see a pattern? What is it?
>
> Where does this word go? Why?
>
> Why doesn't this word fit here?

Eyes: openclipart.org/Prawny; Thought cloud: openclipart.org/rejon; Question mark: openclipart.org/jean_victor_balin.

Find It *The accompanying lesson can be found on page 66 of* Word Study That Sticks.

Pattern Introduction: Nice to Meet You!

Why?
To learn word patterns

You Need:
Word study notebook and a pencil

How?

1. 👀 Watch the teacher begin to sort.

2. 💭 Think: Why is the teacher sorting this way? How are the words alike and different?

3. 💬 Join in! Share your ideas: "I notice . . . " Help sort the words.

Looks Like:

Bonus *The accompanying lesson can be found on page 232.*

Read It! Build It! Write It!

Why?
To become fluent while spelling words

You Need:
Options: Magnetic letters, letter tiles, Wikki Stix, etc.

How?

1. 👀 Look at a word.
2. 💬 Say the word.
3. 🔤 Build the word. Say each letter as you build it.

Looks Like:

Remember: Use the "power of three" and also to clean up respectfully!

Find It *The accompanying lesson (an adapted version of Multisensory Fun) can be found on page 70 of* Word Study That Sticks.

Word Wall *This routine can also be done with high-frequency words.*

Eyes: openclipart.org/Prawny; Speech bubble: openclipart.org/PrinterKiller; ABC: openclipart.org/mazeo.

Word Scavenger Hunts—Books

Why?

To remember words we know *and* use word learning while reading and writing

You Need:

Word study notebook, a pencil, and a book

How?

1. 📖 Reread a book.

2. 👀 Look for pattern words.

3. ✏️ Write down the pattern words you find.

Looks Like:

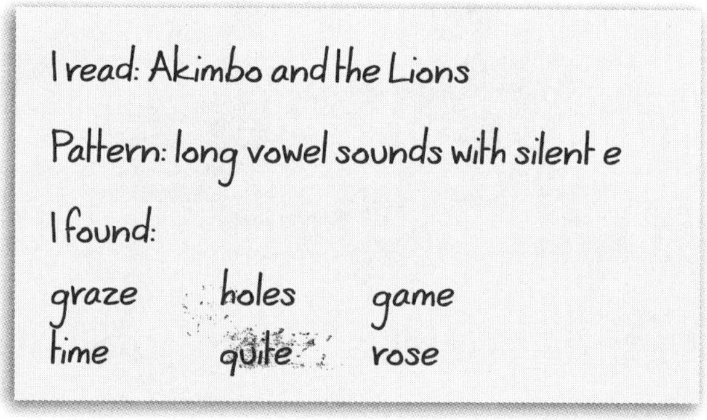

I read: Akimbo and the Lions

Pattern: long vowel sounds with silent e

I found:

graze	holes	game
time	quite	rose

Book: openclipart.org/sonoftroll; Eyes: openclipart.org/Prawny; Pencil: openclipart.org/pascallpalme.

Find It *The accompanying lesson (an adapted version of Word Scavenger Hunts) can be found on page 83 of* Word Study That Sticks.

Word Wall *This routine can also be done with high-frequency words.*

Word Scavenger Hunts—Around Me

Why?

To remember words we know *and* use word learning while reading and writing

You Need:

Word study notebook, a pencil, and a book

How?

1. 👀 Look around you. Think: Do I see any pattern words?

2. 👂 Listen to people talk. Think: Do I hear any pattern words?

3. ✏️ Write down words you find.

Looks Like:

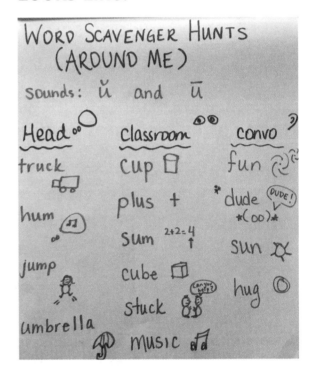

Eyes: openclipart.org/Prawny; Ear: openclipart.org/CCX; Pencil: openclipart.org/pascallpalme.

Find It The accompanying lesson (an adapted version of Word Scavenger Hunts and Stepped Up Word Scavenger Hunts) can be found on pages 83 and 126 of Word Study That Sticks.

Word Wall This routine can also be done with high-frequency words.

How Fast Can We Go?

Why?

To review patterns and become fluent with sorting

You Need:

Word study folder with word cards

How?

1. ◉◉ Look at your word cards.

2. ☁ Think: How can I sort these words based on how they look and sound?

3. 💬 Say each word as you move and sort it.

Hint: Race yourself or work with a partner. Sort your words in the correct columns as quickly as possible.

Repeat many times. Try to get faster every time.

Looks Like:

Find It *The accompanying lesson can be found on page 128 of* Word Study That Sticks.

Eyes: openclipart.org/Prawny; Thought cloud: openclipart.org/rejon; Speech bubble: openclipart.org/PrinterKiller.

Three Key Questions: Reading

Why?

- To check to see if you are reading a word correctly
- To use *all* information to solve words

You Need:

An interesting book

How?

1. 📖 Read a book.

2. 💡 When you get to a tricky word, use what you know to try to solve it!

3. ❓ After a try, ask yourself: Does that *look* and *sound* right? Does that *make sense*? What do I know that can help me?

4. 📖 Yes? Keep reading. No? Try again!

Looks Like:

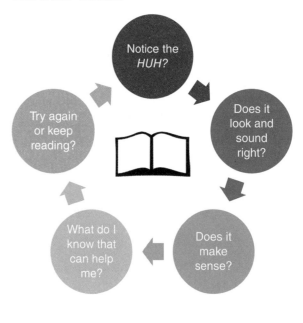

Book: openclipart.org/sonoftroll; Idea: openclipart.org/ousia; Question mark: openclipart.org/jean_victor_balin.

Find It *The accompanying lesson can be found on page 151 of* Word Study That Sticks.

141

Three Key Questions: Writing

Why?

- To check your spelling of written words
- To use *all* information to write words

You Need:

Writing folder (or any writing)

How?

1. 📖 Reread recent writing.

2. 💡 Stop at a tricky word. Use what you know to check the spelling.

3. ❓ Ask yourself: Does that look right? Does that sound right? What have I learned that can help me?

4. ✏️ Yes? Keep rereading. No? Try to spell that word again!

Looks Like:

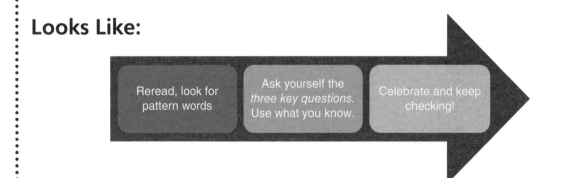

Reread, look for pattern words

Ask yourself the *three key questions*. Use what you know.

Celebrate and keep checking!

Find It *The accompanying lesson can be found on page 151 of* Word Study That Sticks.

Book: openclipart.org/sonoftroll; Idea: openclipart.org/susia; Question mark: openclipart.org/jean_victor_balin; Pencil: openclipart.org/pascallpalme.

Partner Prompting

Why?

To review what we know and to support peers

You Need:

Word study notebook or cards

How?

1.  Sit with a partner.

2. *Say* a word.

3. Ask your partner to *spell* that word.

If your partner is stuck, prompt them with a hint.

Looks Like:

Partners: openclipart.org/piettuk; Speech bubble: openclipart.org/PrinterKiller; Question mark: openclipart.org/jean_victor_balin.

Bonus *The accompanying lesson can be found on page 233.*

Word Wall *This routine can also be done with high-frequency words.*

Look, Say, Cover, Write, Check

Why?

- To check how well you know a word
- To get ready to use words again and again

You Need:

Word study notebook and a pencil

How?

1. 👀 Look at the word.
2. 💬 Say the word out loud.
3. 📄 Cover the word (fold page in).
4. ✏️ Write the word.
5. ✅ Check: Did you spell it correctly?

Looks Like:

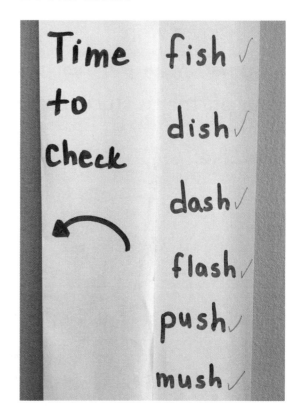

Eyes: openclipart.org/Prawny; Speech bubble: openclipart.org/PrinterKiller; Paper: openclipart.org/PublicDomainArt; Pencil: openclipart.org/pascallpalmer; Green check: openclipart.org/dholler.

Bonus *The accompanying lesson can be found on page 234.*

Word Wall *This routine can also be done with high-frequency words.*

Sound Snapshot

Why?

To look for and explore pattern words out in the real world

You Need:

Camera or device with a camera

How?

1. 💬 Talk about pattern words.

2. 👀 Look around. Think: What do I see that is a pattern word?

3. 📷 Take a picture. Optional: Share or post the pictures.

Looks Like:

I SPY WITH MY LITTLE EYE . . .

We found short *a* and long *a* words.

Bonus *The accompanying lesson (an adapted version of Sound Snapshot) can be found on page 230.*

Speech bubble: openclipart.org/PrinterKiller; Eyes: openclipart.org/Prawny; Camera: openclipart.org/loveandread.

Guess the Pattern

Day ____

Why?

- To think about how words look and sound
- To notice and think about patterns *across* words

You Need:

Word study folder, notebook, and words

How?

1. Lay, Look, Say: Lay out words. Look at the spellings of the words, and say the sounds in the words.
2. Sort words into groups based on the way the words *look* and *sound*.
3. Share or write a few sentences to explain your thinking. What do you notice about your words? Why did you sort this way?

Looks Like:

```
I noticed all the words are verbs and are past tense
verbs (they have -ed at the end).

I noticed that sometimes the endings of these words have
different sounds; -ed can sound like /ed/, it can sound
like /d/, and it can also sometimes sound like /t/.

Since all the words looked the same at the end (they
all had -ed), I sorted them based on the way the -ed
sounded at the end of the word.
```

 Find It *The accompanying lesson can be found on page 78 of* Word Study That Sticks.

 Tech Tip *Remember, any work written in a notebook can also be written digitally. Sometimes students enjoy keeping two-column charts. In the first column (the Before column), students try to guess the pattern, and in the second column (the After column), they write the taught pattern from the Now I Know! routine.*

Pattern Introduction: Now I Know!

Day ____

Why?

- To better understand word patterns
- To prepare to transfer word learning

You Need:

Word study notebook and a pencil

How?

1. Share ideas from Guess the Pattern.

2. Listen and watch as the teacher sorts the words.

3. Think: How is the teacher sorting these words? What similarities and differences do I see?

4. Join in. Share where words belong *and* why the word is being placed into that column.

5. Jot a few key points to remember about the pattern.

Looks Like:

Bonus *The accompanying lesson can be found on page 232.*

Tech Tip *There are templates for SMART Boards (check out Smart Exchange) and other similar interactive whiteboards that can help you create a sorting table and digital word cards. Words can be dragged into the correct columns. If a student tries dragging a word into the incorrect column, the word will "bounce back" to signal that another try is needed.*

Multisensory Fun

Day ____

Why?

- To become more fluent with our spelling
- To have fun and feel playful while we study words

You Need:

Options: Mini chalkboards, Magna Doodles, dry erase boards, magnetic letters, letter tiles, Wikki Stix, shaving cream, etc.

How?

1. Choose a word and say it out loud.
2. Use the chosen tool—write/make/build the word *at least* three times.
3. Repeat with other words.

Looks Like:

Remember to clean up—respect the classroom and materials!

Find It *The accompanying lesson can be found on page 82 of* Word Study That Sticks.

Word Wall *This routine can also be done with high-frequency words.*

Word Scavenger Hunts

Day _____

Why?

- To remember we are studying and learning patterns, not a few particular words
- To apply word learning

You Need:

Word study notebook, a pencil, and a book you have already read

How?

1. *Reread* a book (or part of a book).
2. As you reread, look for pattern words.
3. Write down words you find.

Looks Like:

```
I reread a part of: The Maze Runner, by James Dashner

Pattern: multisyllable words with an open first syllable

I found:

before     remembered
refused    returned
finally    believe
beetle     replaced
begun      crazy
```

 Find It *The accompanying lesson can be found on page 83 of* Word Study That Sticks.

Word Wall *This routine can also be done with high-frequency words.*

149

Stepped Up Word Scavenger Hunts

Day ____

Why?

- To recognize pattern words beyond those currently on "a list"
- To extend word learning outside of word study

You Need:

Word study notebook and a pencil

Optional: Nontraditional word hunt "texts" (infographics, videos, podcasts, etc.)

How?

1. Name and review the pattern being studied.

2. Think: What other words do I know with this pattern? Where might I find other words with this pattern?

3. Go on a "stepped up" scavenger hunt for words containing that pattern.

4. Try searching: your head (prior knowledge), around you (classroom displays, charts, notebooks), and all kinds of texts (print, digital, visual, audio, etc.).

Looks Like:

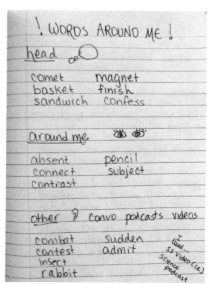

Find It	*The accompanying lesson can be found on page 126 of Word Study That Sticks.*	
Tech Tip	*Students love searching digital infographics, video clips, conversations, content area articles and assignment postings, their own digital writing, blog posts, etc.*	
Word Wall	*This routine can also be done with high-frequency words.*	

How Fast Can We Go?

Day ____

Why?

- To solidify pattern understanding
- To strengthen word fluency

You Need:

Word cards

Optional: Timing device

How?

1. Lay out all word cards.

2. Sort word cards into columns/ groups according to the pattern (the way the word looks and sounds).

3. Repeat several times, trying to increase your speed in each round.

   Hint: Work alone or with a partner.

   Remember to say the words out loud as you move them.

Looks Like:

Find It *The accompanying lesson can be found on page 128 of* Word Study That Sticks.

Tech Tip *There are templates for SMART Boards (check out Smart Exchange) and other similar interactive whiteboards where you can create a sorting table and digital word cards. For those who enjoy added challenges, digital timers can be added to encourage students to work collaboratively to "beat" previous sorting times.*

Partner Prompting
Day _____

Why?

- To review the spelling of pattern words
- To prepare to easily use learned words in writing

You Need:

Word study notebook

How?

1. Find a partner.

2. Switch notebooks.

3. Orally "quiz" each other on the spelling words being studied.

   Hint: Do not correct your partner if they are stuck. Instead, prompt your partner with a helpful hint they can use to get themselves "unstuck."

   Challenge: Can you also talk about the meaning of the word?

Looks Like:

Bonus *The accompanying lesson can be found on page 233.*

Word Wall *This routine can also be done with high-frequency words.*

Look, Say, Cover, Write, Check

Day____

Why?

- To become fluent and confident spellers
- To prepare to use this word (with ease) when we write

You Need:

Word study notebook and a pencil

Optional: Word cards

How?

1. Look at the word.
2. Say the word out loud—while looking at it.
3. Cover/flip over the word so it is not visible.
4. Write the word.
5. Check: Compare your jot to the actual word. Were you correct?

Looks Like:

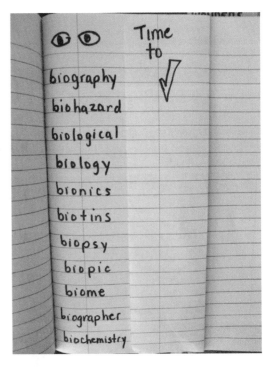

Bonus *The accompanying lesson can be found on page 234.*

Word Wall *This routine can also be done with high-frequency words.*

Pumpin' Patterns

Day____

Why?

- To practice spelling words fluently

- To use active, kinesthetic learning to help you remember how to spell new words

You Need:

Words

Optional: Ball, jump rope, hula hoop . . .

How?

1. Say a word.

2. Spell the word one letter at a time. As you spell the word, incorporate body movement (throw and catch a ball, touch your toes, march in place, etc.).

3. Say the word again.

4. Challenge: Assign each specific pattern a different body movement.

Looks Like:

Bonus *The accompanying lesson can be found on page 235.*

 Word Wall *This routine can also be done with high-frequency words.*

Tying It Together

PATTERN PROFICIENCY

IT'S ALL ABOUT THE ACCESS!

Spelling pattern prowess is empowering. When we build a deep understanding of the *why* behind words and *how* they work, the opportunities that follow are infinite.

PERSONALIZED AND RESPONSIVE

We use assessment formatively to make responsive instructional choices about the types of patterns we prioritize for different learners. Check out Appendix B for guidance in matching students to patterns and words.

FASCINATING!

The inquiry and discovery involved in student explorations of how words work build interest and curiosity. When we provide opportunities for not only direct instruction but also the inquiry-driven practices this chapter supports, students become interested in and passionate about the exciting world of words.

FLUENCY = AHHHH . . .

The spelling pattern fluency routines supported by tools in this chapter help take the more cumbersome work (that often leads to frustration) out of reading and writing. These practices enable students to decode and encode with greater ease, thereby promoting greater enjoyment in both reading and writing.

SPELLING PATTERN ROUTINES IN ACTION

Photo by Katie McGrath

Now I Know! helps teachers introduce the why and how behind a pattern.

Students think about how words look and sound as they sort words in different ways—and ask each other questions to think more deeply about the words and how they are both similar and different.

While engaging in the How Fast Can We Go? routine, students sort with fluency.

This primary student lifted the level of her Word Scavenger Hunts by then using found words in a second word study routine.

An upper-grade student also used their Word Scavenger Hunt words in a second word study routine.

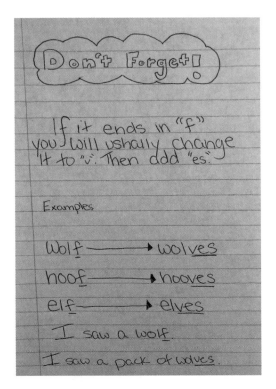

This student used an assessment routine to show off recent spelling pattern learning.

CHAPTER SEVEN

Habit and Hybrid Routines

> My teacher trusts us. We make choices about supplies, routines, workspaces, and so much more. Knowing she trusts us to make decisions means a lot. I think we are all extra responsible because we want Mrs. K to know she was right. We are ready, we got this!

The past few chapters have provided tools to nurture the different facets of word study. In this chapter, we begin to put it all together. The tools you will find here support the habits and culture of a classroom that moves beyond compliance. As such, many tools included in the upcoming pages of this book set out to help students ask thoughtful questions; develop a collaborative mindset; build fruitful talk; be resourceful in their use of classroom materials; and, yes, even seek out new learning risks. By doing so, students are likely to move beyond the zone of "musts" or "shoulds" into the not-so-magical but oh-so-relevant world of student-driven learning. Additionally, there are other tools to support routines that invite students to put all they know about words together. These hybrid routines are a first step toward transfer, as students integrate different aspects of word knowledge as they engage in meaningful practice.

Why Are Habit and Hybrid Word Work Routines Important?

Authors Ross Cooper and Erin Murphy (2016) begin *Hacking Project Based Learning* by providing recommendations for "building relationships, fostering learner agency through our physical environment, creating a resource-rich classroom, teaching students to ask good questions, and promoting risk-taking" (p. 19). This groundwork is essential for *all* types of learning. Word study offers additional opportunities to teach students how to navigate these kinds of learning spaces and nurture these essential learner habits.

Taking the time to teach into these invaluable habits—habits of one who is interested in and actively studies words—supersedes any one realm of learning. Students will develop agency, and as one of my educational heroes, Peter Johnston (2004), writes in *Choice Words*, "Developing in children a sense of agency is not an educational frill or some mushy-headed liberal idea" (p. 40). Johnston goes on to prove this idea with research citing that children with this kind of strong belief work harder, focus their attention better, are more engrossed in their studies, and are less likely to quit when things become challenging (Skinner, Zimmer-Gembeck, & Connell, 1998, as cited in Johnston, 2004, pp. 40–41).

Over time, students will develop a repertoire of studying words, choosing to engage in the routines that best facilitate this deep exploration and discovery. Taking the time to teach into responsibility, respect, talk, and teamwork cultivates excitement about the process of learning. Moreover, by incorporating the use of learning tools (like those in this chapter), students implement these practices with greater ease and success. The culture of the classroom shifts as students become invested and independent!

Few rich learning routines are "only one thing." No one aspect of word study or any one lesson will help students achieve our collective lofty, yet attainable, word study goals. Tim Rasinski (2017) reminds us that there are several key elements to a successful approach to word study: Instruction needs to be authentic, intentional, intensive, consistent, and synergistic. So, the other tools included in this chapter support "hybrid" routines, and these types of practices are a first step in helping students blur the lines between the different facets of word study. These tools help students realize that word study is all about connections and transfer. This type of integrated practice is what turns any one aspect of instruction or learning into the approach inherent in robust word study.

I encourage you to use research-backed best practices to explicitly teach about words. . . on a consistent (daily or near-daily) basis. Moreover, the authenticity of words needs to be respected. Students need to be doing *real* reading in *real* texts and *real* writing on their own. I often say that learning done in isolation tends to stay in isolation. The tools in this chapter support the habits, practices, and routines that move students beyond a narrow definition of isolated word learning.

How Do Habit and Hybrid Word Work Fit a Range of Learners?

In the *primary grades*, the habit routines are of paramount importance! In these early years, we teach students to be respectful, responsible members of a classroom community. Youngsters learn how to manage materials and time with greater independence, starting to monitor themselves and take ownership of their learning. The hybrid routines bring a starting awareness to the fact that learning is not parroting; we want students to begin to apply and integrate learning.

Many *upper-elementary grade* teachers recognize the need to sustain (and bolster) these efforts as students become even more capable. These are the years when kids, tweens, and early teens explore greater independence and responsibility—in and out of school. By teaching and supporting learning habits, we help students make more thoughtful, intentional choices they can feel proud of—and that are effective. We also use hybrid routines to help students transfer learning and infuse gained expertise into all they do. As these practices become second nature, they enrich and enliven the deep exploration of words.

Having worked in support settings, I have witnessed (and to be honest, I have perpetuated) *over*scaffolding. I have also heard utterances of dangerous thoughts like *this type of instruction may work for some kids but not these kids*. However, as professionals in this field, we know nothing could be further from the truth! We can teach and trust all students to take on more independence. This builds confidence and motivation to keep trying and keep growing. At times, points of access *might* vary—and the gradual release used *might* be a bit more gradual—but learning habits are a core component of the work done in support settings. Additionally, the "high-utility" nature of hybrid routines serves the learners we work with so well. Being able to know, rely on, and use gained expertise in a variety of settings serves as a monumental "ahhhh!" for learners. Hybrid routines help learners understand that each setting does *not* require an entirely new skill set and that current expertise can be applied and used at a variety of times and in a range of places.

When Do Learners Engage in Habit and Hybrid Word Work?

Habits are always taught, practiced, and nurtured. Habits transcend any one type of word study practice. Here are two of the many examples of how a word study cycle might look. Please note that habits are always included in other cycle routines, and hybrid practices begin happening after both the meaning and spelling pattern have been introduced.

Day 1	Day 2	Day 3	Day 4	Day 5	Day 6
Meaning	Meaning	Pattern	Pattern	Hybrid	Check-In/ Transfer

Day 1	Day 2	Day 3	Day 4	Day 5	Day 6
Meaning	Meaning	Pattern	Pattern	Phonemic Awareness and Phonics	High Frequency

Cut, Not Styled

Why?

To get ready for sorting!

You Need:

One crayon, scissors, and a word card bag or envelope

How?

1. Do a five-second scribble on the back. Use "your color."

2. *Quickly* cut your word cards (P-C-S, or picture frame, columns, singles).

3. Put word cards in your bag or envelope.

Looks Like:

Crayons: openclipart.org/Dug; Scissors: openclipart.org/nicubunu; Envelope: openclipart.org/kuba.

Find It   *The accompanying lesson can be found on page 60 of* Word Study That Sticks.

What Do You Think?

Why?

To practice speaking, listening, and using new words

You Need:

Your ears, mind, and voice

How?

1.  Listen to the teacher or a partner.
2. Think: Do I agree or disagree? Why or why not?
3. Say your ideas.

Looks Like:

Ear: openclipart.org/CCX; Thought cloud: openclipart.org/rejon; Speech bubble: openclipart.org/PrinterKiller.

Find It   *The accompanying lesson can be found on page 61 of* Word Study That Sticks.

Mirror, Mirror

Why?

- To think more about the parts of word study that are going well

- To think more about the tricky parts of word study

You Need:

Notebook

How?

1. 💬 Talk about a word study goal—what it means *and* what it looks like, sounds like, and "feels" like.

2. 💭 Think and talk: What parts have been going well? Where have I improved? What will I keep doing?

3. 💭 Think and talk: What parts have been hard? What parts still seem tough? What else could I try?

4. 🎉 Celebrate!

Looks Like:

What do I do well?
What can I work on?

I am proud of ___.
___ has been tricky.
I plan to try ___.

Find It *The accompanying lesson can be found on page 85 of* Word Study That Sticks.

Speech bubble: openclipart.org/PrinterKiller; Thought cloud: openclipart.org/rejon; Confetti: openclipart.org/mi_brami.

Word Webs

Why?
To show *all* we know!

You Need:
Word study notebook and colored pencils

How?

1. Choose a word.

2. Think: What do I see, hear, and know about this word?

3. Add bubbles to the web, each one teaching about the word.

Looks Like:

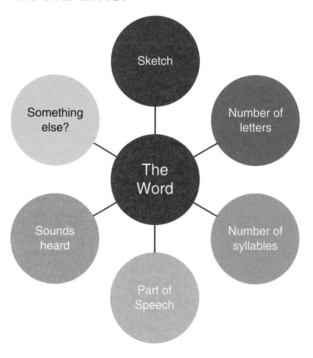

Find It *The accompanying lesson can be found on page 130 of* Word Study That Sticks.

Word Wall *This routine can also be done with high-frequency words.*

Word Riddles I

Why?
To learn about how words sound, how words look, *and* what words mean

You Need:
Word study notebook and a pencil

How?

1. Choose a word.
2. Think: What do I see, hear, and know about this word?
3. Create a riddle with clues about the word.

**Share with a partner. Can they guess?

Looks Like:

> RIDDLES
> 1. I start with the same sound as in *bat*.
> 2. I end with a *g*.
> 3. I am used to pack food at the store.
> 4. Who am I?
>
> BAG

 Find It *The accompanying lesson can be found on page 130 of* Word Study That Sticks.

 Word Wall *This routine can also be done with high-frequency words.*

 Arrow: openclipart.org/GDJ; Question mark: openclipart.org/jean_victor_balin; Pencil: openclipart.org/pascallpalme.

Copyright © 2020 by Pamela Koutrakos. All rights reserved. Reprinted from The Word Study That Sticks Companion: Classroom-Ready Tools for Teachers and Students, Grades K–6, *by Pamela Koutrakos. Thousand Oaks, CA: Corwin, www.corwin.com. Reproduction authorized for educational use by educators, local school sites, and/or noncommercial or nonprofit entities that have purchased the book.*

Word Riddles 2

Why?

To learn about how words sound, how words look, *and* what words mean

You Need:

Word study notebook and a pencil

How?

1. Choose a word.

2. Ask yourself: What do I see, hear, and know about this word?

3. Create a riddle with clues about the word. Share with a partner.

**Hint: Use a Word Web to help you choose clues for your riddle.

Looks Like:

```
Line 1: A "sounds like" clue
Line 2: A "looks like" clue
Line 3: A "means" clue
Line 4: WHO AM I?
```

```
Starts with a B and ends with a G.
Sounds like /ă/ - like in CAT.
I am used to pack food at the store.
WHO AM I?
BAG
```

Arrow: openclipart.org/GDJ; Question mark: openclipart.org/jean_victor_balin; Pencil: openclipart.org/pascallpalme.

 Find It *The accompanying lesson can be found on page 130 of* Word Study That Sticks.

 **Word Wall** *This routine can also be done with high-frequency words.*

Write With It

Why?

To use what we know about words

To share our words with others

You Need:

Word study notebook and a pencil

How?

1. 👀 Look at your words.

2. 💭 Think: What kind of writing do I want to do? What will be my topic?

3. ✏️ Write a story, riddle, poem, fact book— anything you like! Include pattern words.

Looks Like:

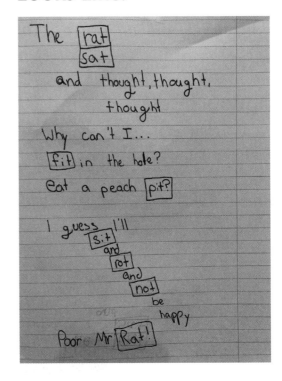

Eyes: openclipart.org/Prawny; Thought cloud: openclipart.org/rejon; Pencil: openclipart.org/pascallpalme.

Bonus *The accompanying lesson can be found on page 240.*

Word Wall *This routine can also be done with high-frequency words.*

Word Games

Why?

- To practice using learned words in social settings
- To talk with others about words

You Need:

Notebook or word cards and game/app of your choice

How?

1. Choose a word game.
2. Play.

Options: Online games, iPad apps, board games (Scrabble, Boggle, Bananagrams, Hedbanz, Upwords, Zingo! Bingo, etc.), classroom games, Puzzle Station

Looks Like:

Be sure to clean up when you finish

Find It *The accompanying lesson can be found on page 82 of* Word Study That Sticks.

Word Wall *This routine can also be done with high-frequency words.*

Arrow: openclipart.org/GDJ; Confetti: openclipart.org/mi_brami.

Creating Word Ladders

Why?

- To play with words
- To help us notice word parts and use word learning

You Need:

Word study notebook and a pencil

Optional: Coloring materials

How?

1.  Study a word ladder. Think about what the creator did. Name what you see.

2. Choose a word. Place the word at the bottom of your ladder.

3. Switch one part of the word to make a new word.

4. Sketch or write a clue for the new word. Keep going!

Share with others! Can they solve your ladder?

Looks Like:

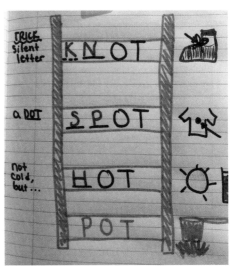

Bonus *The accompanying lesson can be found on page 237.*

Word Wall *This routine can also be done with high-frequency words.*

Thought cloud: openclipart.org/rejon; Arrow: openclipart.org/GDJ; Switch: openclipart.org/bnielsen; Pencil: openclipart.org/pascallpalme.

Nature Knowledge I

Why?

- To be surrounded by nature
- To combine the beauty of words with the beauty of natural materials

You Need:

"Building" supplies from nature (pebbles, rocks, twigs, shells, etc.)

How?

1. 💬 Choose a word. Say the word.
2. 🅰🅱🅲 Build the word using nature "loose parts." Say the letters as you build the word.

Looks Like:

Photo by Grace White

Speech bubble: openclipart.org/PrinterKiller; ABC: openclipart.org/mazeo.

Bonus *The accompanying lesson can be found on page 238.*

Word Wall *This routine can also be done with high-frequency words.*

Nature Knowledge 2

Why?

- To be surrounded by nature
- To combine the beauty of words with the beauty of outside

You Need:

Word study words

How?

1. Choose a routine.
2. Do *that* routine while out in nature.

Looks Like:

Photo by Ellen Calamito

Bonus *The accompanying lesson can be found on page 238.*

Word Wall *This routine can also be done with high-frequency words.*

Arrow: openclipart.org/GD); Pencil: openclipart.org/pascallpalme.

Cut, Not Styled

Day _____

Why?

To prepare word cards for repeated use

You Need:

One crayon, scissors, and word envelope or baggie

How?

1. Scribble on the back of your sort using your color (five seconds).

2. Cut out your word cards (P-C-S).

3. Put all scraps in the recycling bin.

4. Hint: Store word cards in an envelope or baggie.

Looks Like:

  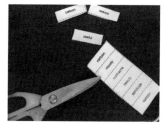

Find It *The accompanying lesson can be found on page 60 of* Word Study That Sticks.

Mirror, Mirror: Look at Me Now!

Day ____

Why?

- To remind ourselves of prioritized next steps
- To see and reflect on any progress toward set goals
- To remember that word learning continues and grows over time and across subject areas

You Need:

Word study notebook and a pencil

How?

1. Check back and review word study goals.
2. Search for any evidence of progress toward this goal/these goals.
3. Share or jot about your growth—and next steps.

Looks Like:

SEPTEMBER–OCTOBER GOALS

HABITS: I will work toward using a quiet voice when working with a partner and my word study group.

CONCEPTS: I will work toward spelling pattern words correctly in word study but also in other subjects.

I have been talking quietly. No one told me to *shh* or be quiet.

In my word study notebook, I almost always spell words correctly (see pages with sticky notes). But I do notice mistakes in my writing notebook. To meet this goal, I will spend two minutes each day rereading my writing entries and checking for spelling. Then, I will notice any mistakes and fix them up right away.

 Find It *The accompanying lesson can be found on page 85 of* Word Study That Sticks.

Tech Tip *Chapter 2 provides examples of digital goal setting and reflection. Consider online notebooks, using Google Forms, or student blogs/vlogs for goal setting and reflection. These provide opportunities for class members to support one another in these pursuits.*

Better Together (Talk It Up)

Day _____

Why?
- To build our understanding about words and the why behind how words work
- To use respectful discourse (discussion) in word study

You Need:

Classmate(s)

How?
1. Wonder *with* your partner. Ask meaningful questions that invite discussion and exploration.
2. Listen as your partner speaks. Prepare to say back what you heard, add your thoughts, and/or ask a related follow-up question.
3. Participate actively: Share the work, and strive to balance the talk.

Tip: Sentence stems can help . . . but please feel comfortable and confident using language that feels natural for you!

Looks Like:

Shared Decision Making	Anytime Partner Work	Listening Work
• What routine do you want to try together? • Would you like to start with . . . • Where can we go from here? • How would you like to contribute?	• I'm wondering . . . because . . . • Do you agree or disagree that . . . • A theory I have is . . . because . . . • What do you think? • What if . . . • What else . . .	• What I heard you say was . . . • Based on what you said . . . • In response to that . . . • May I ask a question about that?

Find It *The accompanying lesson can be found on page 76 of* Word Study That Sticks. *A menu of conferring suggestions for coaching into conversation during word study can be found on pages 158 to 160 of* Word Study That Sticks.

Word Games

Day ____

Why?

- To become more fluent with our spelling

- To remember the play in wordplay

You Need:

Options: Scrabble, Bananagrams, Hangman, word cards—any game that highlights words!

How?

1. Choose a word game with a partner/group.

2. Use studied pattern(s) as much as possible while playing the word game.

3. Clean up.

Looks Like:

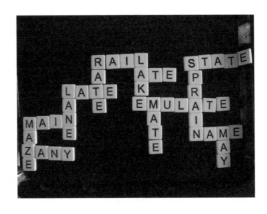

Find It *The accompanying lesson can be found on page 82 of* Word Study That Sticks.

Tech Tip *Many websites provide options for focusing on different patterns, roots, and affixes. Other websites let teachers input the current words being studied. Check the safety and quality of any games students play to make sure that there are clear word study benefits.*

Word Wall *This routine can also be done with high-frequency words.*

Word Webs

Day ____

Why?

- To think about the spelling, parts, meaning, and origins of words
- To get a more complete and well-rounded picture of a word

You Need:

Word study notebook and a pencil

*This can also be done digitally as a visual map or word splash.

How?

1. Choose a word, and put it in the center bubble.

2. Think of what you know about that word, and put different types of information into outer bubbles.

3. Repeat with other words.

Looks Like:

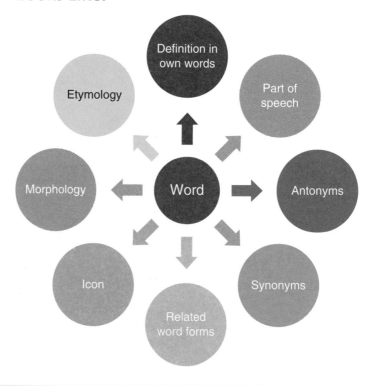

Word Riddles

Day ____

Why?

- To think about words and their spelling, parts, meaning, origins, etc.

- To get a more complete and well-rounded picture of a word

You Need:

Word study notebook and a pencil

How?

1. Choose a word.

2. Create a three-clue riddle with that word.

3. Share riddles with a partner or small group.

Hint: Use Word Webs to help you create riddles.

Looks Like:

```
SAMPLE FORMAT:

Clue 1: Pattern (auditory clue)

Clue 2: Pattern (visual clue)

Clue 3: Meaning (definition, synonym, antonym)

WHO AM I?

ANSWER
```

Find It *The accompanying lesson can be found on page 130 of* Word Study That Sticks.

Word Wall *This routine can also be done with high-frequency words.*

Word Conversations: Written

Day _____

Why?

- To practice using our words in different contexts
- To apply word learning to writing

You Need:

Word study notebook and a pencil

How?

1. Choose a few words.
2. Think of a topic or context where these words could be used.
3. Start composing a "written" conversation using chosen (and other) pattern words.

Hint: Feeling stuck? Practice out loud with a partner first.

Looks Like:

> **Word Conversation**
>
> **Ratha and Kevin are making dinner for their family . . .**
> **(-ing pattern)**
>
> "Kevin, when you're done <u>cutting</u> those vegetables, can you start <u>marinating</u> the steak?" Ratha asked.
>
> "Sure, no problem. I'm <u>finishing</u> this now. I'm also <u>planning</u> on <u>cooking</u> chicken," Kevin responded.
>
> "Sounds perfect! I've been <u>looking</u> forward to <u>having</u> our family over tonight." Ratha tasted her sauce and smiled. Delicious, she thought.

 Bonus *The accompanying lesson can be found on page 239.*

 Tech Tip *Remember, almost anything that can be done in a notebook can also be done digitally!*

 **Word Wall** *This routine can also be done with high-frequency words.*

Write With It

Day ____

Why?

- To practice using our words in different contexts

- To apply word learning, using studied pattern words more frequently and naturally when writing

You Need:

Word study notebook and a pencil

How?

1. Look over pattern words.

2. Think of a context/ topic where you could appropriately use some of the words.

3. Write—using as many pattern words as possible (appropriately).

Looks Like:

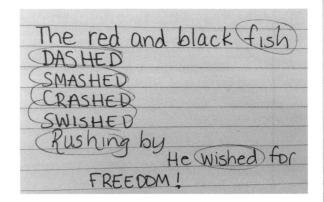

Hints: This writing may or may not be connected to learning in other subjects (math, social studies, etc.).

Free choice? Consider different genres and write whatever you like— fantasy fiction, fan fiction, informational writing, blogs, poetry, songs, lists, etc.

Bonus *The accompanying lesson can be found on page 240.*

Word Wall *This routine can also be done with high-frequency words.*

Creating Word Ladders

Day _____

Why?

To help us integrate word learning

You Need:

Word study notebook and a pencil

Optional: Coloring materials or a device

How?

1. Choose a word. Place the word at the bottom of your ladder.
2. Switch part of the word to make a new word.
3. Sketch or write a clue for the new word. Keep going!
4. Share with others! Can they solve your ladder?

Looks Like:

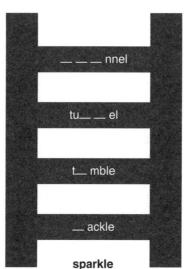

Noun: Water that connects two larger bodies of water; examples: HBO, FX, and NBC — _ _ _ nnel — Verb: To transfer or transmit

Noun: An underground passageway — tu_ _ el — Verb: Dig, burrow, mine

Noun: A fall — t_ mble — Verb: To flip—what gymnasts do on the floor during their routines

Noun: A way to stop a football — _ ackle — Verb: Approach, address, try to deal with

sparkle

Bonus *The accompanying lesson can be found on page 237.*

Word Share

Day _____

Why?

- To share words with others
- To teach others what we have learned about words

You Need:

Word study notebook and other miscellaneous supplies (depends on how you choose to share words)

How?

1. Reflect on recent word exploring and learning.
2. Decide on what you want to share with others and how you will share this knowledge.
3. Plan your "share," and create needed materials.
4. Share with peers.

Ideas: Oral share at the end of word study, anchor chart, quick process-based lesson

Looks Like:

Open and closed syllables

OPEN SYLLABLE:

- Vowel is at the end of a syllable
- Vowel sound is long
- Are not "closed" by a consonant

EXAMPLES:

o/pen   pa/per   ba/sic   lo/cate

Knowing if a syllable is open or closed will help you spell a word when you write and pronounce a word correctly when you read.

Created by Shaila Das

 Tech Tip *Students* love *creating digital Word Share postings to share with peers. Screencastify, ShowMe, Flipgrid, Educreations, Explain Everything, and Snagit work beautifully for this.*

Bonus *The accompanying lesson can be found on page 241.*

HABIT AND HYBRID HOW-TOS

HABITS MATTER

Taking the time to teach, practice, and provide feedback on habits counts. We want learners of all ages to build independence and feel greater ownership of their learning. Habits are the key to making this happen. There is a direct relationship between what students manage and monitor on their own and the amount of time (and energy) we have for providing personalized instruction and feedback.

TRUST MATTERS

Students will rise to the challenge! Once we take the time to explicitly model, teach, practice, and nurture habits, we need to trust students to make these moment-to-moment choices. They will not get it right 100 percent of the time, but that's okay. Neither do we! Even occasional missteps and mistakes have the power to be learning opportunities.

TIMING MATTERS

The different facets of word study are interconnected. Authenticity results from integrating different sources of knowledge about words. Hybrid routines begin to happen mid-cycle, after meanings and spelling patterns have been introduced to learners.

HYBRID PRACTICES BUILD *OTHER* HABITS

Hybrid routines encourage students to integrate their word knowledge. This is a first step toward transferring word knowledge to other subjects. Hybrid routines help students recognize that word knowledge does not exist in isolation. We can integrate different facets of word learning into all we do, connecting the dots between content areas. Application is what makes knowledge meaningful.

HABIT AND HYBRID ROUTINES IN ACTION₁

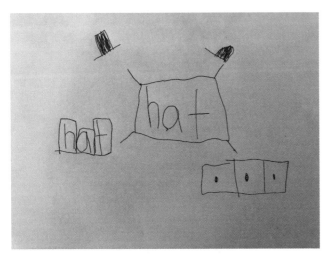

A kindergartener creates a simple Word Web using a combination of Picture It, Configuration Station, and Sound Search.

Students can manage word study materials with independence. Teachers no longer need to hand out folders and notebooks or cut out word cards for students (of any age!).

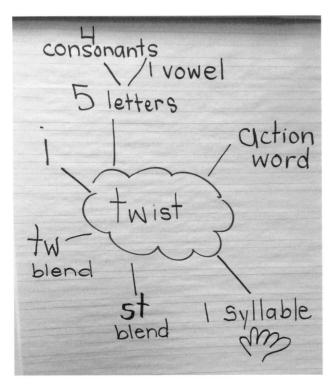

A first-grade class uses Interactive Writing to create a Word Web. Students participate by providing ideas for what could go in the web and by writing some letters and blends on the chart.

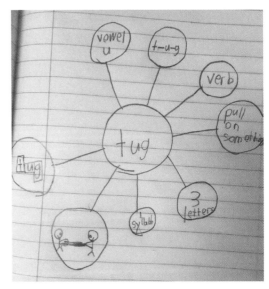

Students show off different aspects of word knowledge when completing Word Webs.

Photo by Katie McGrath

Here, sixth graders are talking over ideas for a collaborative version of Write With It.

A fifth-grade teacher teaches a small group of students all about word riddles.

Write With It—with a math theme!

CHAPTER EIGHT

Check-In and Assessment Routines

In my class, we pick how we show what we know and understand about words. You might think that 6th graders would choose the easiest and quickest ways. But, we end up challenging ourselves _more_ when we get to decide. I NEVER thought I would say this, but we look forward to word study assessments and sharing what we learned with everyone else in the class. I wish my other teachers would do this too.

Numerous tools to support wide and varied exploration of words have been shared throughout the past four chapters. This chapter aims to provide a clearer vision of how to check in on learning. The assessment suggestions provided on the following pages will absolutely help us (teachers) glean information about student growth and progress. However, these charts will also help _students_ step up, reflect on their own processes, and begin to use this gained understanding in future word endeavors. I am personally inspired by seeing students reflecting, checking in, and making thoughtful choices about where to head next as learners. I bet you will feel the same!

Why Are Check-In and Assessment Routines Important?

In *Growing Readers*, Kathy Collins (2004) reminds us of the importance of balance: specifically, balancing time on assessments *with* time getting to know the learners in the room. Over a decade later, Beers and Probst (2017) again ask us to rethink our priorities—encouraging us to look beyond short-term goals (like tests) and instead consider a more important, long-term purpose. They inspire us to contemplate how to encourage each student to become a "lifelong, passionate, curious learner" (p. 109). This steadfast advice is relevant in every grade, in every school, and in every subject area. Students come first and consequently, the choices we make about assessment have the capacity to be as learner-centered as our instruction. Moreover, we can also nurture and develop students' role in assessment. I full-heartedly believe that these kinds of aspirations are very important and are *absolutely* attainable.

I know that in order to feel comfortable making these kinds of shifts, we might first want a clear understanding of what this entails. Katherine Bomer (2016) expresses this vision perfectly when she writes, "Effective assessment helps students name and celebrate what is working . . . and also see what needs revision" (p. 154). The resources in this chapter aspire to align with this very idea. These tools support first steps toward more varied and student-driven assessment practices. *We* know different kinds of assessment provide different kinds of information. The included selection of check-in routine minicharts also enable *students* to see that there are multiple ways to gauge recent learning, show understanding, and apply knowledge to contexts that extend beyond word study. A great first step to take: Look through the tools in this chapter and corresponding lessons. Reflect on student interests, strengths, and next steps. Then use this information to decide which routines you will try out to check in on learning. Once that feels comfortable, find ways to empower students to have greater choice and voice in this process.

How Do Check-In and Assessment Routines Fit a Range of Learners?

Assessment should vary and match our purpose. Informal assessment happens daily and is on a nonstop, continuous loop—in all grades and in all kinds of instructional settings. The last thing today's students need is more testing. I encourage you to intentionally choose assessments that match the learners in the room. This means asking ourselves these questions:

- What am I hoping to find out? What type of assessment can help me glean this information?

- What is developmentally appropriate? What is academically appropriate?

- When was the last time I assessed this group of students and their work?

- How will this experience empower students? How might we invite learners to have choice, voice, and ownership of specific parts of this process—or this whole process?

Here is a final idea to consider: Any previously taught and practiced word study routine can be used as an assessment. Goal reflection and self-assessment are also meaningful ways to build deep, metacognitive thought about practices. The student-facing tools in Chapter 3 help students set goals, reflect on work toward goals, and self-assess their current work habits and word knowledge.

> **Find It**
>
> There is a helpful assessment chart on page 100 of *Word Study That Sticks* that can help you decide if the assessment you plan to use will provide the information you are hoping to get. The different sets of student-facing checklists in Appendix F will enable students to set, reflect on, and celebrate goals with greater independence.

When Do Learners Engage in Check-In and Assessment Routines?

Check-in and assessment routines often happen more formally at the end of a cycle. It is important to note two things. First, that formal check-in/assessment is not needed or required at the end of every word study cycle. Second, informal assessment happens every single day; we can use observations, conversations, and *any* student work to check in on student progress. Here are two of the infinite examples of how a word study cycle might look.

Day 1	Day 2	Day 3	Day 4	Day 5	Day 6
Meaning	Meaning	Pattern	Pattern	Hybrid	Check-In/ Transfer

Day 1	Day 2	Day 3	Day 4	Day 5	Day 6
Meaning	Meaning	Pattern	Pattern	Phonemic Awareness and Phonics	High Frequency

Interactive Writing

Why?

- To use what we learned
- To remember our spelling smarts while we write

You Need:

Chart paper and markers

Optional: Mini dry erase boards, markers, and erasers

How?

1. 👀 Look through words as a group. Choose a writing topic.

2. 💬 Share ideas that include pattern words. The teacher will write.

3. ✏️ Get to a pattern word? Students write the pattern words.

Looks Like:

Eyes: openclipart.org/Prawny; Speech bubble: openclipart.org/PrinterKiller; Pencil: openclipart.org/pascallpalme.

Find It *The accompanying lesson can be found on page 95 of* Word Study That Sticks.

Word Wall *This routine can also be done with high-frequency words.*

Find and Fix Up

Why?
To use what we know about words—*all* the time

You Need:
Writing folder and a pencil

How?

1. ◎◎ Look through your writing. Hunt for pattern words.
2. ✅ ↻ Celebrate correct spelling, and fix up incorrect spelling.
3. Challenge: Add more pattern words to your writing.

Looks Like:

Eyes: openclipart.org/Prawny; Green check: openclipart.org/dholler; Redo: openclipart.org/PERCE-NEIGE.

Find It   *The accompanying lesson can be found on page 93 of* Word Study That Sticks.

Word Wall   *This routine can also be done with high-frequency words.*

Shared Reading and Hunt

Why?

- To practice using word learning while reading
- To stretch our word learning to *new* words

You Need:

Books you already read

How?

1. 👂 Listen and watch as the teacher reads a text.
2. 👀 Hunt for pattern words in the text.
3. 💬 Talk to your partner about the pattern words.
4. 📖 Reread a different text on your own. Look for more pattern words as you read.

Looks Like:

Photo by Linda Day

 Find It The accompanying lesson can be found on page 96 of Word Study That Sticks.

Word Wall This routine can also be done with high-frequency words.

Ear: openclipart.org/CCX; Eyes: openclipart.org/Prawny; Speech bubble: openclipart.org/PrinterKiller; Book: openclipart.org/sonoftroll.

Next-Level Sorting Challenge

Why?

- To notice what is similar and different about words
- To sort words by how they look and sound

You Need:

Pencil and paper

How?

1. 👂 Listen as the teacher says a word.
2. 💭 Think: Where does this word fit best?
3. ✏️ Write the word in that column.

Looks Like:

👂 👀	-at	-it	-ot
Words	cat hat splat	bit hit sit	hot lot shot

Find It *The accompanying lesson can be found on page 97 of* Word Study That Sticks.

Ear: openclipart.org/CCX; Thought cloud: openclipart.org/redo; Pencil: openclipart.org/pascallpalme; Eyes: openclipart.org/Prawny.

193

Show Off

Why?

- To use word learning
- To share word learning

You Need:

It depends! Possibilities: Notebook, paper, coloring materials, or a device

How?

1. 👀 Look through your notebook, and talk about recent learning.

2. 💭 Think: How can I show off my learning?

3. 💡 Plan it, create it, and then share it.

Looks Like:

Eyes: openclipart.org/Prawny; Thought cloud: openclipart.org/redo; Idea: openclipart.org/ousia.

 Find It The accompanying lesson can be found on pages 98 and 99 of Word Study That Sticks.

 Tech Tip *There are countless user-friendly options for digital movie editing: Powtoon, Toontastic, Animoto, STROOM, WeVideo, and YouTube Editor.*

Find and Fix Up

Day ____

Why?

- To transfer and apply word study learning
- To help us remember that we are studying patterns and word parts, not only a few words

You Need:

A notebook or work from any subject area (reading, math, social studies, science, word study) and a pencil

Optional: Highlighter

How?

1. Review pattern.

2. Choose a notebook . . . any notebook (any subject).

3. Look through your work. Hunt for and find pattern words.

4. Correctly spelled? Celebrate. Incorrectly spelled? Fix up and celebrate.

5. Keep going!

Looks Like:

Find It | The accompanying lesson can be found on page 93 of Word Study That Sticks.

Word Wall | This routine can also be done with high-frequency words.

Tech Tip | Some students choose to ignore red and blue squiggles under typed words. Others may think just because there is not a squiggle that the piece has no errors. Teach students how to "find and fix" digitally.

Interactive Writing

Day ____

Why?

- To transfer and apply word study learning when writing (in any subject area)

- To help us remember that we are studying patterns and word parts, not only a few words

You Need:

Word study notebook or slates and different colored markers or pencils

How?

1. Meet with the teacher.

2. Decide together on a topic to write about.

3. Talk with classmates and generate ideas for composing the writing. Try to include pattern words.

4. When prompted, jot pattern words. Remember to apply word learning.

Looks Like:

Tech Tip *1:1 classrooms may choose to engage in digital interactive writing. Begin by composing student ideas on a shared document that is visible to all. At planned stopping points, invite different students to use their own device to type in targeted words and word parts. Not 1:1? Have students pass the keyboard. Finally, if you are 1:1 and want to see how all students attempt spelling targeted words, use whiteboard apps (like Aww App).*

Find It *The accompanying lesson can be found on page 95 of* Word Study That Sticks.

Shared Reading and Hunt

Day ____

Why?

- To transfer and apply word study learning while reading (in any subject area)
- To help us remember that we are studying patterns and word parts, not only a few words

You Need:

Access to enlarged text

Optional: "Follow-up" texts to hunt in

How?

1. Gather with the teacher, and follow along as the teacher reads an enlarged text.
2. Hunt for pattern words in the text.
3. When prompted, talk to a thinking partner about these words.
4. Optional: Follow up with word scavenger hunts in individual or partner texts.

Looks Like:

Photo by Linda Day

Find It *The accompanying lesson can be found on page 96 of* Word Study That Sticks.

Word Wall *This routine can also be done with high-frequency words.*

Tech Tip *Classes can use any type of digital text for shared reading. News articles, primary documents, math word problems, poems, infographics, and subtitled videos are a few of the abundant resources available.*

Next-Level Sorting Challenge
Day ____

Why?

- To recognize and sort words according to their similarities and differences
- To apply pattern knowledge beyond "list words"

You Need:

Word study notebook/paper and a pencil

How?

1. Think back to the pattern recently studied. Set up a chart that reflects the pattern studied.

2. Listen as the teacher reads aloud a pattern word.

3. Jot the word. Try your best to spell the word correctly, and place the word in the correct column/part of the chart.

4. Note: Not all words will be from a particular list. The teacher may include any word that follows the studied pattern.

Looks Like:

Words Studied	walked jumped watched	skipped flipped clapped	studied carried emptied
New Words	bumped	trapped	married
Because...	-ed sounds like /t/ and I just added -ed	-ed sounds like /t/ and I doubled the final consonant before adding -ed	-ed sounds like /d/ and I changed the y to an i before adding -ed

Find It *The accompanying lesson can be found on page 97 of* Word Study That Sticks.

Show Off

Day ___

Why?

- To transfer and apply word study learning
- To share our learning with others and to teach others all we have learned

You Need:

Materials vary—likely word study notebook and a pencil to start

How?

1. Look through recent notebook work and/or talk with others about recent word study learning and experiences.

2. Think about how you can highlight, share, and show off recent learning.

3. Plan it, create it, and then share it.

Hints: Quick, in-notebook ideas: Write a few sentences about word learning or create a chart or infographic to show what you have learned.

Digital ideas: Consider the ideas shared in class. Stay focused on showcasing word learning and not "sparkles and sprinkles" unrelated to word learning.

Looks Like:

 Find It *The accompanying lesson can be found on pages 98 and 99 of* Word Study That Sticks.

 Tech Tip *Use any of the previously mentioned Tech Tip ideas to help students show off digitally. Also, encourage students to create or explore ways to digitally showcase their learning that you may have not yet considered.*

Tying It Together

ASSESSMENT ANSWERS

FORMAL VERSUS INFORMAL

Assessment does not need to be formal. Consistent, informal assessment can provide the information we need to support students.

ASSESSMENT ≠ TEST

Assessment can vary and can be fun! Assessment is not synonymous with test or grade. Students often enjoy and find value in the check-in routines supported by the resources shared in this chapter.

FORMATIVE USE OF ASSESSMENT

Assessment is meaningless if it is not used to guide next steps. We can study and discuss formal and informal assessments. By doing so, we will feel ready to follow up with appropriate, responsive instruction.

ASSESSMENT LOOKS DIFFERENT AT DIFFERENT TIMES AND IN DIFFERENT SETTINGS

Formal assessment does not need to happen at the end of every word study cycle. Some teachers decide to include an end-of-cycle assessment but vary the type of check-in routine used. Other teachers choose instead to use more comprehensive, integrated assessments once every four to six cycles. There are many other teachers who rely solely on their meticulous, consistent record keeping. Finally, daily informal assessment and the goal setting, reflection, and self-assessment used by class members consistently across the year provide plenty of information.

Teachers might ask themselves these questions:

- What were our goals?

- What evidence do I have of student growth and progress toward these goals? Have I met with students and reviewed their work?

- What do these conversations and work samples lead me to believe is now in place—and what might be an appropriate next step?

CHECK-IN AND ASSESSMENT ROUTINES IN ACTION

Student partnerships can informally assess each other's recent word learning.

Photo by Katie McGrath

A sixth-grade class shows off their science and word study knowledge by participating in a student-run Edcamp. Students create, plan, and facilitate their sessions—and then teach their classmates. Here, students model credible "expert talk" using both science vocabulary and word study pattern words.

Reflection is an important part of checking in. Students can write quick reflections of recent work toward goals, and the class can celebrate as part of the closing "share" time of word study.

A kindergarten class shows off recent learning about digraphs (/sh/ and others) by creating a class mural of a marine habitat—and labeling their sketches of words containing digraphs.

I can:
Read new words

My Goal is:
To use new words when I talk

My plan is:

1. Write pattern on a post it
2. Bring post it when I meet with Mario
3. Tally up when I use pattern words

A first-grade student uses self-assessment to help plan his own next steps.

WORD STUDY CONCEPTS GOAL	
A success I am celebrating is...	Spelling correctly on word study Assessments.
A worthwhile next step might be... because...	Spelling correctly when I write because I don't think of patterns when I write.
A goal I am interested in working towards is...	I will use what I know about words all day.
I plan to accomplish this goal by...	I will reread my working just for spelling before partner time every day I will also ask my partner for help.

This upper-elementary student recognizes that spelling correctly during word study is a first step—and then commits to working toward applying learning all day long.

PART III

Extending Word Learning

Photo by Linda Day

Photo by Linda Day

CHAPTER NINE

Connecting With Caregivers

> My dad gets really excited when I bring home my word study notebook. He likes when I give him a tour of my work and talk about all the things we have been learning about words in school. My favorite part is reading the compliments he writes after I finsh sharing. I could only wish every kid could have somthing special moments like this.

Part I included information and resources for getting word study going. Part II centered around tools to foster engagement and independence. In these chapters, over 100 minicharts for each area of word learning were shared. Now, we are ready to explore additional ways to extend word learning. We all know that home-school partnering has a huge impact on student success. As parents, grandparents, aunts, uncles, siblings, and/or cousins ourselves, we may also (from the other side of this type of relationship) recognize the value of having families feel included in what's happening at school. In this chapter, advice for connecting with caregivers is provided. Additionally, there are resources for extending learning beyond the dismissal bell. Keep reading to discover ways teachers and students can include and celebrate with caregivers.

We're Better Together: Tools to Reinforce Home-School Partnership

Taken as a whole, these studies found a positive and convincing relationship between family involvement and benefits for students, including improved academic achievement. This relationship holds across families of all economic, racial/ethnic, and educational backgrounds and for students at all ages. (Henderson & Mapp, 2002, p. 24)

I have heard this said many times: "I can't believe what I used to think and say before I became a parent. I just didn't know." Well, I *definitely* don't think we need to be parents to understand the ins and outs of teaching—and I don't think that my own professional perspectives changed *too* much once I became a parent. However, since "parent" has become central to my own personal identity, I will admit to worrying (perhaps too much?) that others won't see, accept, and appreciate my children, Colby and Peyton, for who they are and hoping every single day that they are in a physically and emotionally safe space. As such, each day I am in a classroom studying beside countless unique and special students, I remember my commitment to learning about, wholeheartedly accepting, and caring for each of these people—*and* striving to form the kind of learning community I most want for Colby and Peyton. How could I not try to provide the same for each of these students?

We know caregivers and families play an essential role in learning and all that happens in school. According to the NEA Education Policy and Practice Department (2008), family and community involvement in education is positively correlated with higher academic performance and school improvement. When schools, caregivers, and communities collaborate to support learning, students earn higher grades, attend school with greater regularity, stay in school longer, and enroll in higher-level programs (Belfield & Levin, 2007). One of our most important roles as educators is to actively seek out information, advice, and support from the prominent people in the lives of our students. We also need to withhold judgment and develop greater compassion and understanding for why caregivers may choose or be unable to play the part *we* may hope for or feel is best. Building respectful, reciprocal relationships— even when it is tough—is part of our job. These efforts can become a joyful aspect of what we do, and the results of these efforts also make many parts of our work more meaningful and lasting!

A Brief Word on Homework

I've spent a lot of time sifting through the research. The results are nothing short of stunning. For starters, there is absolutely no evidence of any academic benefit from assigning homework in elementary or middle school. For younger students, in fact, there isn't even a correlation between whether children do homework (or how much they do) and any meaningful measure of achievement. At the high school level, the correlation is weak and tends to disappear when more sophisticated statistical measures are applied. Meanwhile, no study has ever substantiated the belief that homework builds character or teaches good study habits. (Kohn, 2007)

Over the years I spent in the classroom, I cut back on and eventually ceased assigning word study homework. I was pleased to see that even when there was no officially assigned word study homework, student learning continued to progress and caregivers were supportive of this shift. However, since homework was not being sent home, I wanted to do something to keep families in the loop about the learning currently happening in the classroom. I created After-Hours Activities Letters to help caregivers understand the why behind the shifts in word study instruction. These letters also provide ideas for ways school learning could be supported at home. Based on the well-substantiated research referenced previously by Alfie Kohn, the caregiver letters are intentional in not assigning or describing word study homework. Annotated versions of these letters can be found later in this chapter. I also tried out many of the digital ideas detailed below. Although certain options were more popular than others, each effort was appreciated by caregivers. No matter what decision *you* make about homework, any of the digital or print options in this chapter can be incorporated to enhance the ongoing communication with the adults in students' lives.

There are a number of ways to involve caregivers using digital tools, which often saves time for both teachers and caregivers alike. Many teachers choose to upload the After-Hours Activities Letters (see pp. 209–210 and online) to a classroom website. Other teachers bolster home partnership by regularly posting a different word study "routine of the week" on the class website. Additionally, when permitted, social media has become a more popular forum for sharing with families. With permission, teachers can post photos of students engaged in word study practices on Instagram, Twitter, or on Facebook. This helps provide greater vision to caregivers as to what these kinds of word study practices look like. They also serve as helpful discussion starters for when children insist they did "nothing" at school all day. When use of social media is not permitted or preferred, apps like Remind and TalkingPoints serve as increasingly popular options that use a closed network to easily and regularly communicate

Tech Tip

with families. Finally, many teachers like to periodically have the *class* create digital newsletters for families. Here, small groups of students work collaboratively to write up summaries and highlights of recent classroom happenings—across and beyond all subject areas. Not only are families kept in the loop but teachers can also use these write-ups as an additional, authentic assessment.

After-Hours Activities Letters

There's no doubt this communication and partnership make a difference! As Johnson, Leibowitz, and Perret (2017) write, "Culture involves not merely action but also interaction, not merely learning but also relationship. It stretches far beyond any one person" (p. 11). Interaction and relationships *are* key to a school culture—and I believe that this kind of culture extends beyond the walls of the school building. This kind of culture actively seeks and welcomes home participation. As such, we can imagine how many caregivers appreciate information and guidance in ways to support all that is being done at school. The After-Hours Activities Letters strive to open lines of communication between home and school. They provide basic information on the stepped-up approach to word study used in school and explain how and why it might look different from when we adults were in school. Additionally, these letters provide low-stakes, low-effort *suggestions* for how caregivers can support word study efforts at home should they choose to do so. There are three different versions of this letter (in both English and Spanish) available for download on the companion website, **resources.corwin.com/wstscompanion**. An annotated version of one of these letters can be found right in this chapter:

eTool

The After-Hours Activities Letters available online include information and *options* for simple and meaningful ways to support at home the learning that's happening in school. No "home teaching" or homework required! The companion website includes letters aimed at three different grade-level bands: Grades K–1, Grades 2–3, and Grades 4–6. The letters are available in both English and Spanish.

ANNOTATED AFTER-HOURS ACTIVITIES LETTER (EARLY-ELEMENTARY)

Dear Caregivers,

Not every child lives with parents. *Caregivers* is more inclusive.

Word study is no longer the rote spelling we may remember from when we were in school! Today, word study aims to build communication skills by providing greater access to and interest in words. In word study, students focus on the sounds, letters, spelling patterns, and meanings of words. Students learn the *why* behind how words work, and the emphasis is on examining and manipulating words. This shift is light-years beyond the memorizing once emphasized, which often didn't "stick" long term or transfer beyond a weekly spelling test. By learning the *how* and *why* inherent in the ways words work, students not only learn to spell, but they are also more likely to transfer this knowledge as they read, write, speak, and listen. The end goal is to become proficient readers and writers that apply knowledge of the inner working of words to all that's done—both in and out of school. Today's word study is not only research-supported, but it is also designed to increase curiosity, confidence, and capability.

Start by stating it clearly: Word study has changed and does not look the same as it did years ago. Families will be interested in why and how this refined approach is helping the children in their lives.

At home, you can support these efforts by having fun talking, playing, and reading with your child. No "formal" work is necessary. The following are a few suggestions that may seem intuitive, but yield extremely fruitful results:

- Talk with your child. Don't shy away from using new and interesting words in your conversations. Explain the meaning of new words using child-friendly language and share different times and places where this word might be used.

- Provide access to all kinds of books and texts. Make frequent trips to the library. Read to, with, and beside your child as frequently as possible.

The first set of bullet points in each letter lists the most accessible suggestions. These ideas may already be an existing part of a family's routine. We are naming the benefits of these common practices.

- Encourage your child to write, even if she or he does not *yet* spell conventionally. Shopping lists, cards, letters, stories, notes . . . it all has a positive impact! There is no need to correct spelling, but do encourage your child to use what is known about letters and sounds for assistance! Mistakes are parts of the learning process, and it is important that we encourage effort and risk taking.

- Play games together—"word-themed" games bring an added bonus! A few favorites include Zingo, Story Cubes, Tall Tales, Sequence Letters, Charades, Spot It! Alphabet, Headbanz, Heads Up, What's Gnu?, and so on.

In those little moments here and there (while driving in the car, waiting for a bus, waiting at a sibling's practice or in a doctor's office, cooking a meal, etc.), try the following suggestions that are "just right" for early-elementary students:

- Chant rhymes and poems in different silly voices and sing songs together.

- Create a challenge: How many words can we think of that rhyme, start with the same sound or letter, or end with the same sound or letter? For instance, "How many words can we think of and say that rhyme with *mug*? How many words can we think of and say that start with the /p/ sound? How many words can we think of and say that end with the /t/ sound?

- Stretch out and separate the sounds of words you see around you—for example, "cat; cccaaattt; c - a - t; cat."

- Read environmental print (street signs, store names, etc.).

- Play "I Spy!" Look for—and, when appropriate, highlight or cut out—specific letters or words (that start with ___, that end with ___, that sound like ___, that have two sounds/three sounds, etc.) in newspapers, magazines, circulars, catalogs, and junk mail.

- Make letters, build words, or write words with something fun! For example, depending on availability, preferences, and/or allergies, a few options include sidewalk chalk, shaving cream, whipped cream, sand bins, magnetic letters, toy building bricks, cereal—the options are infinite!

- Play "I'm Thinking of a Word" and provide sound, letter, and meaning clues to guess the answer to each other's riddles—for example, "I'm thinking of a word that starts with the __ sound and ends with the __ sound. I see this/do this when ___. It means ___. What's my word?"

- Get physical: Sing the alphabet song, spell out words, or separate the sounds in words while hopping, doing jumping jacks, running in place, hula hooping, jump roping, bouncing a ball, throwing and catching a ball, hitting or shaking a homemade instrument—whatever seems fun!

- Play "Sound Switcharoo"—for example, "If I know **H**AT, I also know **C__** and **P__**" (cat and pat), **OR** "If I take the /h/ off HAT and change it to /m/, I now have ___" (mat), **OR** "The CAT slept on a m — (mat). His name was P — (Pat)."

Partnering together, we can support your child as they become a more confident and competent communicator. Thank you for all you do. Please reach out with any questions or concerns.

Warmly,

Student-Caregiver-Teacher Communication Tools

Timely, reciprocal communication is essential to maintaining successful home-school partnerships. The Student-Caregiver-Teacher Communication Tools included on the next pages provide an additional way to help families better understand the work happening in school. These tools celebrate the learning *process* and *progress* toward learning goals. You'll notice these protocols have very close ties to the resources in Chapter 3 and Chapter 8 of this book.

Periodically throughout the year (often two to five times), students in Grades 1 and up will reflect on recent learning, prepare to share that with a caregiver, and then actually lead a conference with a caregiver not only to tell but also show recent word learning. Essentially, it goes like this:

1. Students reflect on recent learning. They recall letters, sounds, patterns, and/ or words learned. They recollect the routines practiced over the last several weeks/few months. Students jot a few reminders of this work on the communication tool.

2. Students reflect on their word study goal(s) and work toward this goal. They *may* put sticky notes on three to five pages of notebooks or flag specific digital entries that are evidence of work toward this goal. Students may even quickly jot specific highlights of recent learning.

3. Students give themselves a little written feedback on the communication tool.

4. Students hand in their mostly completed tool. The teacher then provides brief written feedback and returns communication tools to students. Optional: The teacher may choose to briefly meet face-to-face with some or all class members to also share face-to-face feedback.

5. Students each bring the tool and their notebook home. Each student leads an informal conference at home with a caregiver explaining recent learning and showing evidence of learning (marked pages in notebook/flagged digital entries). The student will facilitate a short discussion on highlights and accomplishments. The caregiver can then look over the tool, read the feedback provided by the students *and* the teacher, and provide some of their own feedback to the child.

Often teachers have the students bring back the communication tools, and these are added to student folders or portfolios. And, before doing this the *first time*, the teacher often models an exemplar caregiver conference in class and lists out a few tips. Students may even practice their conference with a partner so they feel prepared to share with someone outside of school.

The next few pages show you how to use these tools. All these forms (and more concise, "streamlined" versions) are also available for download from the companion website, **resources.corwin.com/wstscompanion**.

ANNOTATED STUDENT-CAREGIVER-TEACHER COMMUNICATION TOOL (PRIMARY)

Students list letters, sounds, patterns, or a few examples of learned words.

Students jot the one to two goals they worked toward. Students copy this from the goal section of their notebook. Students then use sticky notes to mark three to five different work samples/notebook pages that show progress toward this goal.

Learning	
Words:	Habits:

Students list a couple of learning habits (teamwork, material management) or new routines they learned and practiced.

Goal:
(Mark three to five pages with sticky notes.)

Students share something they can now do . . . that they were unable to do earlier in the year.

Students share something they think they now feel ready to work on. This may be tied to the next goal they want to set.

When My "Not Yet" Turned Into a Yep!:

Shining Moment:

Students share something they are particularly proud of—a favorite moment they want to share.

Next Up?:

Students write one to three sentences giving some honest, constructive feedback.

Teacher writes two to four sentences to share specific, strength-based feedback.

Self-Feedback: Teacher Feedback: Caregiver Feedback:

A caregiver is welcome to write one to three sentences to share feedback and compliments for the student and his or her efforts.

ANNOTATED STUDENT-CAREGIVER-TEACHER COMMUNICATION TOOL (UPPER-ELEMENTARY GRADES)

Learning

Students list patterns studied here.

Patterns Studied:

Routines Taught:

Students list a couple new routines learned and practiced.

Students jot the one or two goals worked toward. This is copied from the goal section of the notebook.

My Goal Was . . . /My Goals Were . . .

Actions Taken to Work Toward Goal(s):

Students use sticky notes to mark three to five different work samples/ notebook pages that show progress toward goal. If using digital notebooks, students can flag those entries. In lieu of marking entries, students can list evidence here.

Students record the steps taken to work toward the goal(s). This may or may not reflect the original action plan.

Evidence:
(List, mark notebook pages with sticky notes and/or flag digital notebook entries.)

Shout-Outs!

Favorite Area:

Most Improved Area:

Students jot a favorite part about recent word study.

Students jot an area where a lot of recent improvement is shown.

Most Challenging Area:

Shining Moment:

Students name what has been tricky.

Students name a moment or accomplishment that makes them feel proud.

Students consider and write one to three sentences about possible next steps, goals, or areas of focus.

Looking Ahead:
(Thoughts, priorities, goals, wonders.)

Feedback

Students may provide one to three sentences of honest, constructive feedback.

Self:

Teacher:

Caregiver:

A caregiver is welcome to write a few sentences to share feedback and compliments for the student and their efforts.

Teacher provides specific, strength-based feedback.

PARTNERING WITH PARENTS

RELATIONSHIPS YIELD SUCCESS

There is a direct relationship between home-school partnership and student success. As one increases, so does the other.

OPTIONS, NOT ASSIGNMENTS

The After-Hours Activities Letters (available online in both Spanish and English) offer caregivers options for how they might choose to support word learning at home.

CELEBRATING THE PROCESS AND PROGRESS

The Student-Caregiver-Teacher Communication Tools offer ways to help caregivers see and understand the important word work being done in school each day. These could even be used as assessment, reflection, and celebration tools.

INVITE INPUT

Just like we aim to be student-centered in our approach to classroom learning, we can also strive to be family-centered in our approach to home-school partnering. Ask caregivers about the methods, tools, and types of communication they would most easily access and fully appreciate. Then, match your communication methods to family interests and priorities.

HOME-SCHOOL PARTNERING IN ACTION

A student applies her knowledge of the Switch It, Change It routine—to practice word study pattern words while at a local playground.

Photo by Viviana Tamas

Pumpin' Patterns is a favorite home word study routine.

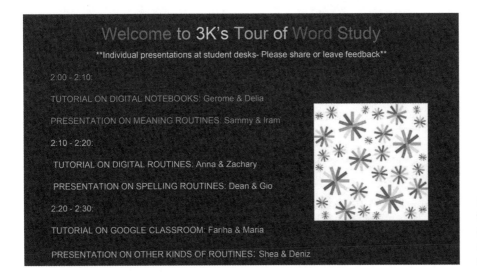

Welcome to 3K's Tour of Word Study

Individual presentations at student desks- Please share or leave feedback

2:00 - 2:10:

TUTORIAL ON DIGITAL NOTEBOOKS: Gerome & Delia

PRESENTATION ON MEANING ROUTINES: Sammy & Iram

2:10 - 2:20:

TUTORIAL ON DIGITAL ROUTINES: Anna & Zachary

PRESENTATION ON SPELLING ROUTINES: Dean & Gio

2:20 - 2:30:

TUTORIAL ON GOOGLE CLASSROOM: Fariha & Maria

PRESENTATION ON OTHER KINDS OF ROUTINES: Shea & Deniz

By inviting caregivers in for an informational and celebratory session run by and starring the students, everyone wins!

Wordplay at home is easier
than one might think—and
a little goes a long way!

Word-themed games are
a great way to support
language learning at home.

CHAPTER TEN

Bonus Lessons to Bolster Word Study Engagement and Success

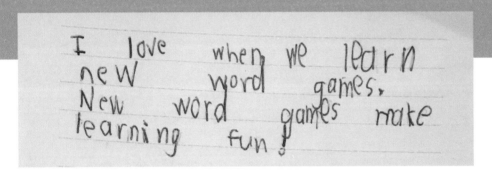

Word Study That Sticks introduced over fifty lessons and routines, and this companion book has provided minicharts for each of these routines. Here, in the pages that follow, are lesson ideas for an additional twenty routines, which I hope will offer even more ways to explore and study words. Educators work with incredibly unique learners—all with diverse and varied next steps. As teachers, we often feel more confident and prepared to support each of these students when we have more "hows" in our toolbox. The lessons in this chapter introduce routines that help us do all this and also keep students engaged in and excited by word study from the first day to the last day of school.

Bonus Meaning Lessons

PART-OF-SPEECH CHART

Bonus Lesson 1

What?

While working on this routine, students identify the part of speech of each word being studied.

How?

1. Post a mentor sentence from a familiar text. Discuss the structure of the sentence, identifying (previously taught) parts of speech and the role of each part of speech.

2. Share the name, what, and why of this routine.

3. Show a partially completed chart, and explain the work done. Then, use think aloud as you identify the part(s) of speech of other pattern words.

4. Invite students to turn and talk with a partner, identifying the part of speech of the last few words. Use student input to complete the chart.

5. Remind students when they might choose this routine. Provide a minichart (p. 79) for students to glue into the Resources section of notebooks or access digitally.

Optional: Send students off to try this routine with the words *they* are currently studying. Coach and provide feedback as students work.

Why?

- Knowing the part of speech of words helps students correctly use words while speaking and writing.

- Students benefit from talking about words and grammar across the day. This supports deeper understanding and greater transfer.

Tips:

- Challenge students to think past initial definitions of words, and explore other lesser-known meanings of words. It can be quite powerful for students to discover that the part of speech *may* change depending on meaning.

- This routine can be written in notebooks or on a digital document, like Google Docs.

- Students can also complete this routine without writing by sorting word cards (or using sorting circles, a pocket chart, or a digital sorting template).

This student is proudly showing off his first Part-of-Speech Chart.

ACT IT OUT

Bonus Lesson 2

What?

Students use their bodies to show their understanding of the meaning of studied words.

How?

1. Ask if anyone has played charades. Play a couple of rounds of charades. Hint: Choose words/topics that are not related to academics. Use pop culture references (video games, movies, TV shows, book titles, etc.) to spark student interest.

2. Model choosing a word study word, thinking of its meaning, considering what you might sketch for Picture It, and then how you could act out the meaning of the word.

3. Act out the word. Invite students to demonstrate additional possibilities.

4. Act out two to four more words, using the same process described above. Encourage greater student participation in each subsequent round.

5. Remind students when they might choose this routine. Provide a choice chart icon or minichart (p. 75) for students to glue into the Resources section of notebooks or access digitally.

Optional: Invite student partnerships or small groups to go back and try this routine with some of the words they are currently studying. Afterward, reflect on the experience together.

Why?

- Kinesthetic movement is engaging and beneficial for many students.
- Acting out the meaning of a word requires a deep understanding of the word.

Tips:

- Use conversation to lift the level of the routine. This may sound something like "I think the word is ___ because it means ___ and when you ___ it showed this." Or, have students reflect on their process: "When I chose the word, I first thought___. I knew this word meant __ and I chose to ___ because___."

- If students find acting the word out to be challenging, encourage them to first make a quick sketch to generate ideas. They might also think: When do I do this? Where do I do this? or How do I do this?

Learners enjoy challenging classmates to figure out what word they are acting out.

SYNONYM AND ANTONYM CHART

Bonus Lesson 3

What?

Students create a simple chart and brainstorm synonyms and antonyms of studied words.

How?

1. Briefly review synonyms and antonyms.

2. Model setting up a quick three-column chart and conventionally writing the words currently being studied down the left-hand column. Use think aloud to model considering synonyms and antonyms for the first word. Jot ideas on the chart. Invite students to help you do the same with another few words. Reflect on and name the process used.

3. Look back at the completed portion of chart. Ask this: What is the part of speech of each word we found a synonym and antonym for? Through conversation and reflection, facilitate the discovery that it is easier to find synonyms and antonyms for certain words: although *some* nouns may have a synonym, nouns do not typically have antonyms.

4. Remind students when they might choose this routine. Provide a minichart (p. 97) for students to glue into the Resources section of notebooks or access digitally.

Why?

- Research shows that students often remember (and use) new words when they connect or attach them to other words they already know.

- This routine encourages the discovery of lesser-known meanings of words.

Tips:

- Encourage those who might need support to choose this routine *after* first identifying the part of speech of each word or completing the Part-of-Speech Chart routine.

- Online tools like WordHippo.com provide support to students who feel "stuck" and students who want to continue to explore additional synonyms and antonyms.

- Students can use this routine to prepare for the Shades of Meaning, More or Less?, and Word Continuums routines.

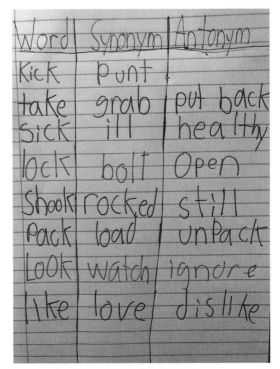

Word	Synonym	Antonym
Kick	punt	
take	grab	put back
sick	ill	healthy
lock	bolt	open
shook	rocked	still
pack	load	unpack
Look	watch	ignore
like	love	dislike

Students begin to discover the "job" of certain prefixes—even before this is taught in word study.

WORD FAMILY TREES

Bonus Lesson 4

What?

Students generate and identify related words and word forms.

How?

1. Explain that knowing one word can help you spell and better understand many other words. Share that today's routine helps students explore the family trees of different words.

2. Model choosing one word. Write the word in the "trunk" of a tree. Use think aloud to consider different affixes that can be added to the word. Brainstorm other miscellaneous words that can be made (using a root, creating compound words . . .). Add each word to a different branch of the tree.

3. Ask students to help you create a second word tree. Ask partnerships to brainstorm related words that you could add as branches and leaves. Review the process used.

4. Remind students when they might choose this routine. Provide a minichart (p. 98) for students to glue into the Resources section of notebooks or access digitally.

Optional: Ask students to go back and try this routine with some of the words they are currently studying. Coach and provide feedback as students work. Reflect on the experience: celebrations and challenges.

Why?

- This routine fosters the transfer of word learning beyond the words currently being studied.

- By delving into affixes and roots, students take word learning to the next level.

Tips:

- Students can write the part of speech of each new word on a "leaf" attached to the word branch.

- Students can create a visual hierarchy of words: grouping similar types of words as leaves on one branch. (The image below shows this.)

- Students can follow up by speaking or writing with the different forms of the word.

So much was learned about the seemingly simple word *note*.

CREATING CONNECTIONS (ANALOGIES)

Bonus Lesson 5

What?

Completing premade analogies encourages critical thinking. Creating analogies takes this work to the next level!

How?

1. Post a simple analogy. Have students work to solve it. Post a more complex analogy. Have students try this one. Share thinking and strategies used. Brainstorm and list common "types" of analogies students are used to seeing. Explain that students are ready for the added challenge of becoming *creators* of analogies.

2. Choose one or two words currently being studied. Use think aloud to mull over the different analogy structures that might work with these words. Consider ideas that don't work before creating a successful analogy. Check to see if analogy structure is clear.

3. Invite partnerships to work together to create another analogy using the same words *or* different words. Invite partnerships to share their analogies and see if other classmates can solve them.

4. Remind students when they might choose this routine. Provide a minichart (p. 101) for students to glue into the Resources section of notebooks or access digitally.

Optional: Invite partners to try this routine with greater independence. End by listing out helpful hints for creating analogies. Post this chart, or invite students to quickly jot these helpful reminders.

Why?

- Exploring relationships between words increases word comprehension.

- Challenging students with enriching learning tasks strengthens problem-solving skills, collaboration, and reflection.

Tips:

- Teach this routine *after* students have seen and practiced solving analogies.

- By working to include more than one pattern word in a single analogy, the level of complexity grows even more.

- Invite students to share analogies with a larger audience—in the classroom, around the school, or digitally.

> **CREATING CONNECTIONS BY PAUL**
>
> prefix : suffix : : prelude : epilogue
>
> predict : guess : : postpone : delay
>
> preheat : stretch : : warm up : cool down

This sixth grader created analogies with the prefixes pre- and post-.

CONCEPT STRETCH

Bonus Lesson 6

What?

Students choose a word being studied and delve into the what, when, where, and/or how of the word.

How?

1. Explain there are times we might want to do a little work with a lot of words and times we want to explore just a few words in greater depth. Share that today's routine represents an in-depth exploration of a few selected words.

2. Model choosing a word and then thinking of a concept to explore, keeping the word in mind. For example, if the word *kind* was selected, you might name "acts" as the concept. Then, you would brainstorm and jot kind acts *and* unkind acts. Further, if the concept was characters, you could then jot book, TV, or movie characters you consider kind *and* unkind.

3. After modeling two examples, send students off to work in partnerships or small groups to try Concept Stretch. Come back together to share out additional examples.

4. Remind students when they might choose this routine. Provide a minichart (p. 102) for students to glue into the Resources section of notebooks or access digitally.

Optional: End with a short debate of some of the choices made. (Does *everyone* believe that character is annoying? Does *anyone* disagree that a selected setting is dangerous?)

Why?

- By taking the time to deeply explore words, students' understanding and readiness to apply knowledge are bolstered.

- By connecting current learning (words) to prior knowledge (different concepts), students are more likely to connect and retain learning.

Tips:

- Students can use a related word form—for example, if *danger* is being studied, the student might change the word to *dangerous* and then think of a concept they want to explore related to *dangerous*.

- Encourage students to connect ideas to other content area learning. For example, students might consider dangerous and safe settings in books recently read, dangerous and safe times in history, or dangerous and thoughtful decisions that could affect their health.

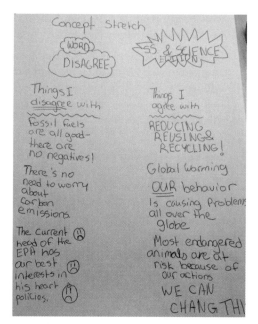

A fifth grader combined a word study Concept Stretch (Disagree) with her content area learning about global warming. Way to go!

Bonus Phonemic Awareness and Phonics Lessons

CONFIGURATION STATION

Bonus Lesson 7

What?

Students focus in on the shape of different words, building muscle memory of the visual appearance of words being studied.

How?

1. Show an image created by a simple outline. Ask students to shout out what they see. Repeat a few more times with additional simple sketches/outlines of images. Explain that when we know the shape of something, we then easily recognize it. We also notice when something seems "off." (You may also choose to show an example of this too—for example, a rabbit with a long, thin tail instead of a short, fluffy tail.) Share that today's routine does this for words.

2. Model writing a word and then creating a box around each letter (or the word). Point out how the boxes help us notice the *tall, small,* and *fall* letters and how this helps us remember how a word is spelled—and notice when something seems "off."

3. Model this same process using a few more words. Take a moment to reflect on the "shape" of each word after you write it.

4. Remind students when they might choose this routine. Provide a choice chart icon or minichart (p. 117) for students to glue into the Resources section of notebooks or access digitally.

Optional: Invite students to go back and try this routine with a few words they are currently studying. Coach and provide feedback as students work.

Why?

- Knowing and recognizing the shape of a word can help students confirm correct spelling or notice incorrect spelling of a word.

- Focusing on the shape of the word also encourages proper letter formation.

Tips:

- Use Configuration Station to help students practice high-frequency and word wall words.

- Invite primary learners to use colors to differentiate between certain types of letters (e.g., blue for consonants, red for vowels, or blue for tall letters, red for small letters, and green for fall letters).

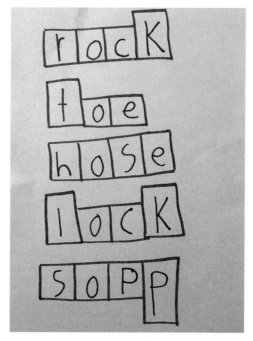

A kindergartener is working to build a visual memory of *rock, toe, nose, lock,* and *soap.*

I SPY!

Bonus Lesson 8

What?

Students search their environment and surroundings for real-life examples of studied letters, sounds, and simple patterns.

How?

1. Play two or three rounds of traditional I Spy! Share that today you are going to teach the word study version of the I Spy! game.

2. Model first remembering and saying the letter, sound, or pattern being studied. Then use think aloud and a bit of acting as you look around the room for something with that letter, sound, or simple pattern. When you find something, excitedly say, "I spy with my little eye . . . something that's ____ and ____" (e.g., "I spy with my little eye, something red that starts with /st/."). Class members participate by guessing the item.

3. Provide the opportunity for students to work in partnerships, and try both I Spy! roles.

4. Remind students when they might choose this routine. Provide a choice chart icon or minichart (p. 118) for students to glue into the Resources section of notebooks or access digitally.

Why?

- Recognizing aspects of word learning in our environments helps content feel worthwhile and relevant.

Tips:

- Consider taking the learning outdoors!
- Students can play I Spy! in print and digital texts—a hybrid of this routine and Word Scavenger Hunts.

- Adding a prop (magnifying glass or laser pointer) can raise the engagement of this work while still protecting the integrity of the routine.

This first grader is a huge fan of I Spy!

SENSORY CYCLE

Bonus Lesson 9

What?

In this routine, students use as many senses as possible to practice spelling words fluently.

How?

1. Quickly review the five senses or read a short passage where the author includes many sensory details. Explain that "learning scientists" believe that when we involve more senses in our learning, we are more likely to remember what we study.

2. Show the available sensory materials (different textured materials such as fabrics, grades of sandpaper, sizes of bubble wrap, or sheets of cotton). Pass items around so students feel each of the materials.

3. Model the Sensory Cycle with a partner: First, look at the word. Then, say the word. Next, listen as your partner says the word. After that, trace or write the letters (with your finger) on the sensory material. Last, look at, say, and listen to the word one more time. Model a second sensory cycle with a different partner and second word.

4. Remind students when they might choose this routine. Provide a choice chart icon or minichart (p. 121) for students to glue into the Resources section of notebooks or access digitally.

Optional: Send students back to try this routine with a partner. If possible, each partnership should have their own sensory surface to "write" the words on. Coach and provide feedback as students work.

Why?

- It's true! Involving many senses helps the learning appeal to a wider variety of students and helps word learning stick.

- Providing a variety of sensory experiences helps to develop not only student understanding of the five senses but also much-needed sensory integration skills.

Tips:

- Some teachers keep all sensory cycle materials in an easily accessible drawer or storage container. Other classrooms create a "touch wall." Here, different sensory materials are hung/attached to a small section of one wall. Kids love touch walls—just be sure to hang materials at student-friendly heights.

- Besides the materials already mentioned, many students also enjoy *any* of the more tactile ideas used for the Multisensory Fun routine (shaving cream, sand bins, gel bags, etc.).

Photo by Laurie Hemmerly

Sometimes, learning gets messy—in all kinds of wonderful ways!

REGGIO ROUTINES

Bonus Lesson 10

What?

Young learners enjoy invitations to use "loose part" materials (and other items) to explore letters, names, and words.

How?

1. Set up a Reggio-styled provocation center (see photo). Gather students to that area of the classroom, and read the invitation provided. Talk with students about what this invitation means, and ask students to consider what they might choose to do with the provided materials.

2. Invite a partnership to accept the invitation. Ask the other students to "study" and name what the partnership does. Invite a different partnership to come up and try something else. Again, ask the other students to "study" and name what the partnership does.

3. Remind students when they might choose this routine. Provide a choice chart icon or a minichart (p. 122) for students to glue into the Resources section of notebooks.

Why?

- The Reggio Emilia process of learning is often credited with building resilience, responsibility, self-confidence, teamwork, and problem-solving skills.

- Whereas integrating some letter- and word-themed provocations does not mean we are using a Reggio "approach," by incorporating these types of learning opportunities, we recognize students as active participants in constructing their knowledge.

Tips:

- Read a bit more about the Reggio Emilia process of learning and loose parts. There are plenty of professional texts but also countless shorter articles and blog posts available online.

- There is no need to purchase loose parts. These are everywhere you might imagine! Loose parts can be natural or synthetic and consist of any materials that could be used in multiple ways: moved, carried, combined, redesigned, lined up, taken apart, and put back together. Sticks, pine cones, shells, pebbles, blocks, manipulatives, recycled materials, buttons, beads . . . there are more loose parts around than we might imagine!

Photo by Danielle Novak

Students use a light board, letters, learning, and their imaginations to respond to this provocation.

SOUND SNAPSHOT AND PATTERN PICTURES

Bonus Lesson II

What?

In this spin-off of I Spy!, students look for particular letters, sounds, or spelling patterns around them. They then take photos of items with these identified letters, sounds, or spelling patterns.

How?

1. Gather students, and play a quick round of I Spy! Share that today you are going to teach a routine that kicks things up a notch. Take out a tablet (or any portable device with a camera), and share that instead of having a partner guess the item they will instead take one photo of the item. The goal is to find several different objects with the sound or pattern being studied.

2. Choose a search topic (e.g., items starting with a /p/). Model searching surroundings for an object that starts with that sound. Take one photo of the object. Ask students to search for additional items, and when they find something to give a signal. When a student shares their ideas, ask the others to confirm it "suits the search." If it does, snap a photo. Repeat a few times.

3. Model again, this time using a studied sound or pattern. Follow the process outlined previously. Provide parameters appropriate for the grade level and age of the students. (Are they only searching inside the classroom? Is a five-minute walk around the halls of the school something they could choose to do?)

4. Remind students when they might choose this routine. Provide a choice chart icon or minichart (p. 127) for students to glue into the Resources section of notebooks or access digitally.

Why?

- Building connections between what's done in word study and what's in the real world helps learning come to life.

Tips:

- If this routine is part of a meaningful word study center, spend time at the center to provide technical assistance and guidance on careful equipment management. If this is a cycle option, prioritize being present the first time a group decides to try this routine. If there is another adult in the room, enlist this person for support.

- Consider what will be done with the photos. Will students share with the teacher or classmates and then delete? Will they be uploaded and available to other class members?

Pattern pictures are fun for students of all ages.

Bonus Spelling Pattern Lessons

PATTERN INTRODUCTION: NICE TO MEET YOU!/NOW I KNOW!

Bonus Lesson 12

What?

In this routine, the teacher introduces the pattern(s) being studied.

How?

1. Set up a pocket chart, or create a digital sorting chart that everyone can see. Gather students. Share that now you will be introducing the word study pattern(s) the class/group will be focusing on for the remainder of the cycle. Tell the students that this will be done as a "game" with three rounds.

2. Round 1: Ask students to watch you sort/ categorize the words. While you do this, they should think about what the words (in the same column) have in common . . . and what makes them different from the words in the other columns. (Have them try to figure out your sorting strategy.) Add a few words to the digital chart or pocket chart.

3. Round 2: Continue to sort additional words, asking students who has a theory about where they think each word belongs. As students are successful, flip over the sort "headers," and unveil the pattern features. Pause to explicitly explain the pattern. Summarize pattern learning as each new word is sorted.

4. Round 3: Finish by having students sort the remainder of the words. Each time a student places a word into a column, they explain why it went there . . . and why it did not go somewhere else.

5. Review the pattern again, and discuss additional words that include this pattern. Remind students when they might choose this routine. Provide a minichart (p. 136) for students to glue into the Resources section of notebooks or access digitally.

Why?

- By gamifying a closed sort and adding an extra helping of inquiry, students are motivated and think deeply throughout the routine.

- Students benefit from the explicit pattern introduction and learning the "why" behind studied patterns.

Tips:

- The pattern is introduced after students have a chance to explore the meaning of words being studied.

- The pattern is introduced *after* students have had the opportunity to sort words in a variety of ways.

Photo by Linda Day

Round 3 of Nice to Meet You! asks students to show their understanding of the introduced pattern.

PARTNER PROMPTING

Bonus Lesson 13

What?

Students orally assess one another's understanding of a word.

How?

1. Gather students. Without saying too much, model this routine with a partner in front of the class. (Your partner could be another adult or a student volunteer.) Ask the rest of the students to name what they saw, what they heard, what they thought, and what they wondered while observing. Use student observations to summarize what this routine entails and how it is done. (The partners switch lists, ask each other to spell words, and provide each other hints—not answers—when stuck or incorrect.)

2. Send students off to try this routine with a partner. Coach and provide feedback as students work together.

3. Remind students when they might choose this routine. Close by reflecting on what students plan to do the same or differently next time. Provide a choice chart icon or minichart (pp. 143 and 152) for students to glue into the Resources section of notebooks or access digitally.

Why?

- Peer support builds community. Students don't always need us there, guiding each step.

- This type of routine could feel like a test, but by working with a peer, it has a more relaxed tone.

Tips:

- Students can also prompt one another to share word information unrelated to spelling. For example, partners might ask each other to share the meaning of a word or to separate the sounds in a word. This routine can be easily adapted to match developmental readiness and instructional priorities.

- I know plenty of teachers who use Partner Prompting as their assessment. They feel this cumulative review with a partner works well. If you like this idea, feel free to take it!

Photo by Linda Day

Students get feedback as they try out Partner Prompting for the first time.

LOOK, SAY, COVER, WRITE, CHECK

Bonus Lesson 14

What?

Students practice spelling words and check in to see how close they got.

How?

1. Gather students. Share that today they will learn an "oldie but a goody." Explain that this routine helps students figure out how much they really know about the letters, word parts, patterns, or words being studied.

2. Demonstrate folding the page and listing the words on one side of the fold (students can also use a preprinted word list). Model looking at the word, saying the word, and then folding in the page to cover up the word. Use think aloud (actively employing strategies) to remember and apply word learning . . . as you write the word. Unfold the page, and check to see if you were correct. Be sure also to explain what to do if the first attempt was incorrect. (Repeat and try again and again until it *is* correct.)

3. Model a few more times, having the students join you when ready. They can look at the word, say the word with you, and write the word on a whiteboard as you write it on your paper. Then, you can all check together, reflect, and decide if the class should move on to the next word or try again.

4. Remind students when they might choose this routine. Provide a minichart (pp. 144 and 153) for students to glue into the Resources section of notebooks or access digitally.

Why?

- Self-assessment is so important! Having an accurate picture of current understanding helps students keep themselves accountable.

- Students can plan "next steps" after using this routine. In this way, students themselves use assessment formatively!

Tips:

- Remind students the "say" is out loud . . . even if in a quiet voice.

- Encourage students to add "other" pattern words to their Look, Say, Cover, Write, Check list. This way, they extend and apply their pattern knowledge.

- If folding paper seems too difficult or time consuming, encourage students to put an object over the list of words while trying to spell them.

- Early learners may benefit from looking at a word, saying it, covering it, writing *part* of the word, and then checking to see if they got that part correct. For example, sometimes students listen for the first sound in a word and write the letter(s) that match that sound. Other times, students try to write the final sound/letter. This routine can easily be adapted to fit prioritized learning goals.

Once students self-assess, they can use this information to help prioritize future practice.

PUMPIN' PATTERNS

Bonus Lesson 15

What?

Students use kinesthetic movement to practice fluently spelling studied words.

How?

1. Engage in a quick brain break or movement break. Ask students how they would feel if they sat in seats all day long . . . and how it helps them learn when they get up and move throughout the day. Share that today's routine will help them stretch their brains and their bodies.

2. Model choosing a word being studied, saying the word aloud, and spelling the word—one letter at a time—while moving your body. Doing jumping jacks, marching in place, and touching toes are all simple kinesthetic options. Spell the word at least three times. Take a short break, and then invite students to join you for the next word.

3. Have students generate and chart other ideas for kinesthetic movement (more ideas are listed in the Tips section). Ask student volunteers to model the routine with different words, each time using different movements.

4. Remind students when they might choose this routine. Provide a choice chart icon or minichart (p. 154) for students to glue into the Resources section of notebooks or access digitally.

Why?

- Moving our bodies regularly throughout the day is important—for so many different reasons.
- Many students are motivated by kinesthetic learning and sustain long-term engagement in these types of routines.

Tips:

- Crossing the midline is a great way to wake up all parts of the brain. Touching elbows to opposite knees and fingers to opposite toes are great options.

- Assign different movements to different patterns (e.g., CVC = jumping jacks, CVCe = jog in place, and CVVC = toe touches).

- Students often enjoy tossing and catching a soft ball (alone or with a partner). Head, Shoulders, Knees, and Toes is also a beloved Pumpin' Patterns movement.

- Students enjoy playing hand games with a partner or showcasing different dance moves. A few years ago, there was a lot of "dabbing" during Pumpin' Patterns. In the past two years, dances made popular by video games have been common.

- As with any routine, make sure to address safety issues and ask students to always check their surroundings before beginning this routine.

This student is crossing the midline while getting physical using the Pumpin' Patterns routine.

Bonus Hybrid Lessons

CREATING WORD LADDERS

Bonus Lesson 16

What?

Students create and share their own word ladders using a combination of visual, auditory, and meaning clues.

How?

1. Display an enlarged premade word ladder. Work together to complete the ladder. Explain that today you are going to teach students not only to be solvers but also creators of their own word ladders.

2. Model choosing a simple word (CVC words are great to start with) and writing it on the bottom rung of a simply sketched word ladder. Decide on one letter or part to change to create a new word. Using think aloud, model different clues you might write along the side of the ladder (purposely consider visual clues, auditory clues, and meaning clues). Choose one or two clues to record. Continue this process, asking students for their input as you work.

3. Remind students when they might choose this routine. Provide a minichart (p. 119) for students to glue into the Resources section of notebooks or access digitally.

Optional: Invite students to go back and try this routine in small groups, creating a word ladder with at least one word they are currently studying. Coach and provide feedback as students work.

Why?

- Word ladders help us create connections between words, comparing and contrasting word parts.

- Creating the clues encourages students to consider and synthesize different facets of word learning.

Tips:

- This routine can be made as simple or as complex as students wish! Three-rung ladders are simpler to create than six-rung ladders. Changing different parts of words is more complex than changing only the first letter on each rung.

- Students enjoy using visual meaning clues along the side of the ladder. In this way, they bring their Picture It skills to word ladders.

- The fun part of creating word ladders is seeing if others can solve them! Consider posting student-created word ladders inside the classroom, outside the classroom, or online. Students can also trade and solve one another's word ladders.

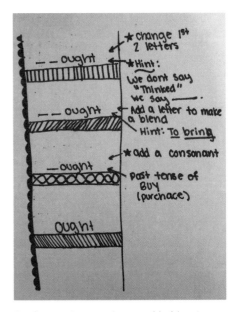

Students enjoy creating word ladders just as much as they enjoy completing word ladders—perhaps even more.

NATURE KNOWLEDGE

Bonus Lesson 17

What?

Students work with letters and words out in nature and/or build words using items found in nature.

How?

1. Head outside! Announce that we can study words anytime, anyplace, and with almost anything. Model a few ways to build words outside (see Tips). Encourage students to add other ideas.

2. Ask students to start engaging in word-themed practice. Coach and provide feedback.

3. Ask students how they enjoyed this routine and if they felt it was a useful way to engage in word learning. Once back inside, provide a minichart (pp. 172–173) for students to glue into the Resources section of notebooks or access digitally.

Why?

- Fresh air does a body good!
- Being out in nature, enjoying nature, and connecting with our surroundings also helps many learn.

Tips:

- Option 1: Build with nature. Collect twigs, acorns, rocks, and other natural resources. Use them as loose parts. Create letters and words using these materials.
- Option 2: Do an outdoor version of a previously practiced routine.

  ○ Fun outdoor Pumpin' Patterns ideas include jump roping (including Double Dutch), hula hooping, and monkey bar crossing as well as playing catch, passing a soccer ball back and forth, shooting baskets, etc.

  ○ Students also like doing virtually any written routine outside using sidewalk chalk, outdoor paint, water, and paintbrushes. Picture It and Write With It are forever favorites. There is a lot of excitement and pride in leaving word poems and six-word stories outside for others to find and read.

- If it is too cold or wet—and even bundling up or covering up won't help—consider using collected nature items and building letters and words indoors.

Photo by Ellen Calamito

Young students write "pattern word poems" while being inspired by nature.

WORD CONVERSATIONS: WRITTEN

Bonus Lesson 18

What?

Students compose written conversations using studied words and other pattern words.

How?

1. Gather students. Remind them of the taught routine: Talkin' the Talk. Explain that today they will learn a written version of this routine.

2. Rehearse orally: Choose a few words, and invite a couple of class members to engage in a short conversation using those words.

3. Use modeled and/or interactive writing to demonstrate how to write the conversation students just had.

4. Remind students when they might choose this routine. Provide a minichart (p. 180) for students to glue into the Resources section of notebooks or access digitally.

Optional: Ask students to try this routine with some of the words they are currently studying. Coach and provide feedback as students work.

Why?

- We want to foster transfer from word study to writing as frequently as possible.

- Students need plenty of practice writing and punctuating dialogue conventionally.

- Conversation (whether oral or written) helps expand students' knowledge of context: when, where, and how these words would fit in a variety of settings.

Tips:

- Teach this routine *after* the oral version has been taught and practiced.

- Students can use oral conversation as a springboard for this written conversation or head straight to the written conversation.

- Students can go to their writing folder or notebooks and add in pattern-word-rich dialogue to their current writing projects.

- Students might enjoy the choice to create comics (on paper or digitally) while engaging in this routine.

A partnership uses oral conversation (Talkin' the Talk) to prepare for written conversations.

WRITE WITH IT

Bonus Lesson 19

What?

Students use and conventionally spell pattern words in *any* kind of writing.

How?

1. Gather students. If already introduced, review the Interactive Writing routine. Explain that today's routine is like this routine and helps make sure students work to meet one of the most important word study goals: to spell correctly *whenever* writing.

2. Choose a few words and a writing topic. Note: Although it is great to tie this routine to other content areas, I suggest the first-time students trying this routine choose a fun, nonacademic topic. Model contemplating different writing ideas and trying to use pattern words in a way that makes sense. Compose some of the writing in front of students.

3. Ask students what they noticed about the process so far. List these observations. Invite students to use these suggestions as they practice this routine. Coach students as needed.

4. Invite students to share their pieces with a partner and tally the total number of times pattern words were used. Gather the class together. Use partner tallies to find the total number of times *the class* used pattern words. Celebrate!

5. Reflect on the steps, and now that students have given this routine a try, extend the chart by adding tips and hints. Provide a minichart (pp. 169 and 181) for students to glue into the Resources section of notebooks or access digitally.

Why?

- Bringing word work to writing is an essential aspect of rich word study.
- This routine helps students prepare to consistently apply their word knowledge while writing.

Tips:

- Pull a small group of students who may need a bit of extra support. Provide small-group instruction focused on this routine.
- Create a class "pull place" with ideas for Write With It: comics, blogs, content area writing, poems, letters, reading long and strong entries, fan fiction, etc.

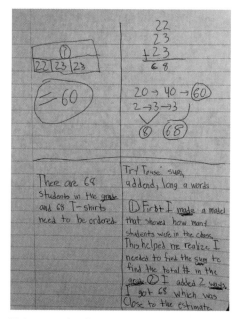

This example of Write With It combines word study and math learning.

WORD SHARE

Bonus Lesson 20

What?

Students share their learning about a word, a pattern, or other recent learning with others.

How?

1. Review the taught Show Off routine, and let students know that today, they will learn a routine that involves a little reflecting, a little teaching, and a little showing off. Reflect together on recent learning. Jot any celebrations and accomplishments mentioned—for example, we are great at putting materials away neatly, we know the sounds each letter makes, we know what open and closed syllables are, we know what these roots mean, we are skilled reflectors.

2. Choose one celebration. Explain that their word shares can be oral or written and that they are often short—about five sentences. Model planning a word share (oral or written). Oral shares are often five "points to know" about the topic listed across fingers. Written shares often resemble mini classroom anchor charts.

3. Remind students when they might choose this routine. Provide a minichart (p. 183) for students to glue into the Resources section of notebooks or access digitally.

Optional: Invite students to go back and work with their word study groups to try this routine. Coach and provide feedback as students work. Interested groups can present their word share.

Why?

- Having an audience to share with is empowering.

- Teaching others is a strong instructional practice: When we teach something, we truly know and understand it. Learning is no longer surface or passive.

Tips:

- For students who like to jot while planning, *box and bullets* is a helpful planning structure. Students can quickly jot a box and bullets in their notebooks to help them plan a word share. Other times, students name the topic being taught while touching the center of their palm and plan things to say while touching each finger on that hand.

- Teachers can use Word Share as an assessment routine. If done this way, the student, partnership, or small group usually presents to the class.

- Word Share can be done at the end of word study to reflect on recent learning. When having all class members engage in this routine at the same time, students typically share with one other student.

This word share became a great learning tool for the whole class!

BONUS ROUTINES IN ACTION

Students can also create Part-of-Speech Charts without any writing.

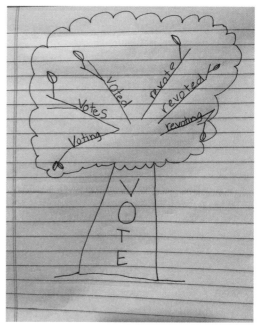

This word family tree was made by a primary student who showed readiness for an upper-elementary routine.

Photo by Linda Day

Teaching a small group a new "bonus" routine is a great way to keep word study fun, lively, and personalized for all classroom learners.

Maya's Written Conversation

Dahlia asked, "Hey Maya, I was wondering if you could help me with this math?"

"Sure, I was thinking the same thing. Division can be tricky. Let's do it together," Maya responded. The girls opened their math journals and grabbed pencils. "Do you think we should start by creating a model?"

"That makes sense. I was considering using a bar diagram. We know the total and the number of groups, we just don't know how many are going into each group." Dahlia began sketching a bar model.

"You do that. I'm going to try using a grid model. Let's see if we get the same answer and then we can start talking about it." Maya got busy. Once the girls finished, they shared their work. "We did it!" Maya and Dahlia did their special handshake and then cleaned up.

In Maya's digital version of a written conversation, the pattern words are highlighted.

A digital version of a word share was made by a sixth-grade student.

Conclusion

Teacher Talk: Tales From the Classroom

As part of a favor for a friend, I was asked to consider what I feel it means to "teach like me." Without thinking, I quickly responded that "we" is the "me" in my teaching. Relationships are *the* core component of any learning community. What most excites me about going to work each day is the knowledge that I am going to have nonstop opportunities to learn, laugh, and connect with educators, students, and families. These connections are both validating and empowering. These relationships are also what makes every day of teaching seem brand new. Teaching is anything but stagnant. We watch, think, plan (and replan), consider (and reconsider), and respond to *what* we see and *who* we see. The people in the room are what brings learning to life, and people (kids in particular) are the ultimate wild card! This is why I can't recommend all teachers use one particular scope and sequence of spelling patterns or teach all routines just as written and in an equally exact order.

Word Study That Sticks and *The Word Study That Sticks Companion* are jumping-off points. The included research, ideas, hints, resources, tools, and guidance intend to help you envision the look and feel of a robust and spirited approach to word study. It is my greatest hope that you will check all this out, make sense of it, and use it in a way that "fits." By making the learning fit learners (not making learners fit some preconceived idea of learning), it *will* stick. And hopefully, connections will be forged and relationships strengthened through the laughter, collaboration, and discovery that happens all along the way.

Although now is the perfect time to start, I understand that for many, buy-in comes once we have proof—seeing positive shifts and changes in students. To that end, I asked some teacher friends to share their thoughts and reflections on recent word study shifts. Check out the "teacher tell-all" confessions and confirmations from those who have recently been in your shoes.

We Hope to See a Shift in the Mindsets of Our Students

I admit it. I found spelling boring. So did my students. Well, things have changed. Word study has become a lively part of the day. We are relaxed, and yet busy. There is often talking, but it is more rhythmic—almost like music—and not noise that makes me uncomfortable. And one of the biggest changes has been in student writing. There is structure, voice, AND conventional spelling. So, yeah. My mindset changed. The mindset of students changed. I am a believer.

—Sasha, Grade 5 Teacher in a Bilingual Classroom

We Hope to See a Shift in Students' Understanding of the Power of Words

I love the pauses I see all around me. The time kids are taking. Sometimes, when students are talking, they stop. I can see the wheels turning. They are searching for—and finding—that exact right word. I see this in their writing too. We have become a community with a strong understanding of how what we say, what we write, and how we express our ideas matters.

—JT, Grade 2 Teacher

We Hope to See Students Using Words to Build Social Comprehension

It's been interesting seeing the students think and talk about words more carefully. We read books and analyze authors' words. But, we have also listened to podcasts, watched interviews, read news articles, and had really amazing conversations about what people say, how they say it, why it matters, and how it impacts us. Engagement is at an all-time high, and so is analytic and critical thinking. We have all experienced some important revelations, me included.

—Michelle, Grade 6 Teacher

We Hope to See Students Becoming More Independent

Photo by Rebecca Johnson

I co-teach in a transitional kindergarten class. The students get, use, and put away their choice charts with independence. They cut out their own word cards. They manage materials with success. Students stay busy while exploring words. I did not totally believe this would happen, but it certainly has. The best part: the students FEEL empowered. As we (slowly) took steps back, the students really stepped up to the plate.

—Melissa, Transitional Kindergarten Teacher

We Hope to See and Feel Joy

My students love word study. This is a first. I feel like this is the part of our day where we exhale. We do such important work and we accomplish a lot, but it does not feel like there is stress or pressure. This has got me thinking about how I can take what works in word study and start bringing it to other subjects.

—Kass, Grade 3 Teacher

We Hope to See Student Success

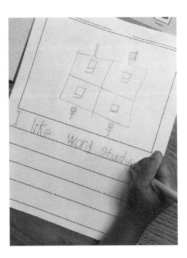

It is incredibly fulfilling to see this culture of words being built in our school. I am in the unique position where I get to work with students and teachers on all grade levels. There have been some affirming upward trends. There is consistent growth on spelling inventories. Student spelling is improving—and not only on inventories or final drafts. As we look at day-to-day student work across subjects, we see evidence of students using what they have practiced. Small shifts bring big success.

—Tatiana, Instructional Coach

I am blown away and inspired by the work of these educators and those in schools near and far. I am eternally grateful to be a part of a larger community of educators who are committed to investing in our own professional growth and joy in learning. I feel privileged to forge connections with administrators, teachers, coaches, and support staff who commit to seeing students, connecting with students, and planning (engaging, discovery-filled, interest-driven) responsive instruction for these students. Margaret Wheatley (2002) tells us, "There is no power for change greater than a community discovering what it cares about" (p. 55). Here's to *our* community and the positive changes I am confident we will bring to each of our classrooms and schools.

Appendix A

Frequently Asked Questions—and Answers

The answers to each of the questions that follow are woven into the pages of both *Word Study That Sticks* and *The Word Study That Sticks Companion*. Throughout the pages of each of these resources, you will find more in-depth information and guidance to more fully support your own professional understanding of word study—and the answers to each of these questions. That said, sometimes we want the more concise and simplified *CliffsNotes* response to a wonder or concern. In that case, look no further—the next few pages intend to be just this!

Where Do I Find Inventories?

Spelling inventories are standardized measures that help teachers see what a student understands about how words work. Sometimes spelling inventories come as part of a spelling program purchased by a school or district. There are also other inventories widely available—no matter what approach a classroom, school, or district is using for word study. Appendix B of *Word Study That Sticks* lists the most commonly used spelling inventories.

Why Didn't You Include Word Study Lists? Where Do I Find the Words?

Word Study That Sticks and *The Word Study That Sticks Companion* are not spelling programs. These professional texts are intended to be resources educators can lean on to start up or step up word study in their classrooms. The approach and routines included in both these texts are meant to be used in conjunction with any existing program—or as a way for teachers who don't have a program to start up word study in their classroom. I made the intentional decision not to provide word lists and sorts. Why? First, words are not hard to come by. Every resource out there offers more word lists than we could ever want or need. Additionally, there are countless books (both hard copy and digital) that exclusively offer word list after word list. Moreover, a simple mind search or Google search will yield all the (free) results we need. In this way, including word lists and sorts would essentially be reinventing the wheel.

Second, I have great respect for educators and the decisions we make each day based on the students currently in our classrooms. You are the expert on your students—not me. Therefore, it would not make sense to outline an "always the same" step-by-step plan that fits every student and every class. To attempt to do so would go against all we know about responsive teaching and personalized learning. I instead purposefully choose to honor the core philosophy and beliefs of a student-centered approach to instruction.

That said, you may still crave confirmation or a bit of guidance. Appendix A of *Word Study That Sticks* lists readily available resources that offer words and patterns. Appendix A also offers one sample "mentor text" of a scope and sequence map to give you greater vision of what this work *could* look like across grades. Chapter 3 of *this* book provides formative assessment tools, protocols, and resources to help you figure out what students have in place and what next steps are most appropriate. Finally, Appendix B of *this* book lays out a simple if/then chart to streamline this process and facilitate a more efficient match of students to patterns and words.

Bottom line: Start with your students. Then use (the listed and included) resources at your fingertips to match students to words and patterns. Kid watching, formal and informal assessment, and trust in yourself will guide you to all the words and patterns you need.

Do I Ever Teach "Spelling Rules"?

Spelling rules are a thing of the past. Why? There are no hard-and-fast spelling rules in the English language—there are *way* too many exceptions. I love providing opportunities for students to discover patterns themselves. The Sort It! Alike or Different? routine facilitates this discovery. I then always follow up with a pattern introduction so that if the students *did not* discover the pattern, they are introduced to the pattern (*and* some of the rebel words that defy the pattern). The Now I Know! and Nice to Meet You! routines help you do just this! By explicitly introducing and reinforcing the pattern being taught, students learn to apply this knowledge to other words and contexts. To sum up, yes, there is a time and place for direct and explicit instruction of a pattern—even when using an approach that highlights inquiry and discovery. But, no, I do not recommend you name these as rules.

How Do I Decide Which Routines to Teach?

Again, your students hold these answers. Use formal and informal assessment to figure out what is in place and what's next for your class. Combine this information with what you know about student interests and developmental readiness. Then, flip through the pages of these two books to select the routines that will engage learners and grow their word expertise. Include some routines to support development in each facet of word study. Teach a few "core" routines as you launch word study. Then, select and teach additional routines (again that match students) throughout the school year.

Is There a Specified Order in Which I Should Teach These Routines?

No. In fact, each year, you may teach different routines at different times. Because these resources are not part of a program, they are meant to be accessed and used flexibly. Say so long to lockstep learning and hello to playful and joyful word exploration that respects *you* as a classroom decision maker. In *Word Study That Sticks*, many lessons are matched to a specific who. In this book, *The Word Study That Sticks Companion,* routine minicharts are separated by "type" of word study practice. These routines are not aligned to a specific scope and sequence and are not meant to be taught in the order in which they appear. So pick and choose the routines that best match students—specifically, student interests and goals.

How Are Choices Built and Added in Over Time?

In the launch to word study, I typically teach five to seven different routines. These become core practices that students can use to study any patterns and any words all year long. Thereafter, I teach additional routines each month. New routines can be taught whole class or in small-group instruction. In the primary grades, I typically introduce one new routine each subsequent month of the school year (sometimes one routine every two months). In the upper-elementary grades, I often teach one to three new routines each month after the launch. This scaffolded process matches the developmental readiness of classroom learners. It also yields word study engagement from Day 1 to Day 180—no more February doldrums.

All of Part II of *Word Study That Sticks* is dedicated to introducing choice to students. In these chapters, you will find in-depth information regarding why we offer choice, what types of choices students have, and how we can help students to become responsible decision makers. You will also find lessons to introduce each new "choice routine." All of Part II of *this* book includes the minicharts that coordinate with each of these routines, thereby making this teaching really stick. Chapter 10 of this book also introduces twenty additional routines you and your students can employ to study and explore words. Chances are, there are so many options provided in these two texts that you will never get to teaching all of them!

What Does a Student Do if They Finish a Routine Before Word Study Is Over?

We all allot different amounts of time to word study. Some of the highlighted routines ask students to do a little work with lots of words; others ask students to do more in-depth work with just a few studied words. In general, if a student feels they have finished a routine before word study is over, they can go back to do more in-depth work or start a new routine. I do recommend that if it is a meaning day, students choose an additional meaning routine and if it is a phonics day, students choose an additional phonics routine. On other days, if a student does not "finish" a routine . . . that's okay too. Because these routines are not traditional written assignments reminiscent of worksheets, we instead prioritize having students make the most of every minute of word study—actively exploring, investigating, discussing, and thinking about words and how they work.

When Are Included Charts Glued Into Notebooks or Made Available Digitally?

I usually provide a minichart to students, whether it is a hard copy to be glued into notebooks or digital access online, on the day I introduce the routine. Traditionally, I introduce the routine, I show the students how it is done, and then the students participate in some kind of guided practice. As we reflect on the why, when, and how of the routine, I make the minichart available to students.

What Are Sound Boxes? How Do We Use Sound Boxes?

Elkonin boxes, also called sound boxes, are named after Russian psychologist D. B. Elkonin. These learning tools build phonemic and phonological awareness. They enable us to segment words into individual sounds (phonemes). Put more simply, sound boxes help students hear the different sounds in a word.

To use sound boxes, we listen to a word, stretch a word, and then separate each sound in that word. Each time we hear a new sound (phoneme), we move a concrete tool or manipulative into a box. Later, when students are ready, we can replace each counter/manipulative with the letter or letters that make each sound. This then becomes a phonics practice as well, helping students solidify their understanding of the alphabetic principle and the relationship between phonemes and graphemes. This work is so purposeful because once fully understood and internalized, both decoding and encoding words become easier and more fluent. What makes this tricky for students (and sometimes us!) is that the number of phonemes in a word does not always match the number of letters in a word. For example, digraphs are composed of two letters that make one sound. A few starting examples to kick-start your growing understanding are included below, but when in doubt, do a little reading or talk to a trained teacher in your building.

This is a typical CVC word.

Blends are separated.

Digraphs go together.

b	oa	t
h	o	pe

Long vowel sounds are often made by more than one letter.

Appendix B

If/Then Chart for Matching Students to Patterns and Words

If I see students are . . .	Then the students may be ready for . . .	A *few* sample patterns include . . .
• interested in words and reading • attempting writing by using letter-like symbols to communicate a message	lots of playful phonemic awareness work beginning to work on the alphabetic principle	n/a Letter recognition—uppercase and lowercase letters
• able to stretch words, separate sounds in words, blend sounds in words, and manipulate sounds in words • recognizing and identifying some letters	continued phonemic awareness work sound–letter correspondence	Letter studies—consonants and vowels beginning sounds ending sounds
• able to recognize and identify letters • able to often match a starting or ending sound to a letter	continued phonemic awareness work and consistent phonics work: short vowels, common CVC word families	-at, -an, -ap, -ad, . . . -et, -en, . . . -ip, -ig, -it, . . . -ot, -og, -op, . . . -ug, -ut, -un, -ug, . . . -ill, -ell, -all, . . .
• able to spell most CVC words conventionally	blends and digraphs	sp, sk, sm, st, pl, bl, fl, sl, cr, fr, gr, pr, tr, dr, br . . . sh, th, ch, wh, . . .

(Continued)

(Continued)

If I see students are . . .	Then the students may be ready for . . .	A *few* sample patterns include . . .
• able to spell most CVC words conventionally *and* many words with beginning and ending blends and digraphs conventionally	long vowel patterns	Long *a* vowel patterns (CVCe, ai, ay) . . . Long *e* vowel patterns (CVCe, ee, ea) . . . Long *o* vowel patterns (CVCe, oa, ow) . . . Long *i* vowel patterns (CVCe, igh, y) . . . Long *u* vowel patterns (CVCe, ew, ue) . . .
• able to spell most one-syllable short and long vowel sounds conventionally	other vowel patterns (such as r-controlled vowels, diphthongs, and ambiguous vowel sounds)	-ar, -are, -air, -ir, -ire, -ier, -or, -ore, -oar, -ur, -ure, -eer, -ear, oo, ou, oi, oy, ow, au, aw, wa, al . . .
	complex consonant clusters	scr-, str-, spr-, -dge, -tch, . . .
• able to spell most one-syllable words conventionally and most high-frequency words conventionally	syllabification and inflected endings	-ed, -ing, -er, -est, -ier, -iest, -ness, -ful, -less, -le, -el, -al, . . .
• displaying a high understanding of the syntactical way words work, including multisyllabic words	a preliminary study of word parts, including prefixes and suffixes	re-, un-, dis-, mis- pre-, post-, fore-, after- -ion, -ian, -tion, -ation, -sion, -ic, -ity, -ty, -ous, -able, -ible, . . .
• spelling most words conventionally and showcasing a strong understanding of how words work	a more in-depth study of word parts, specifically highlighting Greek and Latin roots	inter-, sub-, over-, micro-, macro-, super-, hyper-, -spect, vis-, vid-, scrib-, -script, -graph, dic-, aud-, tele-, . . .

Appendix C

Word Study Routines at a Glance

Meaning Routines

Routine	Description
Act It Out	Students create icons or use their bodies to show understanding of studied words.
Backward Scattergories	Students group words being studied by meaning, and a partner tries to guess the topic or category for each group of words.
Concept Stretch	Students choose a word, consider a concept related to that word, and then generate examples and nonexamples of that word-concept partnership.
Creating Connections (Analogies)	Students create and share analogies using studied words.
Figurative Language Fun	Students create examples of figurative language that include studied pattern words.
Homophones, Homographs, or None (Nun) of the Above	Chart: The students list words being studied, and then list any homophones and/or homographs for these words. Icons: This is like the Picture It routine—only here, the student creates multiple sketches to show understanding of the different meanings of homophones and homographs.
I Might . . .	Students think about (and share or list) the times they might think, feel, do, or say "something" (essentially, the times and places the word would be used).
More or Less?	Students choose a word and then use their understanding to generate a "more" word and a "less" word (synonyms).
Part-of-Speech Chart	Students list words being studied—and then identify the part(s) of speech for each word.
Picture It	Students create icons to show understanding of studied words.
Shades of Meaning	Students choose a word, generate multiple words with a similar meaning, and then order words according to intensity (a little to a lot).
Synonym and Antonym Chart	Students list words being studied—and then synonyms and antonyms for some of the words.

(Continued)

259

(Continued)

Routine	Description
Talkin' the Talk	Students select a few studied words, come up with a topic for discussion, and engage in conversation using studied words.
Word Continuums	Students generate a word, generate other words with similar meanings (synonyms), and then think of other words with very different meanings (antonyms). Students then order words on a continuum—from one extreme to the other.
Word Family Trees	Students choose a word, write the base word on a trunk of a tree, and then think of other word "relatives" to add to branches and leaves of the tree.
Word Introductions: Yep! Maybe . . . Huh? None to Some Tight to Two Fist to Five	The teacher introduces the meaning of words, and the students self-assess prior knowledge of words being introduced.

Phonemic Awareness and Phonics Routines

Routine	Description
Configuration Station	Students box out the letters in studied words to create a stronger visual memory of the shape of the word and how the word looks.
Hold It, Say It, Sort It	Students hold an item, say the name of the item aloud, and then place that item into a specified group (based on either the sounds or letters in the name of the item).
I Spy!	Students name the letter, sound, or pattern being studied and then search for items with that letter, sound, or pattern in their physical environment.
Jumping Beans	Students say a word, stretch a word, and then separate the sounds in that word. Instead of tapping, they jump once for each sound in the word.
Multisensory Fun	Students look at a word, say the word, and use different materials to build or write that word—multiple times.
Pattern Pictures	This routine is similar to I Spy!—only here, students use a camera or device to snap a photo of items/words they see with a particular letter, sound, or pattern.
Reggio Routines	Students accept a Reggio-styled invitation around letters, names, or words and use loose parts, their imagination, and their knowledge to further explore letters, names, and words.

Routine	Description
Sensory Cycle	Students look at a word, say the word, listen to a partner say the word, trace the letters of the word on a sensory (tactile) surface and then look at, say, and listen to the word again.
Singing Sounds	Students reread a poem, chant, rhyme, or song that contains pattern words multiple times—each time reading rhyming or pattern words in different silly voices.
Sound Search	Students say a word, separate the sounds in a that word, and move a manipulative to each square of a sound box to represent each sound in that word.
Sound Search With Letters	Students do the above Sound Search routine but then replace each counter with the letter(s) that make each sound in that word.
Switch It, Change It	Students switch and change one part of a studied word to create new words.
Tap It!	Students say a word, stretch a word, and then separate the sounds in that word. They tap out each separate sound in the word.
Word Ladders (Solving)	Students use provided clues to manipulate sounds and letters in words, thereby making new words.

Spelling Pattern Routines

Routine	Description
How Fast Can We Go?	Students sort—and resort—pattern words multiple times with the goal of becoming more fluent.
Look, Say, Cover, Write, Check	Students look at a word, say the word, cover the word, try to write the word, and then check to see if they spelled the word correctly.
Multisensory Fun	Students look at a word, say the word, and use different materials to build or write that word—multiple times.
Partner Prompting	Partners support one another as they demonstrate their knowledge of studied words and patterns. When stuck, a partner provides a prompt or hint instead of the answer.
Pattern Introduction: Nice to Meet You!/ Now I Know!	The teacher formally introduces the pattern—along with the why and how behind the pattern.
Pumpin' Patterns	Students say a word and then spell the word, letter by letter, while using movement (knee touches, marching in place, etc.).
Question Craze	Students ask each other questions about how a partner or group member has sorted items, picture cards, or words. The goal is to deepen thinking and understanding.

(Continued)

(Continued)

Routine	Description
Read It! Build It! Write It!	Students read a word, build the word using loose parts or word building manipulatives, and then conventionally write the word.
Sort It! Alike or Different?	Students sort and categorize items, picture cards, or words in different ways.
Stepped Up Word Scavenger Hunts	Students hunt in their mind, around them (visual displays and conversations), and all kinds of texts (print, digital, visual, etc.) in hopes of finding other pattern words.
Three Key Questions: Reading	Students apply their word knowledge as they read. When they get to a tricky word, they ask themselves this: Does this look and sound right? Does this make sense? What have I learned that can help me here?
Three Key Questions: Writing	Students apply their word knowledge as they write. When they check their spelling, they ask themselves this: Does this look right? Does this sound right? What have I learned that can help me here?
Word Scavenger Hunts	Students reread a text, looking for other pattern words.

Habit and Hybrid Routines

Routine	Description
Creating Word Ladders	Students create their own word ladders for pattern words.
Cut, Not Styled	Students cut out word cards quickly and efficiently using the P-C-S method (picture frame-columns-singles).
Mirror, Mirror	Students reflect on how things are going in word study—what's a celebration and what's an area to focus on improving.
Nature Knowledge	This routine can be done two different ways. Students may complete any taught routine while out in nature, or students can use "nature's loose parts" for word building.
What Do You Think?	Students ask each other questions with the goal of getting each other to think, say, and understand more.
Word Conversations: Written	Students craft dialogue-rich writing, highlighting pattern words.
Word Games	Students play word-themed games—anything from Go Fish to Scrabble to Hedbanz to Apples to Apples.
Word Riddles	Students create three-clue riddles about studied words, with the first clue hinting what the word sounds like, the second clue hinting what the word looks like, and the last clue hinting what the word means.

Routine	Description
Word Share	Students share their knowledge of particular words, patterns, or routines orally, visually, or graphically.
Word Webs	Students create mind map–styled webs with information about what a word sounds like, looks like, and means.
Write With It	Students write using pattern words.

Check-In/Transfer Routines

Routine	Description
Any Routine	The student completes a taught word study routine—and the teacher uses this work as an assessment.
Conferring Conversation/Guided Reading	The teacher listens in as students read a text to check to see if they apply word knowledge, reading pattern words accurately and fluently.
Find and Fix Up	Students look back to previous writing, looking for attempts at spelling pattern words. They find pattern words in their writing and, when necessary, apply gained knowledge to fix up the spelling of these words.
Interactive Writing	The group generates a topic for writing with the goal of including many pattern words. The students provide ideas, and the teacher does most of the writing. When coming upon a pattern word, everyone pauses. The students all write the pattern word, the teacher checks in, and then the teacher invites one student to add that word to the class-created piece.
Marked Page	The student marks pages in their word study notebook (or flags entries in a digital notebook) that will be used for more formal assessment—or will be used to show progress toward set goals.
Next-Level Sorting Challenge	Essentially, this is a spelling test 2.0. Students both spell words correctly and sort words according to their pattern.
Reflection	Students reflect on recent word study work and progress toward set goals.
Shared Reading and Hunt	The students watch and listen as the teacher reads aloud a short text. The students then hunt for studied letters, sounds, patterns, or words in the text. Students then discuss what they found with a partner before going off to look for additional pattern words in other texts.
Show Off	Similar to Word Share, students show off their recent learning by choosing from a variety of methods.

Appendix D

Word Study Routines and Resources

Routine	Find It (*Word Study That Sticks*)	Bonus (*The Word Study That Sticks Companion*)	Digital** (Tech Tip)	High Frequency (Word Wall)
Backward Scattergories	p. 75		X	
Concept Stretch		p. 224	X	
Configuration Station		p. 226		X
Creating Connections (Analogies)		p. 223	X	
Cut, Not Styled	p. 60			
Figurative Language Fun	p. 125		X	X
Find and Fix Up	p. 93		X	X
Hold It, Say It, Sort It	p. 118			X
Homophones, Homographs, or None (Nun) of the Above	p. 121		X	X
How Fast Can We Go?	p. 128			
I Might . . .	p. 124		X	X
I Spy!		p. 227		X
Interactive Writing	p. 95		X	X
Jumping Beans	p. 147			X
Look, Say, Cover, Write, Check		p. 234		X
Magnificent Material Management	p. 72			
Mirror, Mirror	p. 85		X	

(Continued)

(Continued)

Routine	Find It (*Word Study That Sticks*)	Bonus (*The Word Study That Sticks Companion*)	Digital** (Tech Tip)	High Frequency (Word Wall)
More or Less?*	p. 78		X	
Multisensory Fun	p. 82			X
Nature Knowledge		p. 238		X
Next-Level Sorting Challenge	p. 97			
Partner Prompting		p. 233		X
Part-of-Speech Chart		p. 219	X	
Pattern Introduction: Nice to Meet You!		p. 232	X	
Picture It	p. 123		X	X
Pumpin' Patterns		p. 235		X
Question Craze	p. 66			
Read It! Build It! Write It!	p. 70			X
Reggio Routines		p. 229		X
Sensory Cycle		p. 228		X
Shades of Meaning	p. 78		X	
Shared Reading and Hunt	p. 96		X	X
Show Off	pp. 98–99		X	X
Singing Sounds	p. 149			X
Sort It! Alike or Different?	p. 64			
Sound Search	p. 68			X
Sound Search With Letters	p. 68			X
Sound Snapshot		p. 230	X	X
Stepped Up Word Scavenger Hunts	p. 126		X	
Switch It, Change It	p. 119		X	X

Routine	Find It (*Word Study That Sticks*)	Bonus (*The Word Study That Sticks Companion*)	Digital** (Tech Tip)	High Frequency (Word Wall)
Synonym and Antonym Chart		p. 221	X	
Talkin' the Talk	p. 154		X	X
Tap It!	p. 117			X
Three Key Questions: Reading	p. 151			X
Three Key Questions: Writing	p. 151			X
What Do You Think?	p. 61			
Word Continuums	p. 79		X	
Word Conversations: Written		p. 239	X	X
Word Family Trees		p. 222	X	
Word Games	p. 82		X	X
Word Introductions: None to Some Tight to Two Fist to Five	p. 74			X
Word Introductions: Yep! Maybe . . . Huh?	p. 59			X
Word Ladders		p. 237	X	X
Word Riddles	p. 130		X	X
Word Scavenger Hunts	p. 83			
Word Share		p. 241	X	X
Word Webs	p. 130		X	X
Write With It		p. 240	X	X

*Adapted version of a routine with a different name.

**Almost any routine can be done digitally. Anything that can be done in a notebook can also be done on a digital document. The Tech Tips listed throughout this book offer additional engaging and meaningful methods to digitize word learning.

References

Affinito, S. [AffinitoLit]. (2018, November 8). A7: Privilege pedagogy over technology. We must model how and when to use technology to support learning, as well as how and when to choose not to use it as well. We need to teach students how to make intentional decisions behind their screen time and technology use. #ILAchat [Tweet]. Retrieved from https://twitter.com/AffinitoLit/status/1060711305961725953

Anderson, J., & LaRocca, W. (2018). *Patterns of power: Inviting young writers into the conventions of language*. Portland, ME: Stenhouse Publishers.

Baker, S. K., Simmons, D. C., & Kame'enui, E. J. (1997). Vocabulary acquisition: Research bases. In D. C. Simmons & E. J. Kame'enui (Eds.), *What reading research tells us about children with diverse learning needs: Bases and basics*. Mahwah, NJ: Routledge.

Baron, N. (2016, July 20). Why digital reading is no substitute for print [Blog post]. Retrieved from https://newrepublic.com/article/135326/digital-reading-no-substitute-print

Barron, R. W. (1980). Visual and phonological strategies in reading and spelling. In Uta Frith (Ed.), *Cognitive processes in spelling* (pp. 195–213). London, England: Academic Press.

Bear, D. R., Invernizzi, M., Templeton, S., & Johnston, F. (2003). *Words their way: Word study for phonics, vocabulary, and spelling instruction* (3rd ed). Upper Saddle River, NJ: Prentice Hall.

Beck, I. L., McKeown, M. G., & Kucan, L. *Bringing words to life: Robust vocabulary instruction*. New York, NY: Guilford Press.

Beers, K., & Probst, R. E. (2017). *Disrupting thinking: Why how we read matters*. New York, NY: Scholastic Inc.

Belfield, C. R., & Levin, H. M. (2007). *The price we pay: Economic and social consequences of inadequate education*. Washington, DC: Brookings Institution Press.

Bomer, K. (2016). *The journey is everything: Teaching essays that students want to write for people who want to read them*. Portsmouth, NH: Heinemann.

Butler, R. (1987). Task-involving and ego-involving properties of evaluation: Effects of different feedback conditions on motivational perceptions, interests and performance. *Journal of Educational Psychology, 79*, 474–482.

Butler, R. (1988). Enhancing and undermining intrinsic motivation: The effects of task-involving and ego-involving evaluation on interest and performance. *British Journal of Educational Psychology, 58*, 1–14.

CBS News. (2017, December 17). Too much screen time could be damaging children's eyesight [Blog post]. Retrieved from https://www.cbsnews.com/news/digital-devices-screen-time-damaging-childrens-eyes-vision

Chomsky, C. (1970). Reading, writing, and phonology. *Harvard Educational Review, 40*, 287–309.

Collins, K. (2004). *Growing readers: Units of study in the primary classroom*. Portland, ME: Stenhouse Publishers.

Community. (n.d.). In *Oxford dictionaries online*. Retrieved from https://en.oxforddictionaries.com/definition/us/community

Cooper, R., & Murphy, E. (2016). *Hacking project based learning: 10 easy steps to PBL and inquiry in the classroom*. Cleveland, OH: Times 10 Publishing.

Csikszentmihalyi, M. (1990). *Flow: The psychology of optimal experience*. New York, NY: HarperCollins.

Deevers, M. (2006). *Linking classroom assessment practices with student motivation in mathematics.* Paper presented at the American Educational Research Association, San Francisco, CA.

Dunckley, L. (2017, November 24). Is your child overstimulated from too much screen time? [Blog post]. Retrieved from https://www.psychologytoday.com/us/blog/mental-wealth/201711/is-your-child-overstimulated-too-much-screen-time

Ehri L. C., Nunes, S. R., Willows, D. M., Schuster, B. V., Yaghoub-Zadeh, Z., & Shanahan, T. (2001). Phonemic awareness instruction helps children learn to read: Evidence from the National Reading Panel's meta-analysis. *Reading Research Quarterly, 36,* 250–287.

Elawar, M. C., & Corno, L. (1985). A factorial experiment in teachers' written feedback on student homework: Changing teacher behavior a little rather than a lot. *Journal of Educational Psychology, 77*(2), 162–173.

Evans, M. A., Shaw, D., Bell, M., & Can, J. (2000, June). Home literacy activities and their influence on early literacy skills. *Experimental Psychology, 54*(2), 65–75.

Fountas, I. C., & Pinnell, G. S. (2017). *The Fountas and Pinnell comprehensive phonics, spelling, and word study guide.* Portsmouth, NH: Heinemann.

Ganske, K. (2014). *Word journeys: Assessment-guided phonics, spelling, and vocabulary instruction* (2nd ed.). New York, NY: Guilford Press.

Gentry, J. R. (1982). An analysis of developmental spelling in GNYS AT WRK. *The Reading Teacher, 36,* 192–200.

Goldberg, G. (2016). *Mindset & moves: Strategies that help readers take charge.* Thousand Oaks, CA: Corwin.

Graves, D. (2004, November). What I've learned from teachers of writing. *Language Arts, 82*(2), Retrieved from https://pwpresearch.wikispaces.com/file/view/What+I+have+learned+from+Teachers+-+Graves.pdf

Hattie, J. (2009). *Visible learning: A synthesis of over 800 meta-analyses relating to achievement.* London, England: Routledge.

Hattie, J. (2012). *Visible learning for teachers: Maximizing impact on learning.* London, England: Routledge.

Henderson, A. T., & Mapp, K. L. (2002). *A new wave of evidence: The impact of school, family, and community connections on student achievement.* National Center for Family and Community Connections with Schools, Southwest Educational Development Laboratory. Retrieved from https://www.sedl.org/connections/resources/evidence.pdf

Horn, E. (1954). *Teaching spelling.* Washington, DC: National Education Association.

Howard, M. [DrMaryHoward]. (2018, June 7). A1: Many Ts say time is the challenge, but if we view our schedule by the week rather than just day . . . there is always time. #G2Great [Tweet].

Johnson, J., Leibowitz, S., & Perret, K. (2017). *The coach approach to school leadership: Leading teachers to higher levels of effectiveness.* Alexandria, VA: ASCD.

Johnston, P. (2004). *Choice words: How our language affects children's learning.* Portland, ME: Stenhouse Publishers.

Keene, E. O. (2018). *Engaging children: Igniting a drive for deeper learning.* Portsmouth, NH: Heinemann.

Kirr, J. (2017). *Shift this: How to implement gradual changes for massive impact in your classroom.* San Diego, CA: Dave Burgess Consulting, Inc.

Kohn, A. (2007, January/February). Rethinking homework. Retrieved from https://www.alfiekohn.org/article/rethinking-homework

Koutrakos, P. (2018). *Word study that sticks: Best practices K–6.* Thousand Oaks, CA: Corwin.

Lonigan, C. J. (2003). Development and promotion of emergent literacy skills in preschool children at-risk of reading difficulties. In B. Foorman (Ed.), *Preventing and remediating reading difficulties: Bringing science to scale* (pp. 23–50). Timonium, MD: York Press.

Lonigan, C. J., Dyer, S. M., & Anthony, J. L. (1996, April). *The influence of the home literacy environment on the development of literacy skills in children from diverse racial and economic backgrounds.* Paper presented at the Annual Convention of the American Educational Research Association, New York, NY.

Marzano, R. J., & Pickering, D. J. (2005). *Building academic vocabulary: Teacher's manual.* Alexandria, VA: Association for Supervision and Curriculum Development.

McGee, P. (2017). *Feedback that moves writers forward: How to escape correcting mode to transform student writing.* Thousand Oaks, CA: Corwin.

Mraz, K., Porcelli, A., & Tyler, C. (2016). *Purposeful play: A teacher's guide to igniting deep and joyful learning across the day.* Portsmouth, NH: Heinemann.

Mueller, P. A., & Oppenheimer, D. M. (2014, April 23). The pen is mightier than the keyboard: Advantages of longhand over laptop note taking. *Psychological Science, 25*(6), 1159–1168. doi: 10.1177/0956797614524581

National Reading Panel. (2000). *Report of the National Reading Panel: Teaching children to read.* Washington, DC: U.S. Department of Health and Human Services.

NEA Education Policy and Practice Department. (2008). *Parent, family, community involvement in education* [Policy Brief No. 11]. Washington, DC: Author. Retrieved from https://www.nea.org/assets/docs/PB11_ParentInvolvement08.pdf

Nolen, P., & McMartin, R. (1984). Spelling strategies on the wide range assessment test. *The Reading Teacher, 38*, 148–157.

Payne, A. C., Whitehurst, G. J., & Angell, A. L. (1994). The role of literacy environment in the language development of children from low-income families. *Early Childhood Research Quarterly, 9*(3–4), 427–440.

Phillips, B. M., & Lonigan, C. J. (2005). Social correlates of emergent literacy. In C. Hulme & M. Snowling (Eds.), *The science of reading: A handbook* (pp. 173–187). Malden, MA: Blackwell.

Phillips, B. M., & Lonigan, C. J. (2007, July). *Variations in home literacy environments: A cluster analytic view of an early childhood sample.* Paper presented at the 14th Annual Meeting of the Society for the Scientific Study of Reading, Prague, Czech Republic.

Pulfrey, C., Buchs, C., & Butera, F. (2011). Why grades engender performance-avoidance goals: The mediating role of autonomous motivation. *Journal of Educational Psychology, 103*(3), 683–700.

Rami, M. (2014). *Thrive: 5 ways to (re)invigorate your teaching.* Portsmouth, NH: Heinemann.

Rasinski, T. (2017, March/April). Readers who struggle: Why many struggle and a modest proposal for improving their reading. *The Reading Teacher, 70*(5), 519–524.

Rasinski, T., & Zutell, J. (2010). *Essential Strategies for Word Study.* New York, NY: Scholastic Inc.

Read, C. (1971). Preschool children's knowledge of English phonology. *Harvard Educational Review, 41*, 1–34.

Roberts, K. (2018). *A novel approach: Whole-class novels, student-centered teaching, and choice.* Portsmouth, NH: Heinemann.

Roberts, K., & Roberts, M. B. (2016). *DIY literacy.* Portsmouth, NH: Heinemann.

Schmoker, M. J. (2001). The Crayola curriculum. *Education Week, 21*(8), 42–44.

Sénéchal, M., & LeFevre, J. A. (2002, March/April). Parental involvement in the development of children's reading skill: A five-year longitudinal study. *Child Development, 73*(2), 445–460.

Skinner, E. A., Zimmer-Gembeck, M. J., & Connell, J. P. (1998). Individual differences in the development of perceived control (#254). *Monographs for the Society for Research in Child Development, 63*(2–3), 220.

Snow, C. E., Burns, M. S., & Griffin, P. (Eds.). (1999). *Preventing reading difficulties in young children.* Washington, DC: National Academy Press.

Storch, S. A., & Whitehurst, G. J. (2002, November). Oral language and code-related precursors to reading: Evidence from a longitudinal structural model. *Developmental Psychology, 38*(6), 934–947.

Stuart, M. (Director). (1971). *Willy Wonka and the chocolate factory* [Motion picture]. United States: Warner Bros.

Wheatley, M. J. (2002). *Turning to one another: Simple conversations to restore hope to restore hope to the future.* Oakland, CA: Berrett-Koehler Publishers.

Wilde, S. (1992). *You kan red this!* Portsmouth, NH: Heinemann.

Wiliam, D. (2011). *Embedded formative assessment.* Bloomington, IN: Solution Tree Press.

Yalda, T. U., Michikya, M., Morris, J., Garci, D., Smal, G. W., Zgourou, E., & Greenfield, P. M. (2017, October). Five days at outdoor education camp without screens improves preteen skills with nonverbal emotion cues. *Computers in Human Behavior, 39*, 387–392. Retrieved from https://www.sciencedirect.com/science/article/pii/S0747563214003227

Yates, K. (2015). *Simple starts: Making the move to a reader-centered classroom.* Portsmouth, NH: Heinemann.

Index

Because...

ALL TEACHERS ARE LEADERS

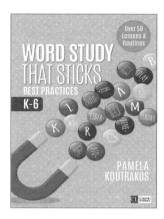

PAMELA KOUTRAKOS

Go back to the source! The book that started it all, *Word Study That Sticks,* delivers challenging, discovery-based word learning routines and planning frameworks you can implement across subject areas.

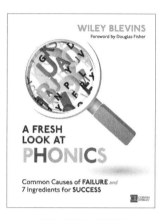

WILEY BLEVINS

Foremost phonics expert Wiley Blevins explains the 7 ingredients that lead to the greatest student gains. This resource includes common pitfalls, lessons, word lists, and routines.

MARIA WALTHER

101 picture book experiences, a thousand ways to savor strategically—this is the book that shows how to use ANY book to teach readers and writers!

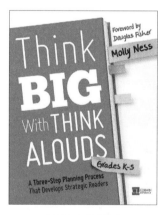

MOLLY NESS

Molly's three-step planning process will help you create dynamic lessons that focus on the five most important think aloud strategies.

Do you have a minute? Of course not.

That's why at Corwin Literacy we have put together a collection of just-in-time, classroom-tested, practical resources from trusted experts that allow you to quickly find the information you need when you need it.

GRETCHEN BERNABEI, KAYLA SHOOK, AND JAYNE HOVER

In 53 lessons centered around classic nursery rhymes, this groundbreaking book offers a straightforward framework for guiding young children in their earliest writing efforts.

PATTY McGEE

Patty McGee helps you transform student writers by showing you what to do to build tone, trust, motivation, and choice into your daily lessons, conferences, and revision suggestions.

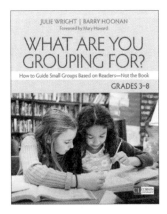

JULIE WRIGHT AND BARRY HOONAN

This book explains the five teacher moves that work together to support students' reading independence through small-group learning—kidwatching, pivoting, assessing, curating, and planning.

NANCY AKHAVAN

With 75 tasks on beautiful full-color pages, this book offers a literacy instruction plan that ensures students benefit from independent effort and engagement.

A SAGE Publishing Company

CORWIN HAS ONE MISSION: to enhance education through intentional professional learning.

We build long-term relationships with our authors, educators, clients, and associations who partner with us to develop and continuously improve the best evidence-based practices that establish and support lifelong learning.

"SLAVES OF THE STAR-SPAWN!

LETTERS
SAM ROSEN

COLORS
TOM PALMER

PENCILS
BRIAN BUCCELLATO

INKS
NEAL ADAMS

X MEN WAR IN THE WORLD BELOW

PENCILS **NEAL ADAMS**
LETTERING **SAM ROSEN**
COLORS **BRIAN BUCCELLATO**
INKS **TOM PALMER**

x men strongers...in a savage land

ON THE WINGS OF DEATH!

PENCILS/INKS
NEAL ADAMS

SAM ROSEN LETTERS
COLORS BRIAN
BUCCELLATO

THE
LAST
X-MAN

4

x men do or
die baby

NEAL
ADAMS
PENCILS/INKS/LETTERS
COLOR
DEREK BELLMAN

PENCILS & INKS **NEAL ADAMS**

COLOR **DEREK BELLMAN**

SAM ROSEN LETTERS

3

x men mission...murder

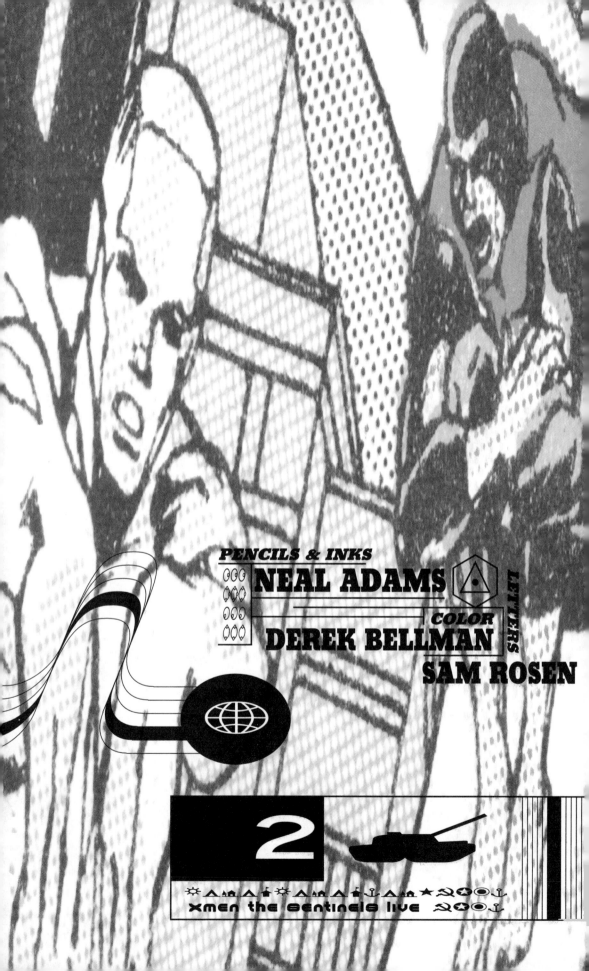

PENCILS & INKS
NEAL ADAMS
LETTERS
COLOR
DEREK BELLMAN
SAM ROSEN

2

xmen the sentinels live

PENCILS & INKS
NEAL ADAMS

NEAL ADAMS &
SAM ROSEN

COLOR
DEREK BELLMAN

PROFESSOR! --PROFESSOR XAVIER!

I'M WEARY... SO *TOTALLY*... WEARY--! PLEASE WHEEL ME TO MY R..ROOM...

AARRHH!

HE--HE SAVED A *WORLD*-- PERHAPS A *UNIVERSE*--!

HAS IT COST HIM... HIS *LIFE?!*

UNAWARE OF THEIR MENTOR'S PLIGHT, THE EXHAUSTED MUTANTS TRUDGE TO THEIR ROCKET, AND BLAST CLEAR OF THE LAST REMNANT OF THE INVASION--

THE Z'NOX... THEY'VE DELIBERATELY *EXPLODED* THEIR VESSEL!

ZOOOOSH

B.WAMM

WHY? WE DIDN'T *DAMAGE* IT--! THEY *COULD'VE* REJOINED THEIR COMPANIONS!

LIKE MAYBE THEY GOT PROF'S MESSAGE--

--UNDERSTOOD WHAT THEY *COULD* BE--

--AND COULDN'T CONTINUE TO *LIVE* WITH WHAT THEY *WERE!*

AMEN, FRIENDS... AMEN!

LOATHSOME THOUGH IT IS, WE MUST ADMIT *DEFEAT!*

--WE ARE, *ABANDONING* THIS SOLAR SYSTEM... AT *MAXIMUM SPEED!*

ATTENTION ALL UNITS! *REVERSE DRIVES!*

THEN, LIKE A CAPRICIOUS COMET, THE *Z'NOX* WORLD VEERS, ACCELERATES, AND IS SWALLOWED UP BY THE INFINITY OF THE UNIVERSE!

X-MEN... YOU MAY RELAX! THE VICTORY IS OURS... AND *HUMANITY'S!*

¿UNNHH!¿

...TOO MUCH *STRAIN!* --BLACKING *OUT!*

EASY, CYKE... LET YOURSELF *UNWIND* WE'LL GET YOU TO THE SHIP!

AND, WITH A FINAL EFFORT, CHARLES XAVIER *RELEASES* THE VALIANT MANY WHOSE COURAGE AND DECENCY QUELLED THE MOST TERRIBLE THREAT OF ALL--!

GO... AND GOD BLESS--!

THEY KNOW NOT WHAT THEY DO... ONLY THAT THEY ARE FILLED WITH BONE-DEEP NEED TO BE *FREE*--

WE CAN NOT *COMBAT* WHAT HAS NO *FACE*... NO *FORM*--!

-- THIS IS AGONY BEYOND *IMAGINING!*

THEY KNOW NOT WHAT THEY *DO...* ONLY THAT THEY ARE GRIPPED WITH AN *URGENCY...* A FIERCE DESIRE TO RIGHT THE WRONGS OF CENTURIES--

TO STAY LONGER WOULD BE *MADNESS!*

NO *Z'NOX* CAN *SURVIVE* SUCH MENTAL CORROSION--!

I SENSE OUR WILL TO *CONQUER* BEING EATEN AWAY!

AND WITHOUT *THAT,* WE ARE *NOTHING!*

THEY KNOW NOT WHAT THEY DO, THESE WHO STRUGGLE... THEY KNOW ONLY THAT SUDDENLY, THEY ARE FILLED WITH AN ALL-CONSUMING *DETERMINATION*--

LEADER-- THE *PAIN!*

WE ARE BEING *ATTACKED*... BUT BY *WHAT?!*

THEY KNOW NOT WHAT THEY DO... ONLY THAT *SYMPATHY* AND *MERCY* WELL UP WITHIN THEM, AND LEAP FORTH--

THESE *IMAGES* THAT BURN OUR CONSCIOUSNESS...

...THEY ARE NOT *NATURAL!*

IT IS MORE THAN WE CAN *STAND!*

AND SO IT BEGINS--!

WITH *SUPERHUMAN WILL,* CHARLES XAVIER FORCES HIS MIND OUT, AWAY.' HIS QUESTING THOUGHTS RANGE OVER THE ENTIRE SURFACE OF THE WORLD--

--PROBING, SEARCHING, QUESTIONING, DEMANDING-- SEEKING *KINDRED SPIRITS*--

--MEN AND WOMEN OF *GOOD WILL!* -- HUMAN BEINGS WHO HAVE IN GOOD MEASURE THE SINGLE TRAIT HE *DESPERATELY* NEEDS--

--COMPASSION! FOR IT IS ONLY THIS WHICH WILL BEST THE ENEMY--!

SOME HE *REJECTS* IMMEDIATELY, BECAUSE TO DISTRACT THEM WOULD BE TO CAUSE IRREPARABLE HARM-- SURGEONS, PILOTS....

--OTHERS HE DISMISSES BECAUSE HE FINDS THEIR PSYCHES TAINTED WITH HATRED, CRUELTY, PREJUDICE, LOVE OF DEATH-- THE SICKNESS WHICH THE *Z'NOX* CHERISH!

THEN, MIRACULOUSLY, THOSE *OTHER* MULTITUDES OF INDIVIDUALS BECOME *JOINED*-- BECOME AS *ONE PERSON!*

"GOOD EVENING... WELL, THE NEWS TONIGHT IS... *DISASTERS!* SEVERAL ASIAN FRONTS HAVE BEEN HIT BY *EARTHQUAKES!* AND ACCORDING TO A REPORT JUST IN, A SMALL PACIFIC ISLAND HAS *SUNK!* DAVID?"

"THERE ARE AS MANY THEORIES EXPLAINING THE *CATACLYSMS* AS THERE ARE *SCIENTISTS!* ONE OF THE MOST INTERESTING HAS BEEN PROPOSED BY DR. THEODORE NORTON'S NOTED ASTRONOMER..."

THEORY? NO, GENTLEMEN, THIS IS *FACT!*

I'VE OBSERVED A *PLANET*-- ABOUT THE SIZE OF PLUTO-- RUSHING TOWARD THE *EARTH*--!

ALREADY IT IS DISRUPTING MANY ECOLOGICAL SYSTEMS!

BARRING A *MIRACLE*, WE ARE... *DOOMED!*

AND, INSIDE THE HOSTILE VESSEL...

HAVE YOU A *REPORT*, EXPEDITION LEADER?

AYE, HIGH COMMANDER-- A MOST *EXCELLENT* REPORT!

WE HAVE ENCOUNTERED *MINOR* RESISTANCE--

--THE *LAST* OF WHICH IS PRESENTLY BEING ELIMINATED!

I FEEL THIS WILL BE OUR MOST *ARTISTIC* TRIUMPH! OUR MOST *EXQUISITE* DESTRUCTION!

NEVER HAVE WE ENCOUNTERED A WORLD OF SUCH *BEAUTY*-- SUCH *POSSIBILITIES* FOR DEFILEMENT!

AND THE PEOPLE ARE *HANDSOME* AND *HARDY!* CAPTIVES WILL PROVIDE *MUCH SPORT!*

AHHH... THIS IS A *HAPPY DAY*--!

OUR VICTIMS LAUNCH YET *ANOTHER* PROJECTILE AT US!

IT IS OF NO CONSEQUENCE! THEIR *ANTIQUES* CAN NOT PENETRATE OUR SCREEN!

--WHEN WE TAKE THEM TO OUR WORLD --AS MERE *SLAVES!*

LET THEM *EXHAUST* THEMSELVES! IT WILL MAKE THE *SURVIVORS* MORE DOCILE--

BUT, LEADER-- THE PROJECTILE *HAS* PASSED OUR SCREEN!

ACTIVATE THE *DISRUPTOR* MISSILES!

UNERRINGLY, THE Z'NOX DEVICES SEEK OUT THE X-MEN'S CRAFT-- BUT CHARLES XAVIER HAS PREPARED *WELL*--

FLOOM

--CONSTRUCTED IT IN *LAYERS* OF INCREDIBLY TOUGH ALLOY! EACH SHELL IS BLASTED AWAY WITHOUT HARM TO ITS PRECIOUS *CARGO*--

FOOM

FAM

--UNTIL IT IS TOO *CLOSE* TO THE ALIEN VESSEL FOR THE Z'NOX TO RISK ANOTHER SHOT!

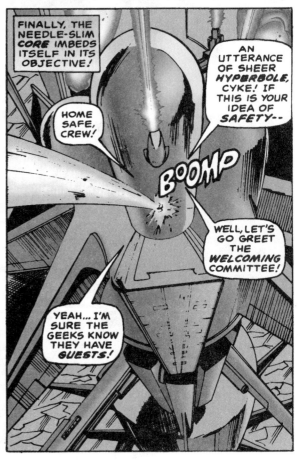

FINALLY, THE NEEDLE-SLIM *CORE* IMBEDS ITSELF IN ITS OBJECTIVE!

AN UTTERANCE OF SHEER *HYPERBOLE*, CYKE! IF THIS IS YOUR IDEA OF *SAFETY*--

HOME SAFE, CREW!

BOOMP

WELL, LET'S GO GREET THE *WELCOMING* COMMITTEE!

YEAH... I'M SURE THE *GEEKS* KNOW THEY HAVE *GUESTS!*

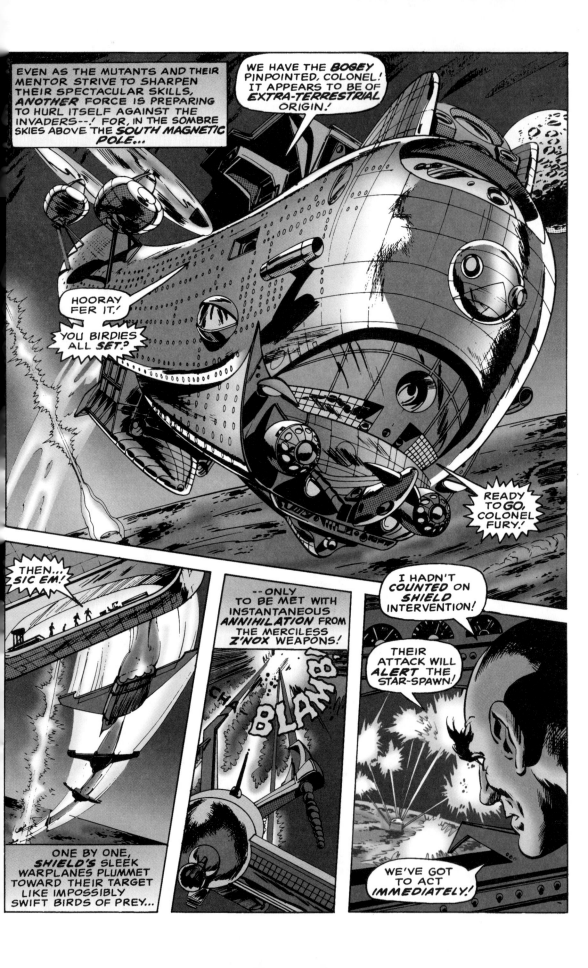

BUT, I *DID* DIVIDE SOME OF MY POWERS BETWEEN HIM AND *JEAN*--AND HE *LED* YOU THOSE FEW WEEKS, UNTIL KILLED BY THE SUB-HUMAN *GROTESK!*

HE... WAS A *FINE PERSON*, AT THE LAST...

I KNOW NOW HOW *HAMLET* FELT WHEN HE SAW HIS FATHER'S *GHOST!*

THEN WHAT ALEX SAID ABOUT THE ALIENS IS *TRUE--?*

YES! THE CHANGELING'S DECEPTION GAVE ME *TIME--*

--TIME TO PREPARE A *COUNTER-ATTACK!* CONCENTRATE...I SHALL MENTALLY ERASE YOUR FATIGUE--

--AND FOR THE NEXT FEW HOURS, YOU SHALL TRAIN AS YOU HAVE NEVER TRAINED *BEFORE!*

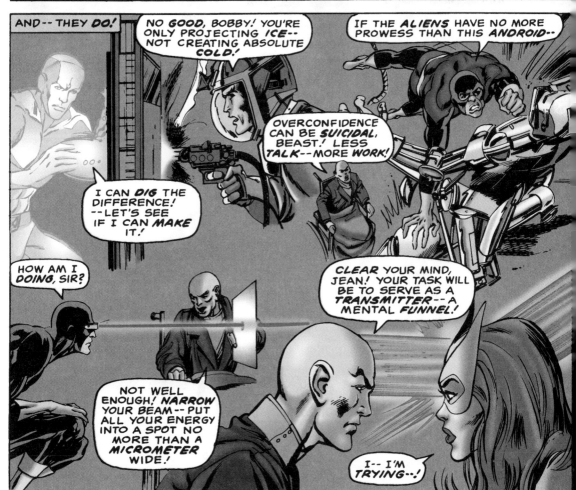

AND-- THEY *DO!*

NO *GOOD*, BOBBY! YOU'RE ONLY PROJECTING *ICE*-- NOT CREATING ABSOLUTE *COLD!*

IF THE *ALIENS* HAVE NO MORE PROWESS THAN THIS *ANDROID*--

OVERCONFIDENCE CAN BE *SUICIDAL*, BEAST! LESS *TALK*--MORE *WORK!*

I CAN *DIG* THE DIFFERENCE! --LET'S SEE IF I CAN *MAKE* IT!

HOW AM I *DOING*, SIR?

CLEAR YOUR MIND, JEAN! YOUR TASK WILL BE TO SERVE AS A *TRANSMITTER*-- A MENTAL *FUNNEL!*

NOT WELL ENOUGH! *NARROW* YOUR BEAM-- PUT ALL YOUR ENERGY INTO A SPOT NO MORE THAN A *MICROMETER* WIDE!

I-- I'M *TRYING*--!

EVERY TIME I PUT *ON* THESE DUDS, I'VE GOT TO WONDER IF I'LL BE *BURIED* IN THEM--

WHICH IS NO WAY FOR A *HERO* TO THINK... MUCH LESS AN *ANGEL!*

THEN--

SNAP IT *UP,* WORTHINGTON!

PAY NO *ATTENTION* TO THE ILL-MANNERED OAF, WARREN!

WHAT KIND OF *NIGHTMARE* IS THAT THING ON THE *SCREEN?*

ACCORDING TO OUR LITTLE TIN HITLER THERE, IT'S *REAL!*

BOTH *REAL*--AND *POWERFUL!* YOU SAW A PRIME SPECIMEN OF THE *Z'NOX*--

A STAR-SPAWNED RACE FROM THE *ANDROMEDA GALAXY*-- UTTERLY DEDICATED TO *PLUNDER* --AND *ENSLAVEMENT!*

FAR BACK IN *Z'NOX* HISTORY, EVOLUTION *SOURED!* IT PRODUCED A RACE ABSOLUTELY LACKING *COMPASSION...*

FOR *EONS,* THEY HAVE PERFECTED THE TECHNIQUES OF *CONQUEST!*

THEIR ONLY ART IS *WAR!* THEIR ONLY JOY-- *DEATH!*

ABOUT A MILLENNIUM AGO, Z'NOX SCIENTISTS DEVISED THE *ULTIMATE WEAPON!* THEY PERFECTED A *GRAVITY TRANSFORMER DRIVE* STRONG ENOUGH TO TRANSPORT THEIR ENTIRE *PLANET* ANYWHERE IN THE COSMOS!

MISTER, IF YOU'RE TRYING TO *SCARE* US WITH THIS HOKEY SCI-FI, YOU'RE NOT *MAKING* IT!

I'VE SEEN SCARIER STORIES ON *STAR TREK!*

AND EVEN IF IT'S *TRUE*-- SO *WHAT?!*

ONE MOMENT, LAD! LET'S HEAR HIM OUT!

SO, EACH OF THE WEARY MUTANTS RETIRES BRIEFLY...TO DON A COSTUME, AND MUSE...

WADDA YA KNOW... LOOKS LIKE NOBODY'S AT *HOME!*

BUT, MY HALCYON HOST'S GOTTA BE AROUND HERE *SOMEWH...*

VOICES!

LET THE *OTHERS* FIGHT THE INFERNAL X-MEN WITH *TOOTH AND CLAW!*

YOU AND I HAVE MORE *IMPORTANT* MATTERS TO ATTEND TO, EH?

WE ARE A *GREAT TEAM,* YOU AND I!

I TURNED *YOU* INTO A MUTANT...

AND NOW, WE CREATE THEM *TOGETHER!*

THERE'S MY SHY, RETIRING RESCUER!

WAIT! WHAT'S THAT THEY'RE *SAYING...?*

AS YOU *WISH,* MASTER!

AND *WITH* HIM...THE BIG-DOMED MUTANT CALLED *BRAIN-CHILD!*

THEN, *THAT'S* THE SECRET YOU'VE BEEN HIDING!

YOU DON'T *SEARCH* FOR MUTANTS AT *ALL!*

YOU CREATE THEM...OUT OF CAPTURED *SAVAGES!*

SO... YOU *KNOW* AT LAST!

STILL, YOU DON'T KNOW THE *WHOLE* TRUTH, X-MAN!

IT'S TIME YOU LEARNED WHO I *REALLY* AM!

MAGNETO!!

STILL, IT WILL SOON MATTER *LITTLE* WHAT THE ANGEL BELIEVES!

WITHIN THE HOUR, I SHALL HAVE PERFECTED MY *GREATEST*... MY *ULTIMATE* MUTANT!

THEN *NOTHING* AND *NO ONE* WILL CHALLENGE MAGNETO'S SUPREMACY IN THE *SAVAGE LAND!*

THE SAVAGE LAND!

TO MOST MEN, SCRAMBLING TO AND FROM THEIR PETTY PURSUITS, THIS NAMELESS CONTINENT BENEATH THE POLAR ICECAP IS BUT A WHISPERED *RUMOR*...A HALF-REMEMBERED *LEGEND* TOLD BY THOSE FORTUNATE FEW WHO HAVE SEEN IT... AND *SURVIVED!*

BUT, TO THE MUTANT *X-MEN*... AND TO THE JUNGLE-BRED *KA-ZAR*... IT IS NOW THE *ONLY* REALITY... AS THEY BEGIN TO SENSE THAT IT IS *HERE*, IN THE *SAVAGE LAND*, THAT THE FATE OF AN UN-WITTING *WORLD* MAY BE DECIDED...!

LOOK! THERE, SWOOPING FROM THE SKY!

IT IS ANOTHER OF THE *STRANGE ONES!*

NO, KA-ZAR... *WAIT!* IT'S ONE OF *US* ...THE *ANGEL!*

IS IT, MARVEL GIRL?

THEN WHY THE ALTERED *COSTUME*... THE SILENT *APPROACH?*

AND, SINCE WE *LAST* BEHELD THE ANGEL RECLINING ON A *SOFA* IN THE WORLD ABOVE...

...THE *BEAST* SUGGESTS WE PURSUE A POLICY OF *WATCHFUL WAITING!*

THE *X-MEN* CAN WATCH!

THE *X-MEN* CAN WAIT!

HOLD IT! THERE'S NO NEED FOR THEM TO BATTLE MY BUDDIES... OR KA-ZAR!

I'LL CALL THEM OFF... I OWE YOU THAT MUCH!

IF ONLY YOU COULD, MY FRIEND...

IT WOULD MEAN PEACE IN OUR TROUBLED LAND!

THEN... PEACE IT WILL BE!

BEAUTIFUL... BEAUTIFUL!

THE ANGEL WILL DELAY THE OTHERS... THUS GIVING ME THE PRECIOUS MOMENTS I NEED!

THE MOMENTS THAT WILL MAKE ME MASTER OF AN ENTIRE PLANET!

THEN, HE DOES NOT SUSPECT, CREATOR?

RRRRRK

NO, AMPHIBIUS!

BUT THEN, WHY SHOULD HE?

THE ANGEL HAS NEVER SEEN ME BEFORE, EXCEPT IN MY OWN ALL-CONQUERING COLORS!

PERHAPS IT IS TRUE WHAT THEY SAY...

...PERHAPS CLOTHES DO MAKE THE MAN!

THERE IS *NO TIME* FOR TALK! *HEED* KA-ZAR'S WORDS, AND *FLEE* THE SAVAGE LAND... WHILE YOU STILL *CAN!*

HE'S OFF LIKE A *SHOT* ...HARD ON THE HEELS OF THAT BEARDED *BARBARIAN!*

SHEESH! WE COME HERE TO RECOVER A *BODY...*

...AND WIND UP IN THE MIDDLE OF A *CIVIL WAR!*

COME, ZABU!!

NOT A MERE *CIVIL WAR,* MUTANTS!

I SENSE THERE IS MORE AT STAKE HERE... THAN *ANY* OF US CAN DREAM! *LISTEN,* X-MEN, TO THOSE *FLUTED STRAINS* FROM NEARBY..!

"I HAVE NEVER *SEEN* THEIR MAKER ...BUT WHISPERED TALES CALL HIM THE *PIPER!"*

"WHEN HE MAKES MUSIC, *DEATH AND DESTRUCTION* ARE HIS DREAD *REFRAIN!"*

VERRRRY INTERESTING, JUNGLE MAN!

BUT WHAT'S THAT GOT TO DO WITH *US?!*

BUT FOR NOW, I MUST RETURN TO MY OFFICE... AND *ALEX SUMMERS!*

HE MUSTN'T BE ALLOWED TO *DIE*...NOT *NOW!*

YOU MAY *LEAVE* ME NOW, ANGEL!

BUT YOU WILL REMEMBER *NOTHING* OF WHERE YOU HAVE *BEEN!*

YOU SHALL HEAR *AGAIN* FROM *KARL LYKOS!!*

KARL...IS THAT *YOU..?*

EH? SOMEONE IN THE *THERAPY ROOM!*

IF IT'S MY *MEDDLING NURSE*...OR ANYONE WHO MIGHT GUESS WHAT I'VE BEEN *DOING*---!

KARL! WHY DIDN'T YOU *ANSWER?*

TANYA!

I THOUGHT...YOU WERE STILL IN *SCARSDALE*, MY DARLING!

YOU KNOW THAT YOUR FATHER HAS *FORBIDDEN* YOU TO SEE ME...!

I...I *HAD* TO COME, DEAR KARL!

I *PHONED* YOU FROM MY HOTEL...BUT THERE WAS...*NO ANSWER!*

SUDDENLY, I HAD A *FEAR*...A *PREMONITION!*...

...THAT SOMETHING *DREADFUL* HAD HAPPENED TO YOU...THAT YOU *NEEDED* ME...AND I WASN'T *THERE!*

...AH...A *LIGHT'S* STILL BURNING!

THEN, DR. LYKOS MUST STILL BE *TREATING* YOUR BROTHER, SCOTT!

I STILL WISH WE'D HAD A CHANCE TO LOOK FOR *ANGEL* FIRST...!

SCOTT... DO YOU *REALLY* THINK... WARREN WAS UNDER OUR ENEMY'S *CONTROL?*

IT'S ONLY A *HUNCH*, JEAN...FOR *NOW!*

FIRST, LET'S SEE ABOUT TAKING *ALEX* HOME!

monsters also weep!

BUT, HERR ANDERSSEN'S PLANS FOR HIS DAUGHTER DID *NOT* INCLUDE A YOUNG MAN OF *PROMISE* BUT NO *MEANS!*

THUS, I *LEFT*...SWEARING TO RETURN AND CLAIM TANYA'S HAND WHEN I POSSESSED THE PROPER *WEALTH!*

WE HAVE SEEN EACH OTHER *SELDOM* SINCE THAT DAY... BUT HER LETTERS TELL ME THAT SHE STILL *LOVES* ME!

AND SO, I'LL DO *ANYTHING* THAT I MUST TO GAIN THE *FORTUNE* THAT WILL MAKE HER MINE!

ANYTHING!

"I LABORED *HARD* AT MEDICAL SCHOOL AND AFTER, TO BECOME A *SUCCESS!* BUT, FATE PLAYED A MACABRE *GAME* WITH ME---FOR, AS I GREW OLDER, MY NEED FOR PURLOINED *HUMAN ENERGY* BECAME GREATER...EVER *GREATER!* ALL MY MONEY...ALL MY RESOURCES...WERE SIPHONED INTO THE EVER-MORE-ELABORATE *ELECTRONIC APPARATUS* NEEDED MERELY TO KEEP ME *ALIVE,* BY ROBBING MY HYPNOTIZED PATIENTS OF THEIR *VITALITY*...THEIR RAW *ENERGY*...!"

BUT ALWAYS, I KNEW THAT *HUMAN MUTANTS* WERE THE *ANSWER* TO MY DILEMMA!

CHARLES XAVIER WISHED TO *FIND* SUCH SPECIMENS AT AN EARLY AGE ...*TRAIN* THEM...!

BUT *I* SECRETLY WANTED THEM FOR A QUITE *DIFFERENT* PURPOSE...

---FOR THE MORE-THAN-HUMAN *ENERGY* WHICH THEY COULD PROVIDE ME!

ALEX SUMMERS MUST BE ONE OF THOSE WHOM XAVIER *SOUGHT*...AND *FOUND!*

FOR, AS NEVER BEFORE, I CAN FEEL ENERGY...YOUTHFUL *VIGOR*...FLOWING INTO MY EVERY *PORE!*

AND...I CAN FEEL POWER... *POWER* SUCH AS NO MAN HAS EVER KNOWN!

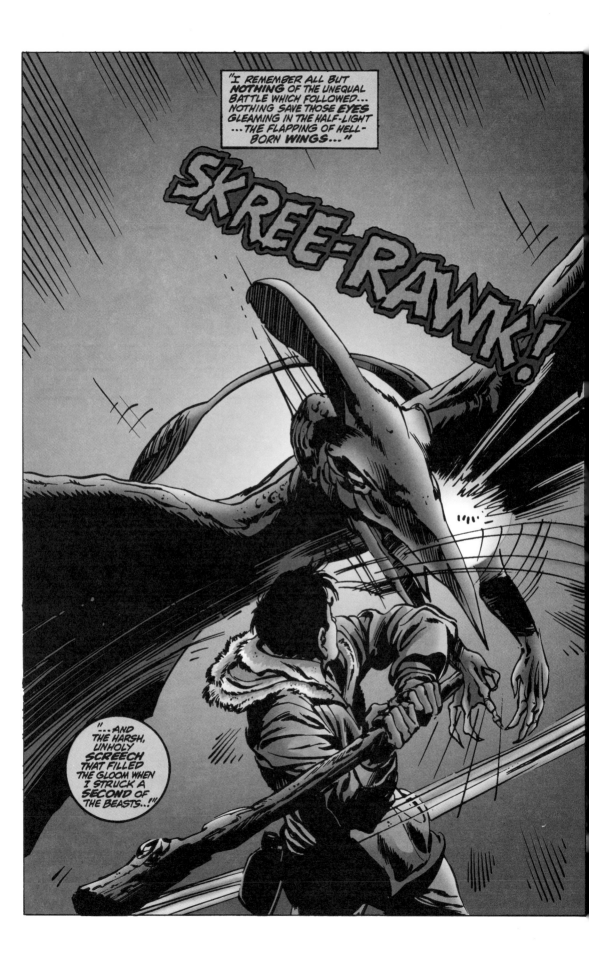

In the shadow of... Sauron

BLAZING ITS PATH THRU SPACE MORE THAN 93 MILLION MILES FROM EARTH, THE SUN POSSESSES A DIAMETER OF 865,400 MILES...ITS SURFACE TEMPERATURE IS 6000° CENTIGRADE...ITS MASS ALMOST 700 TIMES THAT OF ALL OTHER BODIES IN THE SOLAR SYSTEM...!

ON THE SURFACE OF THIS WORLD OF SOLAR WINDS... OF MOMENT-TO-MOMENT THERMONUCLEAR CATACLYSM...A HANDFUL OF HUMANOID FORMS WILL MAKE BUT THE MOST IMPERCEPTIBLE OF RIPPLES...!

AND YET... IT *ISN'T* A GUN!

WHEN I PULL THE TRIGGER, *NOTHING HAPPENS!*

THE MUTANTS ARE STILL *IMPRISONED...* AND THAT SENTINEL STILL *IGNORES* ME!

BUT, LARRY'S EYES *WERE* STARING AT THIS USELESS WEAPON...

...JUST AS THEY *NOW* SEEM RIVETED UPON...

...THE ONE HE CALLS... *HAVOK!*

IS *THAT* WHAT HE WANTS, EVEN *NOW?*

FOR ME TO SOMEHOW *KILL* THAT MUTANT?

I WON'T DO IT! *I WON'T!*

WHILE, ONLY A FEW STEEL-PLATED YARDS AWAY...

MUTANTS!

I RECOGNIZE THEIR *CONFIGURATION* ...FROM VISUAL *PROGRAMMING!*

QUICK-SILVER... AND THE *SCARLET WITCH!*

YOU *OVER-LOOKED* THE TERRIFYING *TOAD!*

...WHO, I MIGHT *JUXTAPOSE,* HAS NEVER LOOKED *BETTER...*

...THAN WHEN PORTRAYED BY THE BIT-PLAYING *BEAST!*

BREAK A LEG, ROBBIE!

UH OH! HE'S *REPAIRING* HIMSELF ALREADY, BOYS AND GIRLS!

I'LL STAY *HERE,* AND IMPEDE HIS PROGRESS!

YOU TWO *TODDLE ALONG...* WITH ALL DELIBERATE *SPEED!*

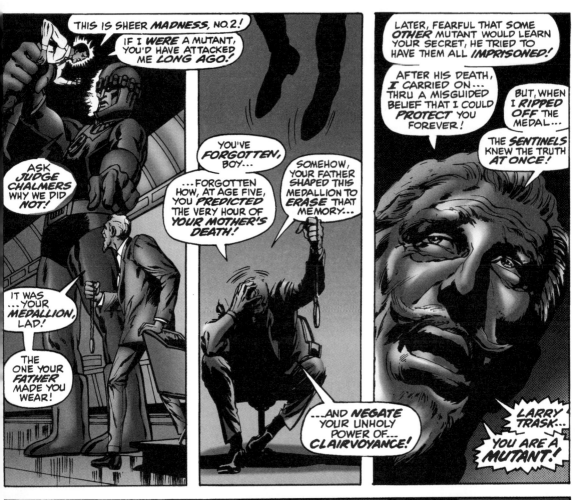

SO, EVER SINCE THAT DAY, I'VE--

THAT NOISE--! WHAT IS IT?!?

IT IS THE MUTANT CALLED...THE BANSHEE, LEADER!

IN HIS NATIVE LAND, HE SURRENDERED TO ME...WITHOUT A FIGHT!

POK

POK

BUT, NOW, HEEEE--!

SIRENS BE PRAISED! I SENT THAT ONE DOWN WITH A SINGLE WAIL!

BUT, TWO OTHERS ASSAULTING ME WITH ANOTHER FREQUENCY--!

UNNHHH!

YOU'VE DONE WELL, MY SENTINELS!

YOU FOUGHT SOUND... WITH SOUND!

PERHAPS THE BANSHEE WAS THE MUTANT PRESENCE THAT 6R DETECTED EARLIER!

LOOK, JUDGE CHALMERS, AT STILL ANOTHER INSTANCE OF MUTANT TREACHERY!

HE SURRENDERED ONLY TO GAIN ENTRANCE TO MY SECRET BASE!

AND YET, I'M GLAD IT HAPPENED--!

FOR, NOW I KNOW WHAT I MUST DO!

HEAR ME, MY SENTINELS!

SECURE ALL MUTANTS IN AREA--AND DESTROY THEM!

NO, YOU YOUNG FOOL-- NO!!

WHY YOUR SUDDEN CONCERN, JUDGE?

...UNLESS YOU'RE A MUTANT-LOVER...

OR PERHAPS... A MUTANT!

CALM *DOWN*, LAD!

YOUR FATHER WAS A *STRONG-WILLED* MAN... BUT A *FAIR* ONE!

HE WOULDN'T HAVE CONDEMNED ANYONE WITHOUT HEARING *BOTH SIDES*...!

AND, I'LL *HEAR BOTH SIDES*...

WHEN *ALL* MUTANTS ARE SAFELY *LOCKED AWAY!*

BUT NOW-- *LOOK!*

IMAGES-- OF ONES WHO CAN ONLY BE THE REMAINING *X-MEN*...!

"I'VE ORDERED MY SCOUT ONLY TO *OBSERVE*... *NOT ATTACK!*"

"THEY'RE MILES AWAY NOW... BUT SOON WILL *DROP* INTO OUR *WAITING NET!*"

Z2-- ACTIVATE SONIC PROBE....!"

...SHIP AND *MINI-CEREBRO* STILL INTACT!

ALL RIGHT, SCOTT... I *WAITED* FOR YOU!

NOW IT'S TIME FOR *ACTION!*

SCOTT... PLEASE BE *CAREFUL* DONNING YOUR VISOR!

IF YOU *OPEN* YOUR EYES... EVEN A *HAIR'S BREADTH*....!

NO ONE KNOWS THE DANGER BETTER THAN *I* DO, JEAN!

BUT, WE'VE GOT TO MOVE *FAST*--

--FIND NOT ONLY *BOBBY*, BUT ALSO *LORNA, ANGEL,* AND-- *ALEX!!*

AND, FIND THEM YOU *SHALL,* CYCLOPS!

THAT I *SWEAR,* BY MY *MEDALLION*...

...THAT SAME MEDALLION WHICH ONCE WAS MY *MOTHER'S*...

AND WHICH MY *FATHER* HUNG ABOUT MY NECK, ON THE DAY SHE *DIED!*

EVEN *YOU* DON'T KNOW ABOUT *THAT,* JUDGE...

...NEVER HEARD THE *OATH* HE MADE ME SWEAR UPON IT....!

YOUR *MOTHER*... WANTED YOU TO HAVE THIS, SON!

AND, I WANT YOU TO PROMISE YOU'LL NEVER *REMOVE* IT-- AS LONG AS YOU *LIVE!*

SWEAR, BOY... *SWEAR!*

I...I *SWEAR,* PAPA....!

...IT'S MIND-STAGGERING, LARRY!

THIS *BASE* WITHIN A *MOUNTAIN*-- THE *GUIDANCE* SYSTEM IN MY JET--!

I HAD NO IDEA OF YOUR TRUE *INVENTIVENESS!*

MOST OF IT IS THE *SENTINELS'* DOING, SIR!

I'M FAST *DISCOVERING* THEY HAVE THEIR OWN BUILT-IN SYSTEM OF *LOGIC!*

THAT LOGIC TOLD THEM THAT SUCH A BASE WOULD BE *USEFUL*...SO HERE IT *IS!*

HOW GOES THE *PUBLIC* PHASE OF THE WAR WITH THE *MUTANTS?*

SOMEWHAT... *UNEASILY*, MY BOY!

MANY PERSONS ARE BECOMING *UNCERTAIN* OF THE *JUSTICE* OF OUR CAUSE...

...INCLUDING, AS I SAID... *MYSELF!*

IF ONLY I WERE *POSITIVE* THAT ALL MUTANTS WERE *MENACES*...!

I HAVE *FILM* FOOTAGE THAT WILL PROVE *THAT*, SIR!

BUT FIRST, COME SEE THE *FACILITIES* I'VE PREPARED FOR OUR... *GUESTS!*

THEY ARE TREATED FAR BETTER THAN THEY *DESERVE!*

GOOD LORD! THEY'RE *ALIVE*... BUT IN SOME SORT OF...*SUSPENDED ANIMATION!*

QUITE *IMPRESSIVE*, LARRY...BUT I DIRECTED THAT THEIR TREATMENT BE *HUMANE!*

HUMANE?

HOW CAN ONE BE HUMANE...

...TO MONSTERS THAT AREN'T EVEN *HUMAN??*

I KNOW I AGREED TO BE YOUR *ASSISTANT*, JUDGE CHALMERS...

BECAUSE I'M AN *UNKNOWN*... AND YOU, A *FEDERAL JURIST!*

BUT, IF YOU GO *SOFT* ON ME... TRY TO *CODDLE* THE ASSASSINS WHO *KILLED* MY FATHER--

MY *SENTINELS* WILL CARRY ON THE *FIGHT*-- ALONE!

CAN'T HOLD HIM *BACK* ANY LONGER!

I'VE DONE MY *BEST*-- ALL THAT ANY MUTANT *COULD* DO!

SAVE ME, MAGNETO --*SAVE* ME!

MASTER--DON'T YOU *HEAR* ME?

WHY DO YOU JUST *STAND* THERE-- SO *SILENT*?

AND WHY DO *YOU*, HAPLESS MUTANT--

--SEEK REFUGE BEHIND A MERE-- *MACHINE*?

MACHINE? WHAT DO YOU M--? *NNOOo*!

MAGNETO *COLLAPSED* --INTO A THOUSAND METAL *FRAGMENTS*!

MY *MASTER* WAS ONLY--

KRASH!

--A *ROBOT*!

THEN, THE *REAL* MAGNETO WAS *NEVER* MY ALLY AGAINST THE *X-MEN*!*

ALL THESE *LONELY* MONTHS--

I SERVED-- A CREATURE OF *STEEL* AND *SYNTHETICS*!!

SO-- MAGNETO HAS TEMPORARILY *ELUDED* ME-- SIMPLY BECAUSE HE HAD AN *ANDROID* DOING HIS DIRTY WORK!

NEVER MIND-- WHAT HAVE YOU TO *REPORT* 6R?

WE HAVE DETECTED ANOTHER *MUTANT* IN THIS VICINITY, O LEADER!

BUT, SOMETHING *PREVENTS* US FROM PINPOINTING THE MUTANT--FOR THE *PRESENT*...!

THE ESCAPED *BEAST*, PERHAPS-- *NOSING ABOUT*!

MEAN- WHILE, I'M SIGNALED THAT *JUDGE CHALMERS* APPROACHES!

MAKE READY TO *RECEIVE* HIM!

"...GOOD EVENING.'
"WELL, THE NEWS TONIGHT IS...MUTANTS.'
"SINCE EARLY THIS MORNING, THE MASSIVE ROBOTIC CREATURES CALLED *SENTINELS* HAVE BEEN SCOURING THE ENTIRE *COUNTRY*, CARRYING OUT SEARCH-AND-CAPTURE MISSIONS FOR THE NEWLY-CREATED *FEDERAL COUNCIL ON MUTANT ACTIVITIES*.'
"*LATEST RUMOR IS...OTHER NATIONS ARE CALLING FOR SENTINELS TO HELP SOLVE THEIR* 'MUTANT PROBLEM'.'
"SOUNDS A BIT FAMILIAR, DOESN'T IT?
"CHET...?"

...THE X-MEN ARE DANGEROUS *CRIMINALS!*

ONLY *HOURS* AGO, THEY TRIED TO *DESTROY* ME!

THEY MUST BE *PUNISHED*... BY INTER-NATIONAL ... LAW...

WHAT'S *WRONG*, PRO-FESSOR *ABDOL?*

YOU SEEM SO *PALE...!*

THEY ARE *RIGHT*... I FEEL AS IF...

YES! I'M *CHANGING* ONCE MORE... INTO THE *LIVING MONOLITH!*

I'M *GROWING* ...BEFORE THEIR VERY *EYES!*

FOOLS! DON'T YOU SEE I NO LONGER *NEED* YOU?

I'LL NEED *NO ONE*...WHEN MY *TRANSFOR-MATION* IS *COMPLETE*...!

NO ONE!!

THEN, YOU SHALL *NOT* COMPLETE IT... *MUTANT!*

SENTINELS!

EVEN *YOU* COULDN'T STOP THE *MONOLITH!*

PERHAPS *NOT*... IF THE CHANGE WERE *DONE!*

BUT, THIS LIQUID *ADHESIVE* WILL KEEP ALL *COSMIC RAYS* FROM YOU... AND THEY ARE THE ONLY *SOURCE* OF YOUR POWER!

-OHHHH--!!

ZKK!

ZKK!

SHRINKING AGAIN-- SHRINKING--!

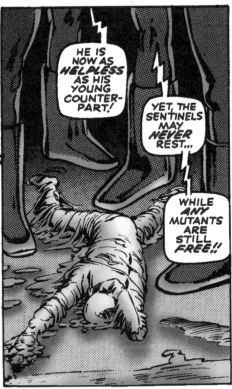

HE IS NOW AS *HELPLESS* AS HIS *YOUNG COUNTER-PART!*

YET, THE SENTINELS MAY *NEVER* REST...

WHILE *ANY* MUTANTS ARE STILL *FREE!!*

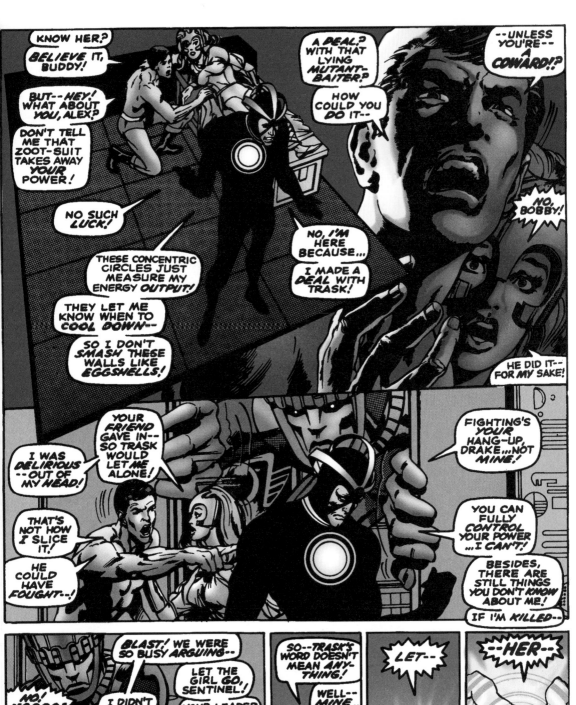

KNOW HER? BELIEVE IT, BUDDY!

BUT--HEY! WHAT ABOUT YOU, ALEX? DON'T TELL ME THAT ZOOT-SUIT TAKES AWAY YOUR POWER!

NO SUCH LUCK!

THESE CONCENTRIC CIRCLES JUST MEASURE MY ENERGY OUTPUT!

THEY LET ME KNOW WHEN TO COOL DOWN--

SO I DON'T SMASH THESE WALLS LIKE EGGSHELLS!

A DEAL? WITH THAT LYING MUTANT-BAITER?

HOW COULD YOU DO IT--

NO, I'M HERE BECAUSE... I MADE A DEAL WITH TRASK!

--UNLESS YOU'RE-- A COWARD!?

NO, BOBBY!

HE DID IT-- FOR MY SAKE!

I WAS DELIRIOUS --OUT OF MY HEAD!

THAT'S NOT HOW I SLICE IT! HE COULD HAVE FOUGHT--!

YOUR FRIEND GAVE IN-- SO TRASK WOULD LET ME ALONE!

FIGHTING'S YOUR HANG-UP, DRAKE...NOT MINE!

YOU CAN FULLY CONTROL YOUR POWER ...I CAN'T!

BESIDES, THERE ARE STILL THINGS YOU DON'T KNOW ABOUT ME!

IF I'M KILLED--

NO! NOOOO!

BLAST! WE WERE SO BUSY ARGUING--

I DIDN'T EVEN SEE THAT CREEP!

LET THE GIRL GO, SENTINEL! YOUR LEADER PROMISED ME--!

SO--TRASK'S WORD DOESN'T MEAN ANY-THING!

WELL-- MINE DOES!!

LET--

--HER--

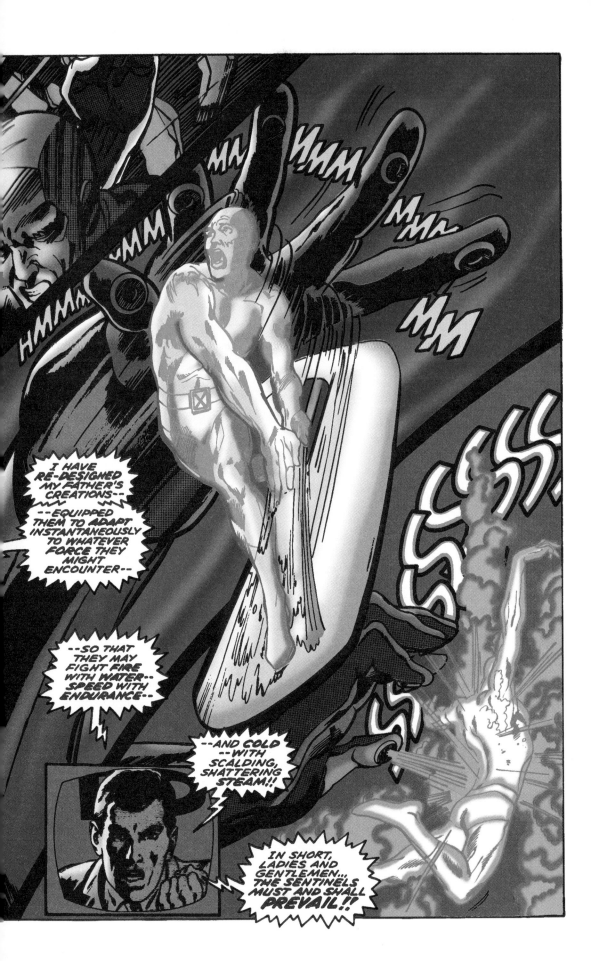

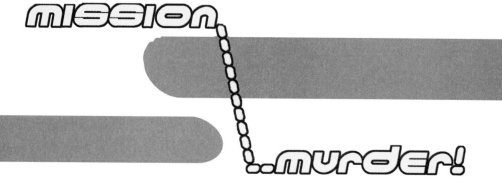

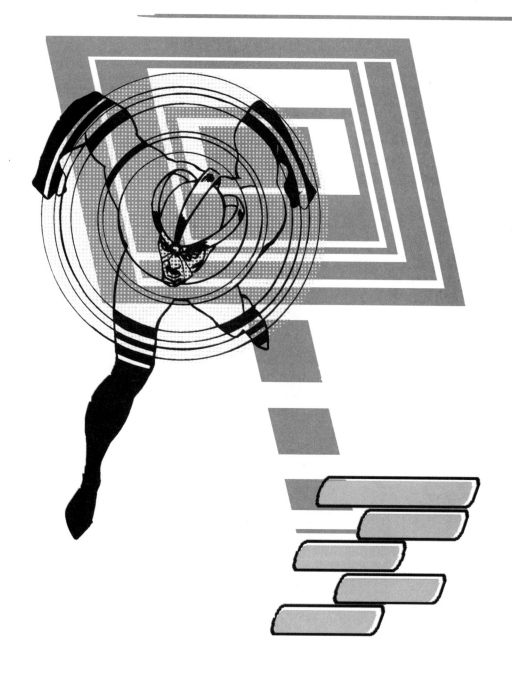

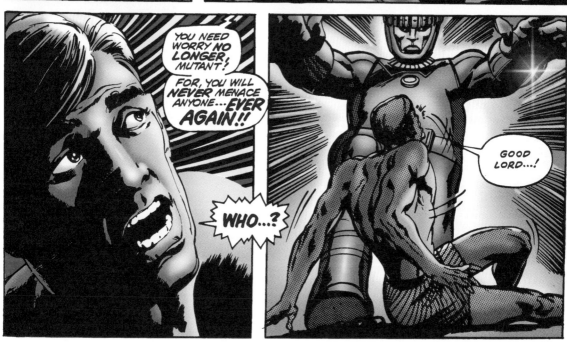

FOR, I STILL CAN'T *CONTROL* MY POWER...

CAN'T TURN IT *ON*...OR *OFF*!

ONE *SECOND* FROM NOW... I MIGHT *DESTROY YOU ALL*!

SO, *BEAT IT*, WILL YOU...

AND LEAVE ME TO MY *NIGHTMARES*--!

WAIT! HERE COMES *ICEMAN*!

WITH THE LOCAL *CONSTABULARY*!

PROFESSOR *ABDOL*...ARE YOU THE *"MENACE"* THE YOUNG ONE SPOKE ABOUT?

YOU TWO... *KNOW* EACH OTHER ??

OF *COURSE*!

AM I NOT THIS LAND'S LEADING *ARCHEOLOGIST*?

BUT NOW, IT IS *MY* TURN TO SPEAK!

THAT *BEARDLESS YOUTH*?

AND I ACCUSE... *THAT MAN*!

THINGS ARE NOT ALWAYS WHAT THEY *SEEM*, MY FRIEND!

THE VERY *HEAVENS* SHRIEK THEIR DEMAND FOR HIS PUNISHMENT!

FOR, I UNEARTHED HERE A *TEMPLE*...AS OLD AS *ANY* IN THE LAND!

HE *DESTROYED* IT...AS SURELY AS HE NOW STANDS AMIDST ITS *RUINS*!

IT SEEMS BEYOND *POSSIBILITY*...AND YET...

WAIT... LISTEN TO *ME*... IT'S *THIS* MAN WHO'S YOUR *MENACE*..!

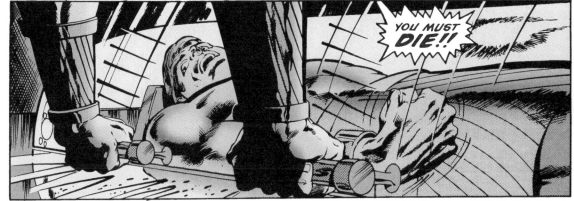

LISTEN, ANGEL...AND LISTEN WELL, AS SINISTER WORDS SWIRL LIKE HARSH WINDS THRU AGE-OLD CORRIDORS...
...YOU GAZE UP IN SULLEN SILENCE, ALEX SUMMERS!
IT IS GOOD!
AND, HOW FITTING THAT YOU SHOULD MEET YOUR RIGHTFUL END HERE--
AMIDST THE RE-DISCOVERED GLORY OF THE KINGS-WHO-WERE... AND THOSE WHO YET-SHALL-BE!
BUT, I SPEAK OF THINGS WHICH CONCERN YOU NOT!
FOR, I DECREED YOU SHOULD LEARN OF THE POWER --IN THE HOUR YOU PERISH!
AND, THAT MOMENT DRAWS EVER NEARER!
I WAS AN ARCHAEOLOGIST... BUT I AM ALSO-- A MUTANT!
YET, YOU AND I ARE BOTH DIFFERENT FROM THE MASKED ONES...FOR, OUR DESTINIES ARE INEXTRICABLY LINKED!
CAN YOU NOT FEEL THEM, INFIDEL--
THE CELESTIAL CHAINS WHICH BIND OUR TWO FATES AS ONE?
THE SAME MUTANT INSTINCT WHICH LED ME TO YOU--
--TELLS ME THAT IT IS COSMIC RAYS WHICH GIVE US EACH... THE POWER!
AS YOURS BEGAN TO AWAKEN ...MINE DID WANE!
YOU ARE THE SOLE THREAT TO MY SUPREMACY!
AND SO--

what is the power?

BOTH STRIVING TO DO OUR BEST, NOT JUST BECAUSE THAT ERA WAS CRUCIAL TO THE SUCCESS OF OUR CAREERS, BUT BECAUSE WE WERE GIVING SOMETHING TO THE ADVANCEMENT OF A BURGEONING INDUSTRY...AND TO YOU, OUR DEVOTED READERS.

I'M STILL TRYING TO UNCOVER THE SECRETS HIDDEN WITHIN THOSE PAGES THAT HAVE ALLOWED THEM TO STAND THE TEST OF TIME AND CHANGING ARTISTIC STYLES AND TASTES. IT JUST MAY BE THAT THE EXCITEMENT WE EXPERIENCED THEN STILL TRANSLATES NOW. IF SO, I CAN ONLY HOPE SOME OF THAT EXCITEMENT IS SHARED WITH YOU AS YOU DELVE INTO THIS UNCANNY COMPILATION.

I HAVE BEEN ASKED ABOUT MY WORKING RELATIONSHIP WITH NEAL ADAMS ON
THE X-MEN. WELL, NOW THAT OUR EFFORTS HAVE BEEN COLLECTED HERE —
IN THE SECOND TRADE PAPERBACK VOLUME DEVOTED TO HONORING THE BEST
ARTISTS EVER TO BRING THE STRANGEST HEROES OF ALL TO LIFE — I
FINALLY HAVE THE CHANCE TO PUT MY THOUGHTS DOWN FOR POSTERITY.

THE WHOLE THING STARTED WHEN I WAS WORKING ON MY FIRST REGULAR
COMIC FOR MARVEL. IT WAS DR. STRANGE, AND I WAS PART OF A TEAM THAT
INCLUDED PENCILER GENE COLAN AND WRITER ROY THOMAS. I WAS A FRESH
FACE, YOUNG IN THE COMICS FIELD, ANXIOUS TO GAIN SOME EXPERIENCE.
ONE DAY, ROY CALLED AND ASKED IF I COULD HANDLE ANOTHER ASSIGN-
MENT. I COULD HEAR THE EXCITEMENT IN HIS VOICE AS HE RELATED THE
COUP OF GETTING NONE OTHER THAN NEAL ADAMS TO PENCIL THE X-MEN! AT
THE TIME, NEAL WAS WORKING AT DC ON A NUMBER OF DIFFERENT PROJECTS
AND WAS GENERATING A GREAT DEAL OF FAN EXCITEMENT. I WAS FLATTERED
WHEN ROY ASKED ME TO INK NEAL'S PENCIL ART, AND AS THE FIRST PAGES
ARRIVED, I WAS MORE THAN EAGER TO GET STARTED.

IN RETROSPECT, I REALIZE IT WAS A SPECIAL TIME IN COMICS WHEN WE BEGAN OUR COLLABORA-
TION ON X-MEN. COMIC BOOKS WERE CHANGING AND EVOLVING VERY RAPIDLY BACK THEN. NEW
ARTISTS WERE JOINING THE RANKS AT MARVEL AND DC, AND NEAL WAS SPEARHEADING A DIFFERENT
APPROACH TO THE MEDIUM. NEAL'S WORK WAS IMPRESSIVE, WITH RENDERING THAT BROUGHT OTHER
DISCIPLINES — LIKE CONTEMPORARY ILLUSTRATION AND ADVERTISING ART PROMINENT AT THE TIME
— TO COMIC BOOKS.

I REMEMBER WORKING CAREFULLY AND SPENDING CONSIDERABLE TIME POURING OVER THE PAGES.
NEAL HAD BEEN INKING HIS OWN WORK AND HAD CREATED A STYLE WITH THE TRADITIONAL TOOLS OF
PEN AND BRUSH, BUT HIS PENCIL LINE WORK ONLY HINTED AT WHAT THE FINISHED ART WOULD LOOK
LIKE WHEN IT WAS INKED. NEAL PUT DOWN A LINE IN PENCIL THAT DEFINED NOT ONLY CHARACTER
ANATOMY, BUT OTHER INCIDENTAL PANEL ELEMENTS IN A METICULOUSLY DETAILED FASHION. TALK
ABOUT A CONSUMMATE ARTIST — NO WONDER IT TOOK HOURS TO INK THE PAGES! NONETHELESS, WORK-
ING OVER NEAL'S PENCIL ART PUSHED ME TO ADVANCE MY OWN EMBELLISHMENT TECHNIQUES, SOME-
THING I AM GRATEFUL FOR.

AND WHILE THOSE THOUGHTS REMAIN FRESH AND OBVIOUSLY IMPORTANT TO ME, THE ACTUAL WORK
HAS TAKEN ON A MYTHIC QUALITY THANKS TO THE PASSAGE OF TIME AND THE SUBSEQUENT PROJECTS
THAT SEPARATE ME FROM THOSE HALCYON DAYS. I CAN'T SPEAK FOR NEAL, BUT I KNOW WE WERE

MONSTERS ALSO WEEP

STRANGERS... IN A
SAVAGE LAND!

WAR IN THE WORLD
BELOW

BEFORE I'D BE SLAVE

WHAT IS THE POWER?

THE SENTINELS GIVE

MISSION... MURDER

DO OR DIE, BABY!

IN THE SHADOW OF... SAURON

penciler:
Neal Adams

writers:
Roy Thomas (chapters 1-8)
Chris Claremont (co-plot: chapter 4)
Dennis O'Neil (chapter 9)

inker:
Tom Palmer

letterers:
Herb Cooper (chapter 1)
Sam Rosen (chapter 2, 4-8)
Art Simek (chapter 3)
Jean Simek Izzo (chapter 9)

original colorist:
Tom Palmer

trade paperback colorists:
Derek Bellman (chapters 1-4)
Brian Buccellato (chapters 5-8)
Gregory Wright (chapter 9)

color separations:
Malibu

original editor:
Stan "The Man" Lee

trade paperback editor:
Ben Raab

editor-in-chief:
Bob Harras

special thanks to:
A. Guillory -- "Grunt"
Melisa Danon, Steve Alexandrov --
    Manufacturing Representatives
Dawn Guzzo
Kevin Tinsley
Darren Auck and The Raiders -- Production

cover art
NEAL ADAMS

cover coloring
GEORGE ROUSSOS

trade paperback design
ELAN COLE AT
BLUE COLLAR WORK ETHIC INC. NYC

X-MEN®: VISIONARIES 2: THE NEAL ADAMS COLLECTION Originally published in magazine form as X-MEN #56-63, 65. Published by **MARVEL COMICS;** 387 PARK AVENUE SOUTH, NEW YORK, N.Y. 10016. Copyright © 1969, 1970, 1996 Marvel Characters, Inc. All rights reserved. X-MEN (including all prominent characters featured in this issue and the distinctive likenesses thereof) is a trademark of **MARVEL CHARACTERS, INC.** No part of this book may be printed or reproduced in any manner without the written permission of the publisher. Printed in the U.S.A. First Printing, 1996. ISBN #0-7851-0198-5. GST #R127032852.
10 9 8 7 6 5 4 3 2 1

X-MEN
VISIONARIES

the neal adams collection